G D
ND.
GH.
AND MY PO-CKETS FULL OF
FAR A- BOVE THE CLOUDS SHE'LL
G
LONG WAY FROM HOME
MOR-NING RAIN DON'T FALL
G D
IN THE
SHE'LL BE
ES
G
WITH NO PLACE TO
IN A - BOUT THREE HOURS
D G D
2. OUT ON
4. THIS OLD
G

Lightfoot

ALSO BY NICHOLAS JENNINGS

Before the Gold Rush: Flashbacks to the Dawn of the Canadian Sound
Fifty Years of Music: The Story of EMI Music Canada

Lightfoot

NICHOLAS JENNINGS

VIKING

VIKING

an imprint of Penguin Canada, a division of Penguin Random House Canada Limited

Canada • USA • UK • Ireland • Australia • New Zealand • India • South Africa • China

First published 2017

www.penguinrandomhouse.ca

LIBRARY AND ARCHIVES CANADA CATALOGUING IN PUBLICATION

Jennings, Nicholas, 1953-, author
Lightfoot / Nicholas Jennings.

ISBN 978-0-7352-3255-6 (hardcover).—ISBN 978-0-14-319920-5 (EPUB)

1. Lightfoot, Gordon. 2. Musicians—Canada—Biography.
3. Singers—Canada—Biography. I. Title.

ML420.L724J54 2017   782.42164092   C2017-900170-1
                                               C2017-900444-1

Cover and interior design: Lisa Jager
Cover images: (front) John Reeves;
(back) Ken Regan/Camera 5 via Contour by Getty Images

Printed and bound in the United States of America

10 9 8 7 6 5 4 3 2 1

Penguin
Random
House

FOR CAROL

Contents

Rolling Thunder

On a hard-backed chair in the upstairs study of his Toronto home, Gordon Lightfoot sat smoking and playing guitar. On what he called his Quebec wicker table were his usual writing tools: a pencil, a pad of yellow lined paper, a cup of coffee and a bottle of whiskey. There was little else in the sparsely furnished room, aside from a telephone, a desk lamp and a large map of Canada on the wall. It wasn't that Lightfoot lacked possessions or was short of money. His house was, in fact, a mansion. "Sundown" had made him rich. In June 1974, the sultry song and album of the same name had simultaneously topped the charts, bumping Paul McCartney out of the coveted number 1 position and taking Lightfoot to the biggest stages in North America. Things had kept rolling with "Cold on the Shoulder" and "Rainy Day People" hitting the Top 10. The momentum carried him across the Atlantic for his first European concerts, followed by a return engagement at London's prestigious Royal Albert Hall. By late November 1975, after two triumphant final dates at New York's Avery Fisher Hall, Lightfoot was back home. But there was no time to rest. With another album due, he had to come up with a new batch of songs.

Lightfoot was deep into his writing session when the phone rang. It was Bob Dylan. Lightfoot and Dylan went back a long way. They'd both come up during the folk boom, shared a manager in Albert Grossman, had hung out together and respected each other as songwriters. "What are you doing for the next two nights?" Dylan asked. He was in town with his Rolling Thunder Revue. Would Lightfoot like to join the two shows at Maple Leaf Gardens? Although his writing and recording usually took precedence, Lightfoot couldn't resist.

Rolling Thunder was an entirely different way of touring. It began with the idea of Dylan, his buddy Bobby Neuwirth and mentor Ramblin' Jack Elliott playing small venues while traveling around in a station wagon, then accumulated a larger, illustrious cast of characters that included Joan Baez, Roger McGuinn, Ronee Blakley, who'd just appeared in Robert Altman's *Nashville*, and a stellar band featuring gypsy violinist Scarlet Rivera, future Americana star T Bone Burnett and ex–David Bowie sideman Mick Ronson.

Dylan's tour had opened on October 30, 1975, in Plymouth, Massachusetts, and rolled through New England in two buses: one called Phydeaux, for the musicians, and the other nicknamed Ghetto, for friends. Dylan, his wife, Sara, and their kids traveled in a lime-green camper called Palm Beach. It was a wild, theatrical affair, with Dylan performing in white greasepaint, Allen Ginsberg along for the ride as resident poet and actor-playwright Sam Shepard documenting the antics, impressionistically, in a journal. Cameras shooting footage for a planned film called *Renaldo and Clara* captured the giddy spirit of the tour. It was as if a bunch of kids had run away and joined the circus. Spontaneity was the order of the day. During one stop, Dylan and Ginsberg visited Beat writer Jack Kerouac's grave to sing a tribute to their *On the Road* hero. At another, John Prine and Bruce Springsteen showed up just to be in the audience.

Like a traveling Woodstock, Rolling Thunder was shaping up to be a major pop event. Who could resist a psychedelic musical caravan?

The tour's destinations were being kept quiet, with handbills like advertisements for an old-timey roadshow getting distributed only at the last minute. But word quickly spread. Lightfoot knew all about it. Fans were thrilled to learn that Dylan had new songs and that he and Baez were performing together for the first time in a decade. Then there were all the famous musicians onstage at once. Additional guests were hopping on and off like passengers on a train. Joni Mitchell was supposed to appear only at Niagara Falls, but she enjoyed the tour's communal feeling so much she stayed on for several dates. Now Dylan was inviting Lightfoot to take part in the crazy, star-packed shows scheduled for Toronto.

Dylan and his entourage dropped by Lightfoot's house the night of November 30 to discuss it. Things got a little testy with Baez, Lightfoot recalls. "Bob and I had to negotiate with Joan right there on the second floor of my house, because she was worried about the running time. She kept saying, 'There isn't enough time, Bob. There isn't enough time.' Joan was kind of uptight but a great lady. In the end, Bob just said to me, 'You're booked anyway.'" Lightfoot was officially on board. As he casually told a newspaper reporter the next day, "They gave me a buzz when they got to town, to come down and do a few tunes, and that's just what we're gonna do." Like it was no big deal.

Maple Leaf Gardens, home of Lightfoot's favorite team, the Toronto Maple Leafs, was Canada's most storied hockey shrine. But the arena also hosted plenty of concerts, including Dylan's last Toronto appearance, when he shared the stage with the Band. The fifteen-thousand-seat venue quickly began filling up for the first Rolling Thunder show. Backstage was buzzing. The scene was a who's who of rock nobility. Elton John was there. So too were David Clayton-Thomas, of Blood, Sweat & Tears fame, and Ronnie Hawkins, the man who'd groomed the Band for stardom.

Up to this point, the concerts had been running close to four hours. Dylan was in charge, orchestrating everything. He was clearly pleased to have Lightfoot along. On the first night, before singing a stark duet of "Dark as a Dungeon" with Baez, Dylan dedicated the traditional ballad to Lightfoot, who'd first sung it while still a member of the Two Tones. "We're gonna do this one for Gordon tonight," Dylan announced. "Gordon Lightfoot, is he still here?" Then, looking around, he whimsically added, "Thought I saw him walking toward the door—stop him!" During his next set, before a mesmerizing solo performance of "Love Minus Zero / No Limit," Dylan called Lightfoot "one of my favorite songwriters in the world."

Rolling Thunder's cast shone brilliantly as well. Mitchell delivered a riveting version of her song "Coyote." Elliott paid warm homage to Woody Guthrie with "Muleskinner Blues." And Baez sang the haunting "Joe Hill" and two moving songs in tribute to the Band, "Long Black Veil" and "The Night They Drove Old Dixie Down." Then she joined McGuinn for a soaring rendition of the Byrds' epic "Eight Miles High."

Dylan had given Lightfoot an important slot in the show, right before his own final set. It took a long time for Lightfoot to come out; he was backstage tuning guitars, his usual pre-concert ritual. Baez, acting as emcee, entertained the crowd with her impressions of comedian Lily Tomlin's best-known characters. Then, when it finally came time, Baez introduced Lightfoot. As he walked onstage, Lightfoot looked every inch the handsome hometown hero, clad in denim with sleeves rolled up, ready to work, the spotlight illuminating his blond curls. He'd started out a decade earlier, playing a small room at Steele's Tavern, a few blocks away on Yonge Street. Now he had the prime spot at the hottest concert of the decade.

Backed by his usual sidemen, bassist Rick Haynes, guitarist Terry Clements and pedal steel player Pee Wee Charles, Lightfoot launched right into a brand-new song: "Race Among the Ruins." It was his latest poetic take on a tumultuous romantic life. "The road to love is littered by the bones of other ones," he sang, "who by the magic of the moment were mysteriously undone." The audience loved it. Lightfoot's songs always took listeners on a journey, drawing them into stories rich in emotion and without a trace of artifice. Next up, he sang "The Watchman's Gone," one of his many songs steeped in railway imagery. By the time he closed with "Sundown," his taut tale of sexual jealousy, Lightfoot had everyone cheering wildly. The following night, he added "Cherokee Bend," about injustices suffered by First Nations people, and finished with "High and Dry," an upbeat number he liked to call a "toe-tapper." Meticulously crafted, the songs were nonetheless instantly accessible and sounded entirely natural. With the audience screaming for more, Neuwirth stepped to the mike and urged Lightfoot back. Once again, a simmering "Sundown" enthralled the crowd. Both shows ended with Lightfoot and Mitchell joining tour regulars, friends and family, including Dylan's mother, Beatty, for a jubilant round of Guthrie's "This Land Is Your Land."

The December 1 show broke the four-hour mark. Everyone was ecstatic. Swept up in the euphoria, Lightfoot invited Dylan and the entire cast of more than seventy people back to his place for a party. The Rolling Thunder circus pulled onto Beaumont Road, a quiet cul-de-sac by a ravine in Rosedale. What took place in Lightfoot's mansion was a rock-and-roll bacchanal. His blue-and-silver Seeburg jukebox was working overtime, pumping out a steady stream of Cream, Zeppelin, Doobies and Flying Burritos. Everyone was either drinking, snorting or inhaling something, and smoke floated freely about the sprawling house—past the grand piano, the slate billiard table and the Tiffany lamps all the way up to the master bedroom, with its Frank Lloyd Wright stained-glass window. The heavy consumption may explain why memories of the event are so fuzzy. Most people think there was one big noisy party; others believe there were two. Some recall one of Lightfoot's friends, a six-foot-ten banjo player named Tiny, acting as security and greeting Mitchell, McGuinn, Rivera, Ronson and all the others as they arrived.

But almost everyone remembers Dylan's buddy Neuwirth throwing his leather jacket into Lightfoot's fireplace and filling the house with thick black clouds. Says Ramblin' Jack, "Bobby was a very enthusiastic partier. I don't remember all that transpired at Gord's, because we drank to excess. But we were told we had quite a lot of fun." Ronnie Hawkins, another Rolling Thunder addition, certainly recalls the fireplace incident. "Dylan was into drinking carrot juice at the time, and he and Neuwirth got into an argument. . . . Neuwirth just lost it and threw his jacket into the fire. It was like a smoke bomb going off."

While revelry raged on the main floor, Lightfoot and Dylan were alone upstairs with their guitars, in a parlor room with a leaded bay window and floral wallpaper. Lightfoot had stripped down to a singlet, jeans and sandals. Dylan was still wearing his leather coat and fur hat. They seemed a mismatched couple, a study in contrasts. Here were two songwriters at the top of their games. But neither was comfortable in conversation, despite their friendship and mutual respect. Too guarded, or maybe too competitive. They did, though, share the common language of music. As others partied wildly below, Lightfoot and Dylan quietly traded songs. A recording made that night of Lightfoot playing Dylan's "Ballad in Plain D" can be heard on the *Renaldo and Clara* soundtrack. A few photographs captured the historic exchange.

Each of them had started out the same way—alone in a room with a guitar, pencil and pad of paper. The discipline of that hard, solitary work created timeless songs that reached millions. Dylan had become the greatest songwriter of his era. Lightfoot was close behind. Although more workmanlike and straightforward, Lightfoot's songs had an artful structure and poetic resonance that made them accessible in ways that Dylan's weren't. Both were highly prolific and idiosyncratic. After selling out the largest venue in the city, attracting a constellation of music's brightest stars and hosting a fabulously decadent party, all these two artists wanted to do was retreat to a room and trade songs over acoustic guitars. For Lightfoot, as for Dylan, it was always about the song.

ONE

By Lake Couchiching

*The beautiful thing about Orillia is that you
get on your bicycle and after two or three miles
it's all the streams and hills a boy could want.*

The "Town on Two Lakes," situated between Lake Simcoe to the
south and Lake Couchiching to the north, is certainly in an
idyllic setting. When Gordon Lightfoot was growing up, the wilderness at the edge of Orillia offered endless possibilities for adventure:
go-karting down hills, mushroom-hunting in the woods and fishing
in the dozens of nearby lakes, rivers and streams. Lightfoot's father,
Gordon Sr., introduced his son to fishing at an early age. During the
summer, young Gordie's favorite spot was a bridge over North River,
where suckers and rock bass were plentiful. In the winter months, he
and his father would often go ice fishing on Couchiching or Simcoe.
Together, they'd build a wooden hut in the backyard and haul it out
onto the frozen lake. Most weekends, they'd fish through holes
drilled in the ice. Typically, the herring, lake trout and whitefish
would start biting at dawn, so Gord Sr. and his son would stay in the
hut overnight, keeping warm with a small wood-burning stove.

Gordie fished all through his childhood. When he reached his teens, his parents allowed him and his friends to go out on the frozen lakes themselves. Gord Sr. would drive them, towing their huts to whatever spot they fancied. If the boys were successful, they'd take their catch downtown to the Buehler Bros. market and sell the whitefish to the guy who ran the place. For a fourteen-year-old, it was an easy way to earn some decent pocket money. One weekend evening in the winter of 1952, Gord Sr. dropped Gordie and his cousin Peter Townsend off at Carthew Bay, in the northwest corner of Lake Simcoe. They'd heard the herring were in good number there. Gord Sr. wished them luck with a terse "Hope they're biting."

Peter and I set up our huts about two hundred yards from shore. Then we walked back to fish off the mouth of a little stream. It was dark and getting late, so after a while we decided to walk back across the ice to our huts. We started heading toward some lights, which we assumed were the lights of other nearby huts. It turned out to be fishermen on rafts, because there was still unfrozen water out there. We'd gone the wrong direction. Suddenly the ice gave way and we fell through into freezing cold water, up to our necks in our heavy winter coats and boots. Every time we tried to climb out, the ice, which was only about an inch thick, kept breaking. I was really panicking. I could see the headline: "Two Boys Drown Ice Fishing." The water was so cold, it actually felt hot. And we were getting really tired. Finally, something held, and I managed to climb out. My cousin Peter pulled himself out too, and we started walking very quickly back to shore. The ice kept cracking beneath us from the extra weight of our wet clothing. It was such a close call. I'm still amazed we survived.

He could have died, but his nonchalant description of it today doesn't convey the grim terror he and his cousin faced. Even at four-teen, Lightfoot was showing the kind of dogged determination that would carry him out of Orillia and into international stardom, seeing him through all the ups and downs of a large, messy, wonderful and sometimes troubled life. Says his longtime drummer Barry Keane, "Whenever Gord would be presented with a crisis, he'd simply absorb it, say, 'Okay, that's the way it is'—no whining or trying to weasel out of it. Just deal with it and move on. Very strong-willed and strong-minded. That's his character."

Gordon Meredith Lightfoot Jr. was born on November 17, 1938. He was the second child of Gordon Meredith Lightfoot and Jessica Vick Lightfoot (née Trill). Their daughter, Beverley, had arrived five years earlier. Gordon Sr. grew up on a farm in Alvinston, a village between Sarnia and London in southwestern Ontario, not knowing either of his parents. His mother died giving birth to him, and three years after his father remarried, he too died. Gordon Sr.'s stepmother was left to raise him and his siblings. Her resentment at finding herself in this plight made for a deeply unpleasant home life. As soon as he was old enough, Gordon Sr. bought himself a suit and tie and moved to Paris, Ontario. There, he landed a job as a junior clerk at the Royal Bank of Canada. Quiet, hardworking and disciplined, he impressed his manager enough that within a few years he earned a transfer to the Royal Bank's branch in Orillia.

Gordon Sr. arrived in Orillia just as the Depression began. The town had previously prospered thanks to businesses like the Tudhope Carriage Company, whose factory was the largest of its kind in Canada at the turn of the century. Small manufacturing followed, but it struggled after Tudhope's demise. Before that, a thriving lumber business had given rise to furniture factories and shipbuilding, along with saloons and bars that catered to the thirsty workers. Orillia soon became known as the hardest drinking town in Canada and gained such a rowdy, brawling reputation that in 1874 taxpayers voted 144 to 3 to prohibit stores from selling liquor—then voted again in 1908 to shut down all the bars. There was a long wait for a legal drink: Orillia remained dry until 1967.

During the Depression, a frozen Lake Couchiching proved a financial blessing for the town, supplying ice for much of Ontario in the days before refrigeration. Despite the economic downturn, Orillia remained a friendly and relatively thriving community. It was the "Courtesy Town" or "Sunshine Town." As local historian Allan Ironside told the *Orillia Packet & Times*, "Orillia in the 1930s was large enough to provide for one's interests but small enough to escape the stress of the city life. It offered religion, culture, sports, recreation, politics at all levels, clubs and fraternity societies and much more. It welcomed participation and support. It was a good-natured society, ready to amuse or be amused."

Certainly humorist Stephen Leacock, Canada's Mark Twain, found great amusement in Orillia, where he summered for many years on Lake Couchiching. He based his 1912 classic *Sunshine Sketches of a Little Town* on the comic charms of day-to-day life in Orillia, thinly disguised as Mariposa. Leacock got much of his material about eccentric townsfolk from gossip he heard at Jefferson Short's barbershop and wrote about the foibles and hypocrisies of priests, bankers and miners through the deadpan voice of an unnamed narrator. "Heaven knows Pupkin tried hard to please the judge," wrote Leacock of Peter Pupkin, a bank teller in love with the judge's daughter. "He agreed with every theory that Judge Pepperleigh advanced, and that took a pretty pliable intellect in itself."

While working at the Royal Bank, Gordon Sr. met Jessica Trill, a teller at the rival branch of the Canadian Bank of Commerce. Jessie was one of four sisters born to the descendant of one of Orillia's first white settlers. Leacock was one of her customers at the bank, and she swore he always smelled of alcohol. Jessie and Gord found they had more in common than just counting banknotes. They married, and Jessie quit working, which was expected of a newlywed woman at the time.

At the height of the Depression, in 1933, Gord lost his job. It was around the same time that their daughter, Bev, was born. With a wife and a newborn baby, he needed work right away. Showing determination, responsibility and quiet authority—qualities he'd pass on to his son—he took a job at Wagg's Imperial Laundry, which had just introduced a new dry cleaning service. By the time little Gordie arrived, five years later, Wagg's was thriving and Gord Sr. had become the company's plant manager. Gord Sr.'s new position meant his family could live in a comfortable two-and-a-half-story detached house at 283 Harvey Street. The Lightfoots had only a short drive to St. Paul's United, the church they attended. And when Gordie started kindergarten, it was a just a quick bike ride to West Ward Public School.

Gordie loved the outdoors, and on hikes with his family, with his beloved dog Chip tagging along, he learned his way around the woods of an area known as Marchmont, near Bass Lake and the shores of North River. Often, they'd hunt for morels, a hard-to-find mushroom, when they were in season.

These were war years, but Gordie was untroubled by the conflict overseas. His parents ensured he had a happy childhood, although it was impossible to avoid the sight and sound of Canadian troops as they marched around town on their way to maneuvers at Orillia's army training camp. "The stomp of army boots and the loud marching songs, beer drinking ballads and others caused a great deal of excitement among classroom children," noted local historian Marcel Rousseau. And the town's war effort occasionally pressed students of all ages into service. One of Orillia's many paper drives collected seventeen tons of paper and cardboard and 851 pounds of rags, which were taken to schools to be sorted by students.

The Lightfoots' neighborhood was a close-knit community. Kids played on the street and neighbors got together for Sunday dinners. Jessie had a penchant for orderliness she passed on to young Gordie, who remains a self-described "neat freak" to this day. Once a year, the

Lightfoots visited with Gord Sr.'s relatives. "Sometimes Dad's family came to Orillia, but usually we drove down to Alvinston," Lightfoot says. "They were good people, who loved to play cards." His mother's relatives all lived close by and were highly musical. Jessie's mother, Ethel, played piano, and Jessie and her three sisters, Laura (known as Lola), Mary and Martha (nicknamed Babe), loved nothing more than to sing in rounds and harmonize at family gatherings. At Christmas they would sing carols, and at other times they'd blend their voices in popular hymns or the hits of the day. Bing Crosby was always a favorite with Jessie. Young Gordie, who was present at all those gatherings, soaked it up. Soon, they got him up singing too.

My mum, aunts and other relatives would bribe me, saying, "Here's a nickel. Get up there and sing." Then they'd put me up on Grandma Ethel's kitchen table and pay me to do it. I would've gotten up there anyway! I don't remember what I'd sing, probably something to do with Christmas. Once I sang "Jesus Loves Me." But whatever it was, I'd sing it quite freely, without being self-conscious or going sharp or flat. They'd be all standing around in the kitchen, listening, and I remember getting applause at the end of it. That's when I first realized I had a good voice and could do something with it.

The bribery continued. Jessie enrolled her son in the junior choir at St. Paul's and began buying Gordie small metal cars and trucks made in England as a reward to encourage his singing. "I had quite the collection of Dinky toys after a while," says Lightfoot. Things started getting serious when Ray Williams, St. Paul's choir director, told Gordon Sr. and Jessica that he wanted to train their son as a boy soprano. Gordie began weekly voice training with Williams, who became an influential figure, the first of a number of guiding hands that helped Lightfoot along his path. At the same time, Jessie enrolled Gordie and Bev in piano lessons with Gertrude Lambert. It wasn't long before Jessie's blond-haired boy was being singled out to sing solos for church services at Easter and Christmas and Orillians had their first exposure to the purity of Gordie Lightfoot's voice. Jessie couldn't have been prouder.

Music was becoming a big part of Lightfoot's life, but it wasn't his only interest. Orillia had the largest YMCA of any town in North America, and its annual hobby fairs attracted hundreds of boys and girls who entered their handiwork in competitions. Gordie developed a passion for building model airplanes, and in 1947, when he was nine, he won first prize for his creations (another winner that year was eight-year-old Charlie Baillie, future chairman and CEO of the Toronto-Dominion Bank). "It was all done with glue and sticks and paper back then," says Lightfoot, "and you had to nail the finished frame down on a plank. It was a hobby I kept up for a couple of years."

Jessie's promotion of her son's singing talent soon led to paid gigs at service club functions around town. Usually his sister, Bev, accompanied him on piano. On occasion, they performed at the Shangri-La Gardens. The "Shang" was Orillia's popular Chinese restaurant, run by Jin Seto and frequented by pianist Glenn Gould, whose family had a cottage on the east side of Lake Couchiching. Lightfoot knew nothing of Gould but recalls being crammed into a corner of the Shang once with Bev when they performed for the women's auxiliary. "The place was packed, and there were people practically sitting in my lap," he says. "I remember I started feeling really claustrophobic." With each public performance, young Gordie's reputation grew. Before long, it seemed the whole town knew about the local boy with the golden voice. While all of this made Jessie proud, none of it sat well with Gord Sr., a quiet, no-nonsense man, who worried about the effect all this attention might be having on his son. "I remember at one point," Lightfoot says, "when I was doing so well, my dad saying to my mother, 'I hope he doesn't get a swelled head over this. He's just a boy and he's already getting paid to do this.'" The growing attention soon spread to West Ward Public School. One fall day when he was in Grade 5, Gordie heard an announcement summoning him to the principal's office.

I was called down to the office of Mr. Dobson, thinking I'd done something terribly wrong. That was very serious in those days, because you'd get the strap if you had. But when I got down there, it was nothing like that at all. Mr. Dobson had heard from Mrs. Murphy, the singing teacher, that I had a good voice. He said that if I sang a song, he'd record it on this new device he had. The machine would seem pretty primitive now, but it was the latest technology at the time. So he set me up with a microphone and I sang "Irish Lullaby" [also known as "Too-Ra-Loo-Ra-Loo-Ral," the Tin Pan Alley song popularized by Bing Crosby]. Mrs. Murphy accompanied me on piano. It wound up being cut onto this red plastic disc. Then, when Parents' Day came around a short while later, the school played it over the public address system for everyone to hear, including my mother and father. That was the first time I ever heard my voice coming back at me.

That red platter, cut on Mr. Dobson's portable Wilcox-Gay recording machine on November 16, 1948, just one day before Lightfoot's tenth birthday, was his recording debut. The ten-inch 78 rpm disc had his name and the song title handwritten on its label. Lightfoot still owns it. As one of his most treasured possessions, the old, slightly cracked piece of plastic-coated cardboard is safely stored in a box in the basement of Lightfoot's home. He would go on to record music for the next sixty years using the industry's most sophisticated equipment in the world's finest studios. And Lightfoot's first recording, although crude, was the catalyst.

———

Lightfoot got along well enough with his father. But Gordon Sr. could be difficult to read and a little intimidating. A man of few words, he also possessed a temper that could explode like a sudden thunderclap before a storm. Gordie, Bev and Jessie learned to navigate their way around his deceptively quiet waters. What he lacked in free and easy conversation, Gordon Sr. made up for by his disciplined approach to work. His son remembers him as a tireless man who did whatever needed to be done and could fix anything.

He was the plant manager, but he'd clean out the furnace, because no one else would do it. It was run by coal. I remember him taking me down there while he was doing it. It was kind of cool. There was dust everywhere. And I remember him showering afterwards, the only time I stood naked with my dad, washing the dust off. They had all this machinery around the place, some of it dangerous. They had belts whirring and wheels turning, and I remember him lying underneath one of these big extractors, trying to fix something underneath. It scared the hell out of me. He was the only guy in that place who could do that.

Gordon Sr. was a conscientious and active member of the community, something his son greatly admired. Along with teaching Sunday school, he was an avid golfer and president of the Couchiching Golf and Country Club. He also curled, and Gordie was soon trying his hand at both sports. At Wagg's, Gordon Sr. coached the company's women's baseball team, and his son would go along to watch the Wagg's Aces play. One summer night after a game, the younger Gordon experienced something that shook him to the core. He and his dad, on their way back from driving one of the players home, were going over a railroad crossing that had no signal lights. They didn't see the train that was bearing down on them, and they narrowly avoided getting hit. For Lightfoot, coming so close to dying in such a startling way caused the otherwise carefree boy to question his own existence.

"I came face to face with my mortality at age ten," he told journalist Nick Krewen years afterward. "With some people, it happens a little later in their lives. You realize you're gonna die. It hits everybody between the eyes like a big stone. It hit me when I was ten, and I've been depressed ever since." Whether it was actually depression or some kind of fatalism, there's no doubt that Lightfoot experienced something that would color his life. The close call—one of several he'd face over the years—may have sparked in him a determination to make his mark with music, the one thing he knew he could do really well. His brushes with death, and the resulting wonder of why he was spared, could well have contributed to the tinge of melancholy that later crept into his songs.

Gordie, realizing that the best way to stay happy was to keep singing, pressed on. Using what his mother said was his God-given talent, he continued to participate in the junior church choir and, under Ray Williams's guidance, developed more vocal range and control. All of his early musical training came from the church. "I even learned how to sing with emotion at that point," says Lightfoot. "I remember there was a piece from Handel's *Messiah* that got me. I said, 'Hey, this feels good to really put your heart and soul into something.'" At church, he learned a tremendous number of hymns. When the Orillia Opera House held an amateur talent contest, sponsored by local radio station CFOR, Lightfoot won second place, singing "Bless This House," the hymn popularized by England's Vera Lynn, the "Forces' Sweetheart."

He looked the part, dressed in his formal white cassock, with his neatly combed blond hair, but Lightfoot was no angel. Like most pre-teenage boys, he had a rambunctious streak. The Lightfoots and their neighbors the Spencers took turns having each other over for Sunday dinner. Jessie was godmother to the Spencers' daughter Marylou. Marylou remembers the party she and Bev held for their friends when they were fifteen. "Gordie was a real troublemaker," she says. "He brought a toilet plunger downstairs, stuck it to the living room wall and wound up pulling the plaster off. When my parents came home and saw the damage, Gordie blamed Clark, a guy who was going to take me to the senior prom. After that, my parents wouldn't let me go out with Clark, so I wound up being dateless for the dance. Gordie sure had the devil in his eyes." Devilish or not, the boy could do no wrong in his mother's eyes. With his heavenly voice, all was forgiven.

Jessie was her son's enthusiastic cheerleader in all things, especially music. Socially, Lightfoot was shy and a little awkward. Jessie's encouragement boosted his confidence, at least when he was performing, and their bond made him feel deeply loved. She also taught him manners, loyalty and the importance of being honest with others. These were lessons that would stay with Lightfoot his whole life. "She wasn't a pushover," Lightfoot says today. "She could be stern to a degree, and I certainly didn't try to get away with anything with her." His closeness with Jessie made up for his more distant relationship with Gord Sr. But mother and son's tight connection left Bev out in the cold. Everything always seemed to be about Gordie. By the time she was fifteen, Bev couldn't wait to get out of the house. While working part-time doing laundry at Wagg's, she met nineteen-year-old Bob Eyers, who worked for her father as a truck driver. Two years later, they were married.

Lightfoot continued to impress Ray Williams, who had big plans for his twelve-year-old prodigy. He arranged Lightfoot's next recording, the choirboy's sweet rendition of "The Lord's Prayer." Then the St. Paul's choirmaster entered his star soprano in the Kiwanis Music Festival at Toronto's Massey Hall. Kiwanis was one of the largest service clubs in Canada, and its annual festival, conceived by celebrated composer and Toronto Symphony conductor Sir Ernest MacMillan, had grown to become a prestigious showcase for young musical talent. Ten-year-old Glenn Gould had won the piano competition at the first Kiwanis Music Festival in 1944.

On a winter day in early 1951, the Lightfoots drove south to Toronto in the family's new Pontiac Silver Streak, down the road that would soon become Highway 400, thanks to Ontario's Orillia-born premier, Leslie Frost. Gord and Jessie Lightfoot arrived at Massey Hall to find the place full of proud and anxious parents just like themselves. They took their seats with Bev and waited patiently for their son's turn. When Gordie stepped out onto the auditorium's stage, a beaming Jessie gave her husband's hand a gentle squeeze. With piano accompanist May Wedlock at his side, Gordie, dressed neatly in a white shirt and tie, was visibly nervous. But his confidence grew as he sang his way through his first selection, John Ireland's "Alpine Song," and at the end he received strong applause. By the time he hit the last note of his second piece, Thomas Arne's "Under the Greenwood Tree," it was clear from the cheers that the Orillia boy had nailed it. Gordie wound up taking first prize in the under-thirteen class. To celebrate, Gord Sr. took the family out for a fancy meal. That was the beginning of Lightfoot's long relationship with the hallowed Massey Hall. The following year, he won again at the same event, coming first in the Boys, Unchanged Voices category with his performance of Schubert's "Who Is Sylvia?" Winning meant he also performed each year at Massey's Stars of the Festival gala concert. Lightfoot now knew his voice was going to take him places.

TWO

Jazz 'n' Jive

In 1952, popular music was safe and unexciting, still reflecting the cautious postwar times. You could turn on the radio and hear lightweight pop from the likes of Doris Day and Perry Como or country songs by Hank Williams and Kitty Wells. Elvis Presley hadn't yet walked into the offices of Sun Records in Memphis to record his first hit and bring the rough-and-tumble sound of rock 'n' roll to the masses. The biggest musical thrill for kids at the time came from the smooth harmonies of vocal groups like the Four Aces and the Mills Brothers. Canada's the Four Lads, a quartet formed at Toronto's St. Michael's Choir School, had hit the charts that year with the harmony-filled ballad "The Mocking Bird."

When Lightfoot entered his Grade 9 science classroom that fall at Orillia District Collegiate Institute (everyone called the high school simply "OD"), his teacher wasted no time in recruiting him to join a singing group—not a pop vocal outfit, but a barbershop quartet. "I was shanghaied right into it by Mr. Wallace," Lightfoot says today. "I simply said, 'When do we start?'" The Collegiate Four was formed right away, with Lightfoot singing tenor and schoolmates Bob Croxall on lead, Wayne Rankin on baritone and Paul Lazier on bass. The four neatly dressed guys made their first public appearance that December during commencement ceremonies at OD. As members of the Society for the Preservation and Encouragement of Barber Shop Quartet Singing in America (SPEBSQSA), the Collegiate Four got access to arrangements for tunes like "After Dark" and "The Old Songs." Wearing matching V-neck sweaters and bow ties, the group was soon singing all around Orillia, at school assemblies, church meetings and service clubs. Not shy of ambition, the quartet got itself bookings in Midland, Toronto and as far away as Sarnia.

Throughout Grade 10, Lightfoot kept his sights firmly set on music. His shyness meant he wasn't yet boldly pursuing girls. In fact, Lightfoot's first date came just two weeks before his fourteenth birthday, when Lois Doble asked him to go with her to the school's Sadie Hawkins dance. More dates with girls would follow for the good-looking Lightfoot, but the Collegiate Four remained his first priority.

All the rehearsing and polishing of harmonies started paying off. First, Lightfoot made his national radio debut with the quartet on *The Dominion Barn Dance*, a locally recorded show broadcast on the CBC network. His national TV debut followed soon after, when the Collegiate Four traveled to Toronto to appear on CBC's *Pick the Stars,* a talent contest with a judging panel that included *Toronto Telegram* critic Clyde Gilmour. Lightfoot and his schoolmates arrived at the studio, warmed up their vocal cords and waited as tap dancers, comedians and country bands worked hard to impress the judges. When their call came, they stepped into the spotlight, gathered around a microphone and delivered their polished four-part harmonies. The Collegiate Four impressed Gilmour and his panelists and took first prize. Lightfoot was thrilled. His group's performance was

---

* Other contestants who later competed on *Pick the Stars* included such future household names as Paul Anka, Rich Little and Robert Goulet.

seen on TV sets across Canada, with most of Orillia tuning in—
Jessie made sure of that. But *Pick the Stars* proved to be the Collegiate
Four's crowning achievement. Nature soon took its course and Gordie's
voice descended a couple of octaves, making him a baritone—a position in the group that was already filled. Lightfoot was out, and the
quartet disbanded shortly afterward.

If Lightfoot was despondent, he didn't show it. He knew another
musical opportunity would come up. He threw himself into more
school activities, joining the curling team and taking part in glee club
productions of Gilbert and Sullivan comic operas. He almost joined
the student council, but Jessie, who encouraged him in most things,
frowned on the idea. "You don't want to get into politics," she told him.

Not content to see his barbershopping days come to an end,
Lightfoot formed a new quartet, the Teen-Timers, in the fall of 1954,
enlisting three fellow OD students: Bill Hughes on bass, Bob Branch
on tenor and Terry Whelan on lead. Whelan proved to be an asset.
He wasn't shy and could speak confidently in public in a way that
Lightfoot simply couldn't. The Teen-Timers stayed busy through the
summer months, rehearsing regularly and performing wherever they
landed gigs, just as the Collegiate Four had done. "We did the same
thing," Lightfoot told the barbershop magazine *The Harmonizer* in
2006. "We went through the contests, practiced, were coached, went
to meetings, sang with the chorus; did everything we were supposed
to do. It became a whole project that lasted all through high school
up until the end of Grade 12." This time, Lightfoot was in charge.
With his unstoppable work ethic, he was determined that the Teen-
Timers would be going places.

Lightfoot's new group became competitive right away. It took
part in barbershop competitions at Toronto's Massey Hall and as far
away as St. Catharines, where the group placed second in the annual

contest of the SPEBSQSA. His father did all the driving, shepherd-ing the boys to competitions and as many as two gigs a week. When Gord Sr. complained about the time it was taking, it prompted an unexpected outburst from his headstrong son.

I had to confront my dad about it. We had an argument in our backyard. We raised our voices. I told him, "You don't have to drive, but somebody has gotta do it. It ain't gonna be Terry's dad, or Bill's dad, because he's a dentist, and it ain't gonna be Bob's, because he doesn't have a dad." I was running the quartet, so it was my responsibility to get us to the shows. It was the first time I stood up to my dad. He listened, saw I was serious, and we got it settled right there.

Locking horns with his father took some nerve. Gord Sr., then forty-four, had a stubborn streak as long as Main Street. But so too did his son. Gordie was beginning to use that Lightfoot bullheaded-ness to further his music career. It wasn't long before he had his driver's license and was able to transport the Teen-Timers himself. When school finished, the quartet spent part of the summer at a lodge in Haliburton, performing twice a week in the resort's floor show as well as at other hotels in the area. With plenty of beer and girls around, it was a sweet deal.

Throughout Grade 12, Lightfoot remained wholly committed to music, less so to academics. He did play guard for OD's junior foot-ball team, alongside classmate Charlie Baillie, and earned the fol-lowing yearbook comment: "Gord [no longer Gordie] has often found the weakness in the offensive team and has made some fine stops." Lightfoot was one of the school's most popular kids, although his shyness remained a handicap. Guys admired his competitive drive and girls liked his gentle manner and blond good looks. He was a local star. His singing—both solo and with the Teen-Timers—was often heard around campus. This led to some teasing from his classmates. "WANTED: Gord Lightfoot," read the yearbook's class notes, "for singing to the endangerment of the public's eardrums." Truth was, Gord was the Orillia boy made good, and everyone enjoyed his voice. Tayler "Hap" Parnaby, who was a teenage DJ at CFOR, heard him sing "Moonlight in Vermont" at the Pavalon, or the "Pav," as the locals called the Couchiching Park dance hall. "He did a masterful version of it," says Parnaby, "a little bit like Crosby, in that velvet voice Gord has when he sings softly. Everyone really sat up and took notice."

Despite his best efforts, Lightfoot could not keep the Teen-Timers together. With bass singer Hughes already graduated and studying at the University of Toronto, and tenor Branch quitting school to work in town, the quartet disbanded in Lightfoot's final high school year. Barbershopping had run its course, and Lightfoot's music tastes were shifting anyway. He and one of his school friends, Buddy Hill, were getting into jazz and traveling to Toronto with other classmates to see concerts.

There'd be a carload of us, and we'd go to catch whatever big name was in the clubs. I remember one time when we went on the bus to hear Dave Brubeck and Gerry Mulligan at Massey Hall. We saw them all—Count Basie, Louis Armstrong, Duke Ellington—when they played the dance halls. I really enjoyed listening to jazz. It really got me interested in studying notation.

Orillia's own swing band, the ten-piece Charlie Andrews Orchestra, was a regular fixture at the Rainbow Room, owned by the Andrews family, and at places like Dunn's Pavilion, in Bala. While Lightfoot was still in Grade 13, he received an invitation—and a challenge—from Andrews.

I got a call from Charlie, the orchestra leader. I'd known about him all through high school and knew what his band was doing. He said to me, "You can sing, but can you play an instrument?" No, I told him. "Can you play the drums?" "Well, I can certainly try," I said, "but I don't have any drums." He had me over to his house, where he had a drum kit. They were quite a musical family and were all in the orchestra. Charlie played bass, his wife, Anne, played piano and their son Ross was a horn player. The band was doing a mix of ballads and jazz tunes. Charlie said to me, "Take the drums home and learn to play them." How do I do that? "You put records on and play along with them." That's how I learned to play drums. I set them up in the basement and started drumming to Louis Armstrong. The next thing I knew, I was up on the bandstand performing with the orchestra.

Supplying the backbeat for the band at places like Orillia's Rainbow Room and Gravenhurst's Muskoka Sands, Gord was also the vocalist when they did Nat King Cole's "Stardust" and the Platters' "My Prayer." Marg McEachern, an attractive teenager from nearby Pefferlaw, caught Lightfoot singing with the Andrews orchestra at Beaverton's Commodore. Like other girls in the dance hall that night, she was instantly smitten. "He sang 'Cry Me a River,' and we all slid under our chairs," she says. "Gordie was like an Elvis Presley in those days. Extremely good-looking and very shy—but he really lit up when he was onstage."

At intermission, Lightfoot came and asked McEachern to dance. The two hit it off. They started a relationship that was somewhere between romance and a musical partnership. Marg played piano, and they jammed at her house and at the Lightfoot home, half an hour away in Orillia. "I can't remember if we actually dated or if we were just best friends," says McEachern, who does remember at least one kiss. "We were kind of platonic. It became a standing joke."

At eighteen, Lightfoot was having the time of his life, trying his hand at everything that came his way. Jessie, always willing to further

her son's interests, had bought him a four-string tenor guitar, and he'd begun dabbling in rock and roll, doing Presley imitations with Brendan McKinnon, another friend and budding guitarist.

Gary Thiess was a schoolmate in awe of Lightfoot's relentless activities. "Gord was such a hardworking guy," Thiess says. "My mom always used to say, 'If only you could apply yourself like Gordon did.' But I couldn't keep up with him." Thiess remembers the determination Lightfoot showed with track and field: "When he developed a passion for pole vaulting, he'd practice over and over in his parents' back garden. He didn't have a proper landing area other than some dirt he'd dug up to make it a little softer. He finally managed to get up to a certain height but came down the wrong way, causing him to tear a ligament when he landed. But that was Gord—a real competitor." Lightfoot got his work ethic from his father. But he developed his competitive drive entirely by himself. Both would become characteristic qualities in Lightfoot throughout his music career.

In early 1957, the Everly Brothers were topping the charts everywhere with sweet melodic hits like "Bye Bye Love" and "Wake Up Little Susie." The siblings' close, expressive harmonies inspired Lightfoot and Terry Whelan, his partner in the Teen-Timers, to form their own Everly-style duo. They called themselves the Two Timers, a roguish play on their quartet's name, and began doing gigs around town. On a Friday night at the Pav, nineteen-year-old Lightfoot and Whelan—wearing sports jackets and ties, their hair swept up à la Elvis or Johnny Cash—sang earnest renditions of the Everlys' songs and Harry Belafonte's "Don't Ever Love Me." They took turns alternating between four- and six-string guitars, but harmonizing was their forte. Whelan handled the between-song patter. Lightfoot was happy to let the songs do the talking, a pattern he followed throughout his career.

Lightfoot finished high school in June 1957. He flunked algebra, having spent more time on harmonies than homework, and had to make up the credit to get his diploma. But he had chosen his career path and there was no deviating from it. By now, he'd already written his first composition, "The Hula Hoop Song," about the popular toy that kids everywhere were twirling around their waists, limbs and necks. "I read about it in *Life* magazine," Lightfoot says. "It was a craze that came before the twist. The magazine showed a picture with 150 people in a vacant lot all hula-hooping at once. It inspired me to write a song about it." Convinced that he had something, and determined to prove it, the teenager borrowed his father's Buick and drove down Highway 400 to pitch the unlikely song directly to the performing rights association in Toronto. Armed with just a ukulele and an unwavering conviction, he bravely played the tune for BMI executives Harold Moon, Whitey Haines and Bailey Bird. They listened patiently but weren't buying. Still, Lightfoot says, they offered words of encouragement. "Harold Moon said it was quite good for a topical song and told me to keep writing." That was all he needed to hear.

That summer, Lightfoot was working for Wagg's, delivering linens to area resorts. On his lunch break, he'd read *Downbeat* magazine, the American jazz bible he subscribed to. One day, in between articles on pianist Dave Brubeck and drummer Max Roach, something jumped out at him: an advertisement for the Westlake College of Modern Music in Hollywood. Westlake was the first academic institution after Boston's Berklee to offer a college diploma in jazz. Lightfoot called his friend Buddy Hill, an aspiring pianist. This was exactly what they needed. Right then and there, they hatched a plan to go to the music school together.* They were both accepted. Why

---

* Legendary jazz bassist Charlie Haden had studied at Westlake after seeing a similar ad in *Downbeat*.

two kids from Orillia were granted admission in the same year is anyone's guess, but Lightfoot didn't question it.

Lightfoot made a deal with his parents: with his wages from Wagg's, he would pay as much as he could toward airfare and tuition if they would make up the difference. His mother and father agreed, and Gord began counting the days before the Westlake semester began in September. When word spread around Orillia that Gord Lightfoot Jr. was going to Hollywood, the news sparked a predictable reaction. Maybe it was jealousy or maybe people thought the kid's success had gone to his head, but Orillians did not take his plans seriously. "They were laughing about it," says Lightfoot, giving the example of how his father's friends responded on the golf course one day that summer. A local boy studying in Hollywood? "People thought that was the most outlandish thing they had ever heard of." Just as Leacock had observed in *Sunshine Sketches*, Orillia's townsfolk loved to cut ambitious locals down to size. It was the same narrow-minded disapproval and small-town Ontario repression that Nobel Prize winner Alice Munro depicts so forcefully in her short stories. *Who Do You Think You Are?*, the title of one Munro collection, was a double-edged question facing Lightfoot or anyone else growing up in a community with Scottish Presbyterian roots.

But Gord Jr. was not deterred. Come September, he said goodbye to his parents, sister and his girlfriend at the time, Shauna Smith, and he and Buddy took a bus to Chicago. From there, they boarded a TWA Constellation to Los Angeles. It was the first time Lightfoot had flown on a commercial airline and the first time he'd been away from Orillia.

Westlake had the perfect location. Surrounded by palm trees and pink stucco buildings, the school was situated at 7190 Sunset Boulevard, not far from Hollywood Senior High School. Every day was a chance to see things he'd only ever read about in magazines. The luxurious Beverly Hills Hotel, where the Rat Pack, Humphrey

Bogart and Marilyn Monroe all stayed, was to the west, while to the east was the celebrated Sunset Strip, home of the city's best nightclubs.

Pat LaCroix, another Canadian student at Westlake that year (as many as twelve out of a total enrollment of fifty), recalls walking a short distance from the small campus and its dormitories to a pack of jazz clubs. "I remember seeing Blossom Dearie just down the street, and we could stroll over to Sherry's and see a great band for the price of a beer. There was so much great music," says LaCroix. "Plus, we'd all go jam down at Ben Pollock's Pick-a-Rib nightclub on Sunday nights."

Like Lightfoot, LaCroix was a singer. He'd later form the Halifax Three folk group with Denny Doherty, future vocalist with the Mamas & the Papas. "Gord and I were both vying to be singers, but it was a friendly rivalry," says LaCroix. "We took turns singing with the school's A band. He was a good vocalist, but trying real hard to sing like Frank Sinatra in those days. Later, when I finally heard Gord doing his original stuff, I thought, 'Man, he's really come into his own.' I had no idea he could write songs." Fact was, Lightfoot spent his time at Westlake studying how to improve his compositional skills, taking courses in orchestration and music theory. He also learned musical notation and how to write in all keys on the piano—essential tools for any versatile songwriter, and he would make full use of them all.

With LaCroix and two fellow students, Lightfoot formed a singing group called the Four Winds. "It wasn't like barbershop," he points out. "We were getting into more of the jazz type of modern, fancy chords." The Four Winds landed a couple of cool gigs through Westlake connections. They were hired to sing backup vocals for a rockabilly-style artist named Johnny Stark, who had a deal with Mercury Records. "We recorded four songs with him," says Lightfoot, "including a good one called 'Cold Coffee.' But we never heard

another thing about it. Never heard about Johnny Stark again either!"
Then the Four Winds were asked to appear on a local TV show
hosted by Bobby Troup, a musician and actor who later starred in
Emergency! with his wife Julie London. LaCroix recalls they sang on
several tunes performed on the show, including Troup's own "(Get
Your Kicks on) Route 66."

There were plenty of kicks to be had for Canadian teenagers
living in Hollywood. One of the students had a big old convertible,
and a carload of them would drive through neighborhoods like Bel
Air stealing oranges right off the trees. LaCroix recalls one night
when they'd partied late and drunk a crazy amount of beer. "No
sooner were we all tucked into our beds, around three in the morning, than the birds start singing, making a real din," he says. "All of a
sudden, we hear *thump, thump, thump*, someone going down the
stairs, and then, s*mash*, the screen door slams. 'Hey, you fuckin' birds,
shut up!' It was Gord, yelling at the birds in the middle of the night.
You could hear everyone in the dorm laughing at that."

Although Westlake was a two-year course, Lightfoot stayed for
only two semesters. But the school had taught him a lot about composition, arranging and sight-reading. He'd also learned how to write
musical notation in his neat penmanship, a skill that would soon
come in handy. Despite the allure of Los Angeles, Lightfoot was
deeply homesick, and he returned home to Canada in the spring of
1958. He had a summer job waiting for him at Wagg's and the chance
to get back to singing with his pal Terry Whelan. But when the
summer job ran out, so too did his tolerance for Orillia. His small
hometown had been idyllic in his youth, but now, after the experience of Hollywood, he found it claustrophobic. Plus, his girlfriend,
Shauna Smith, with whom he'd corresponded while at Westlake, had
started going out with one of his old classmates. It was time to get
out of Orillia. "I just knew I had to go to Toronto," says Lightfoot,
"and get my engine started."

THREE

Movin'

On a clear fall day in 1958, twenty-one-year-old Lightfoot headed south, making the trip to Toronto he had done so many times before. This time was different: he was moving there for good. His parents supported his decision. Gord Sr. had even bought him a car as a leaving-home gift. As he drove down Highway 400 in his secondhand Pontiac, Lightfoot had a flurry of thoughts racing through his head. He remembered the Kiwanis Festival wins at Massey Hall when he was a kid and how he'd driven to Toronto as a teenager to pitch publisher Harold Moon his "Hula Hoop Song." Getting his music career going wouldn't be easy, but he realized that his best shot was to keep working with the Two Timers, the Everly Brothers–style duo with his high school buddy Terry Whelan.

Lightfoot found accommodation at Mrs. Smith's rooming house in Toronto's east end, sharing with Brendan McKinnon, the Orillia friend with whom he'd once sung Elvis songs. But he needed a job. His father, who knew the manager at the Royal Bank of Canada in Orillia, helped him land one as a junior clerk at the bank's Yonge and Eglinton branch. Young Lightfoot's salary was $48 a week—enough to cover his room and board and keep his Pontiac filled with gas.

Toronto in the late 1950s was still a buttoned-down town. Rock 'n' roll had arrived in Toronto the Good to loosen hips and, according to the guardians of morality, corrupt local youths, but the city was still a pretty staid place. The wildest action could be found down on Yonge Street. There, visiting rockers, jazz players and country singers were busy plying their trade in clubs along the neon-lit district known as the Strip. Bo Diddley, Oscar Peterson and Conway Twitty all played there. And Pete Seeger and the Weavers had come to town, performing "Goodnight, Irene" at Massey Hall for college kids, but folk music had not yet exploded.

Lightfoot had little time to absorb all this. By day, he was pushing paper; by night, he was busy trying to find work for the Two Timers. Whelan was still living in Orillia, and gigs weren't frequent. But Lightfoot did manage to get them booked at places like Bloor Street's Collegiate Club, a teenage nightspot that had once showcased 1950s vocal stars the Four Lads, the Diamonds and the Crew-Cuts. Dressed in dark suits and slicked-back hair, the Two Timers were a polished act, with Lightfoot on a four-string tenor guitar and Whelan strumming a baritone ukulele. Their repertoire consisted of crowd-pleasing covers of pop tunes and country ballads, with the occasional calypso and Irish folk song thrown in. Lightfoot's smooth voice carried them musically, while Whelan did the talking. Together they drew on all the experience they'd gained playing for tourists around Orillia. To get his high school diploma, some of Lightfoot's evenings were also spent making up for his failed algebra course. "I went to night school at the same time I was working at the bank," he recalls. "I was certainly an industrious little bugger."

Lightfoot also found time for songwriting. Marg McEachern, his dance partner from Pefferlaw, was now running a music school in Toronto. Her business partner was Art Snider, a veteran pianist with connections in the music world. McEachern made the introduction, telling Snider of her friend's talent. She also insisted that Lightfoot use their studio space to work on his songwriting. One night, while passing by one of the rehearsal rooms, Snider noticed Lightfoot sitting at a piano with pen in hand, putting down some notation. "Can you write lead sheets?" Snider asked. "I think so," replied Lightfoot. "Come over to my studio on Eglinton," Snider told him. "I've got a tape full of songs that need transcribing." Lightfoot's Westlake training was coming in handy.

Soon, Lightfoot was copying scores for CBC musical productions that Snider had arranged. The work was painstaking. "It all had to be written with great care," says Lightfoot. "Ink on onionskin transparencies—that was the process. There were no photocopiers. You'd take the sheets to this guy who'd transfer them onto white sheets of paper using ammonia. I'd be there once a week. The smell of the ammonia was overpowering." Soon, he was copying individual parts for the likes of Rick Wilkins, Lucio Agostini and Bert Niosi, working musicians who were members of CBC orchestras at the network's Sumach Street studios.

Working in the bank by day and copying music scores by night didn't leave Lightfoot much time for socializing. And there was no new girlfriend yet in his life. On one rare night off, Lightfoot ventured downtown to the Yonge Street strip, where he hoped a little romance might be found. Yonge Street could be a dangerous place for a small-town boy, as young Gord discovered that night at a Las Vegas–style nightclub called the Brown Derby. He'd gone to hear the house band, Joe King & the Zaniacs, and was knocking back beers to get his confidence up, hoping to maybe meet a woman, when it all went terribly wrong.

I looked at somebody's girl when I shouldn't have. I looked at her and she returned my gaze. Turned out her boyfriend was a thug, even had a switchblade. He and three or four of his friends played cat and mouse with

me for the next half hour, chasing me through the Brown Derby and its
other room down below. They almost caught me in O'Keefe Lane, the
alleyway behind, but I managed to escape in a taxicab. Scared the hell out
of me. I wouldn't go downtown to a bar for six months after that.

Through his CBC connections, Art Snider learned of an opening
at *Country Hoedown*, the TV network's corny but wildly popular country music series. The show needed another cast member for its square-
dance group, the Singin' Swingin' Eight, and Snider urged Lightfoot
to audition. Lightfoot knew he could handle the singing side of the
job but had serious doubts about the swinging, square-dancing part.
The audition proved him right: the producers liked his voice but felt
his footwork was hopeless. One producer called him "a clumsy son
of a bitch." Still, they were so impressed they figured some intensive
dance training would sort him out. Lightfoot was hired. Rehearsals
began immediately, with the show set to debut in a primetime slot that
October. Lightfoot had to tell his parents and the bank that he was
quitting. Gord Sr., inherently cautious, worried that his son was being
hasty: "You're leaving your job to do what?"

Lightfoot was convinced that *Country Hoedown*, the square dancing notwithstanding, was a good move. The job paid twice as much as
the bank did, and for less work: two days of rehearsals at the Sumach
studios, then a third on Friday at Studio 4 on Yonge at Marlborough,*
where the show went live at 8 P.M. The show's set was a makeshift
barn, complete with wagon wheels and bales of straw, and its host,
Gordie Tapp, played a hayseed character in bib overalls and blackened
teeth. Members of the Singin' Swingin' Eight wore yoked cowboy
shirts or gingham crinoline dresses and usually performed five numbers each week, including such hokey fare as "Heel and Toe Polka"

---

* The former Pierce-Arrow automobile showroom, now a Staples business supply store.

and "Boomps-a-Daisy." The new kid in the cast was soon nicknamed "Gord Leadfoot" because of his tendency to allemande left instead of do-si-do right.

Still, Lightfoot loved the show's colorful characters, especially Gordie Tapp, who was pure cornball, and the redheaded Hames Sisters—Jean, Marjorie and Norma—who were "cute, bubbly and a lot of fun." Regular guests on the show included the Red & Les Trio, who were signed to Snider's Chateau label. Red and Les Pouliot hailed from Prince Albert, Saskatchewan. Red's real name was Laurice Pouliot, a former carny worker and freight train hopper who'd done a stint in prison. No one knew exactly what crime he'd committed. He changed his name to Red Shea to distance himself from his checkered past and became a mean guitar picker. Les could also play and was an aspiring songwriter (the trio was rounded out by bassist Bill Gibbs). In Toronto, Red and Les became known as the gas-guzzling Pouliot boys, siphoning petrol to run their beat-up convertible around town.

Country Hoedown's house band, fiddler King Ganam and his Sons of the West, included a tall, broad-shouldered guitarist named Tommy Hunter. One Friday, Lightfoot and Hunter arrived at the Yonge Street studio early. In the dressing room, Hunter took out his guitar and started playing the Carter Family's "Wildwood Flower," with its distinctive "Carter scratch" style of picking the melody on the bass strings while simultaneously strumming on the treble strings. Lightfoot was transfixed. "Play that again," he said. Hunter obliged, and was impressed that the newcomer showed so much interest. "If you listen to some of Gord's early recordings," says Hunter today, "there's a bit of Carter scratch in there." Lightfoot was learning tons, absorbing ideas at every turn.

Lightfoot and Whelan were now performing under a new name, the Two Tones. Impresario Billy O'Connor got them a few nightclub bookings and a variety and ice-show benefit for the Kiwanis Club. O'Connor boasted to the *Toronto Star* with astonishing hyperbole that the Two Tones had a "better sound than the Kingston Trio," America's popular folk group. The combination of O'Connor's promotional enthusiasm and Snider's industry acumen got Lightfoot and Whelan gigs on CBC shows like *Talent Caravan*. When the Two Tones appeared on the network's *While We're Young*, the duo performed Belafonte's Caribbean song "Don't Ever Love Me," and, with host Tommy Ambrose, tackled the Mexican-flavored "Three Caballeros." But as the *Toronto Star* wrote in a dismissive review, "The guitar-strumming lads kept away from anything even suggesting rock and roll, despite their superficial resemblance to the Everly Brothers."

Lightfoot wasn't about to allow a few snide jabs to derail him. He continued to plug away at his songwriting. Keeping up his *Country Hoedown* duties, and still believing the Two Tones could be a success, he also started moonlighting as a drummer with the Up Tempo '61 revue at the King Edward Hotel. And he kept even busier performing with Jack Zaza's band at its Friday night residency at the Orchard Park Tavern in the city's east end, drumming and singing as he'd done with Orillia's Charlie Andrews Orchestra.

Snider admired Lightfoot's ambition and took the Two Tones into the studio to make their first recording. The single "Lessons in Love," a breezy number written by Sy Soloway and Shirley Wolfe, came out on the Quality label. Its flip side was "Sweet Polly," a cheery tune penned by Les Pouliot. In an effort to boost radio play, the pair also recorded station breaks and safety checks that began with a chirpy "Hi, we're the Two Tones: Gordie Lightfoot and Terry Whelan." It didn't work: the single stiffed.

The sad truth was that the Two Tones were musically out of step with the times. A folk music boom was resounding across North America, sparked by the phenomenal success of the Kingston Trio's

earnest murder ballad "Tom Dooley." Audiences craved traditional
story songs with a ring of truth more than well-polished pop tunes.
New coffeehouses were featuring budding troubadours. And folk
festivals, the biggest being in Newport, Rhode Island, were springing
up everywhere—even in Lightfoot's hometown. There, Ruth Jones,
her husband, Dr. Crawford Jones, her brother, David Major, and
broadcaster Pete McGarvey launched Canada's first folk music festival and called it Mariposa, after Stephen Leacock's fictional name
for Orillia. Lightfoot applied for the Two Tones to appear but
was turned down, despite his duo's local connection. Their music was
judged too polished. Instead, the inaugural Mariposa, held in August
1961, featured the more "authentic" folk sounds of Alan Mills, Bonnie
Dobson, Ian Tyson and Sylvia Fricker and the Weavers-inspired
Travellers. Lightfoot was understandably hurt by the rejection.

By now, Lightfoot was living in a condemned building on Yorkville's
Avenue Road with four other Orillia lads. He continued composing his
own songs, carefully writing out the words and musical notation on
parchment paper and quietly registering them with the Library of
Congress in Washington, DC. In his bedroom in that rundown house,
he wrote "Remember Me (I'm the One)," a forlorn country ballad full
of regret and remorse about forsaking the woman he loves. The lyrics
went, "I'm the one who ran away and left you all alone / I'm the one
who broke your heart and scorned the love I'd known." Although the
story was a figment of his imagination, "Remember Me" was a harbin-
ger of songs Lightfoot would write about failed romance.

Lightfoot played "Remember Me" for Snider, who felt the song
had great potential. Snider convinced his protégé to drive with him
to Nashville to record it. Even better, he arranged for Chet Atkins,
one of the biggest names in country music, to assemble top Nashville
cats like guitarist Grady Martin and pianists Floyd Cramer and
Hargus "Pig" Robbins to play on the sessions at RCA Studios. Atkins
himself dropped in for the recording. "Knowing Chet was there got

me fired up," says Lightfoot. "I even tried to sing it in more of a bari-tone." It wouldn't be the last time Lightfoot would record in Nashville.

Lightfoot returned to Toronto armed with a dozen recorded songs that Snider planned to release on his new Chateau label. But first, Snider agreed to produce a live recording of the Two Tones. The Village Corner was the first club in the Yorkville coffeehouse district to feature live music regularly, promising "folksinging for the discriminating folknik." On the night of January 20, 1962, in the midst of a huge ice storm, Lightfoot and Whelan made their way to the club. While the crowd smoked and drank coffee in the cramped quarters down below, the duo waited upstairs for Snider and engineer Dave Newberry to arrive with the recording gear. The session finally got underway after midnight. Backed by stand-up bassist Howie Morris, the Two Tones performed a mix of traditional folk and country songs, calypso tunes and pop fare courtesy of Les Pouliot. There were also a couple of surprises: a spiritual popularized by Nina Simone, "Children, Go Where I Send Thee," and, more significantly, a brand-new Lightfoot composition, "This Is My Song." It was all captured on tape.

The album proved to be a good move. *Two Tones at the Village Corner* kept the Two Tones busy for much of 1962. Mariposa even booked the duo for its second festival in Orillia, slotting Lightfoot and Whelan (mistakenly billed as the "Tu Tones") into the Sunday afternoon schedule. No sooner were the Two Tones experiencing a little success than Whelan's fast-talking father started pushing for the pair to formalize their partnership. Lightfoot's dad disagreed. In his quiet, measured tone, Gord Sr. told his son, "You need to do this yourself." Lightfoot was caught in the middle.

I just wasn't happy. I was writing songs and Terry wasn't. But Terry's father, Tom, who worked in refrigeration and often acted like our man-ager, was really pressuring us to sign a partnership agreement that was

*going to split everything fifty-fifty. "It's a mutual pooling of talent," he
said, "no matter what."*

Meanwhile, Snider released "Remember Me," and the single was
climbing the charts. *Country Hoedown's* producers asked Lightfoot
to sing it on the show. It was the first time he'd ever performed on
Hoedown without the rest of the Singin' Swingin' Eight. Everyone
praised his smooth, confident performance. Lightfoot knew it was
time to end it with Whelan.

*I went back to Orillia and was so upset by the prospect that I fell face down
in my aunt's living room and had a nervous breakdown. I didn't want to
break up with Terry, but I just knew that I had to. It was just like getting
a divorce.*

While agonizing over ending the duo, Lightfoot moved into a
new rooming house on Admiral Road. It was right around the corner
from the Dupont Street laundromat where homeless busking musician and future Lovin' Spoonful member Zal Yanovsky was sleeping in
a clothes dryer. One of Lightfoot's new housemates was a young blond
woman whose room was down the hallway from his. Brita Olaisson
had arrived from Sweden with the intention of learning English while
working for the Toronto office of M.P. Hofstetter, a Swedish type-
writer and office supply company. Lightfoot was instantly smitten and
invited her out to George's Spaghetti House for some pasta and jazz.
Later, in his room, she listened to him sing his songs and began
advising him about his career that very night. Brita was brainy and
beautiful, with a clear level-headedness that impressed her new boyfriend. With Brita egging him on, Lightfoot delivered the difficult
news to Whelan that he was through with the Two Tones.

Lightfoot and Brita saw each other frequently over the next
several months. They'd get together in the evenings for dinner and

talk about how work had gone for her at the office and for him at the studio. Brita listened intently to Gordon's latest news about upcoming shows and recordings (Snider was releasing two more singles from the Nashville sessions on his Chateau label). And she was able to practice her English as she offered advice or opinions. Brita was full of encouragement and had a confidence that Lightfoot admired. He knew she was only in Toronto for a short time, but he couldn't help himself—he was falling in love with her.

With Snider's help, Lightfoot began getting solo gigs. First, he appeared on CFTO-TV's *Hi Time*, a variety show hosted by Canadian teen idol Bobby Curtola. Then, alongside fellow Chateau recording artist Pat Hervey, Lightfoot performed at the Hull Arena for what was advertised as a "Mammoth Dance Party." Snider's own trio opened, and Hervey and Lightfoot received top billing, highlighted by their respective hits: her "Mr. Heartache" and his "Remember Me." Before the year was out, he appeared at a New Year's Eve dance at Club 888 in Toronto's Masonic Temple, backed by Dave Newberry and His Orchestra. Lightfoot seemed noticeably uncomfortable performing solo. Whelan had always spoken to audiences and handled song introductions; now, Lightfoot had to do that all by himself as well as carry the songs. By the end of the year, he was wondering whether he could make it on his own. To make matters worse, Brita had returned to Sweden.

FOUR

Early Morning Rain

By 1963, Toronto was becoming a hotbed for folk music. Coffeehouses were opening throughout the city's bohemian Yorkville district, all offering stages and attentive audiences for aspiring troubadours. This was good news for Lightfoot, although he'd now have to get used to singing with just his guitar—no band or orchestra backing. The more Lightfoot wrestled with uncertainty, the more he realized how much he missed Brita. Soon, he was phoning, begging her to return. "Brita gave me a sense of security that I lost as soon as she went back to Sweden," Lightfoot says now. "I knew she was going back, but I didn't say anything at the time to make her stay. And the insecurity set in." He had already been booked to make weeklong appearances in February and March at the Village Corner and Fifth Peg coffeehouses. Once he met those commitments, he made his decision: he quit *Country Hoedown* in mid-season and flew to Sweden with a marriage proposal. His parents were dead set against it, but there was no talking Gordie out of it.

On April 6, 1963, Lightfoot, twenty-four, and Olaisson, twenty-six, married in the Seglora Church in Skansen, the open-air museum in Brita's hometown of Stockholm, and left the church in a horse-drawn buggy. None of Lightfoot's family flew over for the nuptials.

After the party, the couple set off on a weeklong skiing honeymoon in the Norwegian town of Lillehammer. The following month, the new-lyweds moved to London, England. Lightfoot had called his producer friend Snider, who'd got in touch with a London agent named Phillip Solomon. On the strength of Lightfoot's *Country Hoedown* experience, Solomon lined up a job for him on *The Country and Western Show*, a summer replacement series on the BBC.

Brita and Gordon moved into a fourth-floor apartment at 56 Gloucester Road, in London's Kensington district. Each day, Lightfoot took the Tube out to the BBC studios in Shepherd's Bush for rehearsals. The producers quickly realized he was not cut out for the hosting job they had in mind, so Gordie Lightfoot, as he was billed, performed with a cast that included names like Dougie Squires and the Hickory Sticks and Pete Stanley and His Tennessee Mountaineers. With live horses and corny scripting, the show was similar to *Country Hoedown*. The producers' idea of country and western had more to do with stage musicals like *Oklahoma!* and *Annie Get Your Gun* than the twanging sounds of Nashville, but Lightfoot tried to make it work. He spent hours in the BBC's record library looking for songs to sing on the show. "I did Buck Owens's 'Foolin' Around,' Johnny Cash's 'The Troubadour' and songs by England's Frank Ifield, who was huge at that time."

Two of *The Country and Western Show*'s most prominent guest stars were pop singer Alma Cogan, Britain's highest paid female entertainer and later a friend of the Beatles, and comedian Frankie Howerd, then also appearing in the network's top-rated satirical series *That Was the Week That Was* and a future star of the popular *Carry On* movies. Lightfoot got to watch these veteran performers up close while earning a decent wage and gaining on-camera experience. At night, he was tuning into pirate radio, unlicensed illegal radio stations that broadcast from international waters, and picking up on some of the licks he heard. All the while, Lightfoot kept up his songwriting.

It was an exciting time to be in London. A youthful look of short skirts and close-cropped hair was sweeping through the fashion world, while sharply dressed Mods on scooters clashed with leather-jacketed Rockers on motorcycles. Late-night coffee bars and music clubs, once swinging to jazz and skiffle, were suddenly rocking to the energetic sounds of rhythm and blues and Jamaican ska. This was the scene, at places like Oxford Street's Marquee Club or Soho's Flamingo Club, where Manfred Mann, Georgie Fame and the Rolling Stones all got their start. But it was the "Fab Four" from Liverpool that caused the biggest sensation in London that summer, topping the charts and sparking the fan frenzy quickly dubbed Beatlemania. Lightfoot was there to witness it.

When the Beatles burst on the scene, I watched it with my own eyes on TV. "I'll give it five [out of five]," the girl on Juke Box Jury *would say. They'd have a panel, and they would rate the singles of the week on the television show. And every time those Beatles came on, everybody in the whole panel would give them a five at the same time. All you had to do was to take one look and—boom—there it was: "These guys can't miss," you thought. Immediately, they had about five other acts imitating them. The Rolling Stones came out about a week after them, and they too were all over the charts.*

The new English beat groups impressed Lightfoot—but not enough to prompt a change in musical direction. Through Phillip Solomon, he hooked up with Clodagh Rodgers, an Irish singer who'd just been signed by Decca Records. Together, they recorded a series of demos, but in swinging London there were no takers for the pair's pop duets. Lightfoot had never intended on staying in England, so when *The Country and Western Show* finished, he and Brita had a cold, wind-swept holiday in Cork, on Ireland's southern coast, and flew back to Canada. The plan? To get Gordie's career on track and start a family. In fact, Brita was already pregnant.

———

While Lightfoot was away, Toronto's club and coffeehouse scene had continued to flourish. On Yonge Street, it was all licensed bars, where the legal drinking age was twenty-one. Rock 'n' roll and rhythm 'n' blues were the drawing cards there, led by a larger-than-life character from Arkansas. A rockabilly contemporary of Elvis Presley, Ronnie Hawkins had migrated north and declared Toronto the "promised land," because Yonge Street's long strip of neon-glowing bars offered sweet salvation for a hungry musician. Hawkins put together the Hawks, a crack outfit of players—Levon Helm, Rick Danko, Richard Manuel, Garth Hudson and Robbie Robertson—who would later form the Band. Their frequent shows at Le Coq d'Or became so popular that lineups snaked around the block.

Up in Yorkville, it was an entirely different scene. More than a dozen unlicensed coffeehouses were operating in the former working-class Victorian houses along the tree-lined streets, all catering to younger audiences. Folk music was the dominant sound in the "village," where singer-songwriters commanded attention and the strongest drink available was espresso. Some of the leading folk musicians, at coffeehouses like the Village Corner, the Purple Onion and the Penny Farthing, included Bonnie Dobson, the Travellers and Malka & Joso. But the biggest stars were Ian & Sylvia. The handsome couple had already ventured to New York and wowed audiences with their gorgeous harmonies and eclectic repertoire, which included Ian's "Four Strong Winds" and Sylvia's as-yet-unrecorded "You Were On My Mind." As soon as Lightfoot heard them, he knew their marriage of folk and country styles was the sound he wanted.

Gordon and Brita stayed initially in a motel on Toronto's lakefront before finding a basement apartment at 413 Arlington Avenue, near Oakwood and Vaughan. Lightfoot was anxious to get back onstage. Oddly enough, he began performing his folk songs not in Yorkville but smack in the middle of the Yonge Street strip. Fran's Restaurant was a family-owned business specializing in affordable comfort food. Lightfoot convinced the manager that his folk songs would be a good addition to the diner's atmosphere. Hawkins dropped in one night and liked Lightfoot's sound. But he was surprised to find him playing at Fran's. "You should be on the east side of Yonge Street," he told Lightfoot. "That's where the action is." Lightfoot took the advice and promptly got himself booked across the street at Steele's Tavern. Says Hawkins, "Gordie had a good ear and played great gee-tar. I used to go see him whenever I could and loved listening to him sing Marty Robbins songs."

On February 1, Brita gave birth to their first child, a boy they named Francis, who'd been conceived on their Norwegian honeymoon. Two days later, the new father began a monthlong residency at Steele's. Run by Greek immigrant Steele Basil, the tavern was sandwiched between Toronto's two landmark record stores, Sam the Record Man and A&A Records, vinyl heaven for music fans. Steele's had a restaurant on the main floor and a bar, exotically named the Venetian Lounge, upstairs. During that bitterly cold February, Lightfoot set up shop in the distinctly un-exotic lounge, singing every night for anyone who would listen over the racket at the bar and the hockey games on the TV.

Musically, Lightfoot was paying close attention to Chicago folk singer Bob Gibson. But it was New York's Bob Dylan who really turned his head. By the beginning of 1964, Dylan had already released three albums. Lightfoot studied all of them in great detail and challenged himself to dig deeper with his own songwriting. He started singing his own material at Steele's. Ian and Sylvia heard about Lightfoot. One night, the couple climbed the stairs at Steele's to see what he was all about. The first thing Sylvia noticed was his stage presence. "He was very contained, but a solid enough performer to clearly get his own songs across." Lightfoot sang "For Lovin' Me," a song with tough-guy posturing that was clearly inspired by Dylan's "Don't Think Twice, It's All Right." But the song that really made Sylvia sit up and take notice was an evocative ballad called "Early Morning Rain."

This old airport's got me down, it's no earthly good to me
'Cause I'm stuck here on the ground, as cold and drunk as I can be
You can't jump a jet plane like you can a freight train
So I'd best be on my way in the early morning rain

Lightfoot had never written anything with such clarity before. Personal and poetic, "Early Morning Rain" expressed a palpable longing while expertly contrasting the rural past and urban present in one brilliant line about freight trains and jet planes. There was real emotion in the song. Lightfoot had placed himself directly in the story, summoning his own experience of travel and homesickness for inspiration. It paid off. Lightfoot's memories of big 707s, a rain-soaked runway and feeling a long way from home had given him his first great song.

Lightfoot had composed it in his cramped basement apartment earlier that month. Brita was out, and baby Francis, just a few weeks old, was asleep in his bassinet next to him. The lyrics, about being broke and stuck on the ground while jets are taking off without him, were drawn from Lightfoot's time at Westlake in Los Angeles. "Some nights, we didn't have much to do and weren't far from the airport," Lightfoot recalls, "so we'd drive out and stand and watch the airplanes landing and taking off. I liked doing that kind of thing. And one time it was raining like crazy, a real steady downpour like they sometimes used to get out in Los Angeles."

Lightfoot played other material for Ian and Sylvia. They could see his growth as a songwriter. "I liked everything about Gord's approach to music and singing," says Ian. Tyson got Lightfoot to put some of his songs on tape and took them to Albert Grossman's office in midtown Manhattan. Grossman was Ian & Sylvia's manager and the dean of the Greenwich Village folk scene. When he first heard Ian & Sylvia he'd promptly added the Canadian duo to a stellar artist roster that included Dylan, Odetta and Peter, Paul and Mary. A powerful, intimidating figure in the music world, Grossman was renowned for his tough negotiating style. Although he was ruthless in his devotion to his clients, he didn't speak much and cultivated an air of mystery and inscrutability that earned him the nickname "the floating Buddha." Dylan described first meeting Grossman at the Gaslight Cafe in Greenwich Village: "He looked like Sydney Greenstreet from the film *The Maltese Falcon*, had an enormous presence, always dressed in a conventional suit and tie, and he sat at his corner table. Usually when he talked, his voice was loud like the booming of war drums. He didn't talk so much as growl."

Grossman listened to Lightfoot's songs and quickly dispatched his partner, John Court, to Toronto to check him out. Court had been with Grossman since their days running the Gate of Horn, Chicago's premier folk club. He was already knocked out by what he'd heard on tape, especially "Early Morning Rain" and "For Lovin' Me," which proved that the Canadian was "one heck of a songsmith." But seeing Lightfoot perform sealed the deal (he remembered it being at Steele's, although Lightfoot believes it was the Purple Onion). "I was really impressed with his voice," Court told this author in 1996. "The truth behind any successful singer is that people must trust the voice, be able to relax with it and go on the singer's journey. And Gord had one of those wonderful voices."

That night, Court approached Lightfoot with an offer. "We'd like to sign you," he told him. Lightfoot couldn't believe his ears. Representation by Court and Grossman would put him in the same stable as some of the biggest names in folk music. The pair could book him into key venues in the States and were promising to land him a record deal with an American label as soon as possible. Lightfoot needed that. Breaking into the US market was crucial to success, and there was no significant record label in the nascent Canadian recording industry capable of doing that. But as attractive as the offer was, Lightfoot hesitated about signing. Like his father, he was inherently cautious. Plus, he tended to shy away from binding agreements, remembering his uneasy partnership with Whelan. It ultimately took Ian Tyson yelling "Don't be an idiot, Gord. Sign!" to force his hand.

One of the first things Court and Grossman did for Lightfoot was place his song "For Lovin' Me" with Peter, Paul and Mary, the folk trio that Grossman put together in 1961. An attractive blonde between two fashionable goatees, the group of Peter Yarrow, Noel Paul Stookey and Mary Travers had already topped the charts with "Puff (the Magic Dragon)" and its cover of Dylan's "Blowin' in the Wind." When they recorded "For Lovin' Me" later that year, it had none of the cavalier quality of the heartless lover in Lightfoot's brisk original, and lines like "I got a hundred more like you . . . I'll have a thousand 'fore I'm through" were no longer a boast. Yarrow had a different interpretation: "It's a wrenching song for me. The singer wasn't gloating about breaking this person's heart, he was in a kind of despair about his inability to be constructive in love." For Yarrow, this was something new. Like Dylan's "Don't Think Twice, It's All Right," it offered "an honest look at life's dilemmas, not just a Pollyanna view of relationships."

Dylan's mentor, a Brooklyn-born Jewish troubadour born Elliot Charles Adnopoz who went by the name Ramblin' Jack Elliott, was renowned in folk music circles. He remembers hearing "For Lovin' Me" for the first time in the fall of 1964, when Stookey of Peter, Paul and Mary sang it to him. Stookey had spotted Elliott on a Greenwich Village sidewalk. Says Elliott, "I needed to get to a gig at Yale University, and Paul kindly offered me a ride. As we're driving along in his brown Jaguar convertible, he starts singing, 'That's what you get for lovin' me.' I said, 'What's that?' He explained that his trio had just recorded it and proceeded to sing it all the way to Connecticut. This was long before I ever met Gordon."

Meanwhile, Lightfoot was busy honing his stagecraft. In April 1964, he performed at Massey Hall for the Canadian Folk Festival, a hootenanny led by Oscar Brand. That same month, he appeared on *Music Hop*, CBC's new *American Bandstand*-style series hosted by future game-show guru and *Jeopardy* host Alex Trebek. In the same Yonge Street studio where he'd worked on *Country Hoedown*, Lightfoot sang Pete Seeger's "If I Had a Hammer" and Ian & Sylvia's "You Were On My Mind." The house band that backed him, Norm Amadio and His Rhythm Rockers, included ginger-haired guitarist Red Shea and a baby-faced bassist named John Stockfish. Lightfoot remembered Shea from the Red & Les Trio on *Country Hoedown*. Little did he, Shea or Stockfish know, but fate would soon reunite them. After the performance, Trebek invited "Gordie" to join him for a chat in the audience. Surrounded by visibly excited teenage girls, Lightfoot shared news that his friends Ian and Sylvia had just recorded one of his songs for their next album.

It was already becoming a busy year for Lightfoot. Then came another TV appearance, this time with Judy Collins and the Clancy Brothers on *Let's Sing Out*. After opening for country music pioneer Ernest Tubb at Toronto's Club Kingsway, Lightfoot began the summer touring season. First stop was the Algoma Folk Festival, up north in Sault Ste. Marie, Ontario, where he appeared in an all-Canadian lineup with Alan Mills, the Travellers, Bonnie Dobson, the Chanteclairs and others. Dobson, who was already making a name for herself with "Morning Dew," her stark ballad of nuclear dread, remembers the weekend festival as being fun but poorly attended. It was the first time she'd heard Lightfoot. "You knew just listening to him what an amazing writer he was," she says. "A great voice, very warm and approachable and not at all full of himself like some people."

But the highlight of the summer circuit in Canada was Mariposa, and Lightfoot was set to make his solo debut at the festival. Relocated to Toronto's Maple Leaf Stadium after rowdies forced its cancellation in Orillia, the festival featured veteran blues star Mississippi John Hurt, bluegrass group the Greenbriar Boys and Buffy Sainte-Marie, who'd just released her debut album, which included the anti-war anthem "Universal Soldier." Lightfoot was booked to perform at the Saturday evening concert and take part in a Sunday afternoon "religious concert," sharing both shows with Sonny Terry & Brownie McGhee. But the duo had mistakenly gone to Orillia, so blind blues singer Reverend Gary Davis, who happened to be in town, took their place. Lightfoot, performing in suit vest and tie, delivered a polished set on Saturday night and contributed a couple of folk songs with a spiritual feel to Sunday's workshop. His accompanist was David Rea, a seventeen-year-old bespectacled guitar whiz from Akron, Ohio, who'd settled in Toronto. When Rea wasn't where he was supposed to be Sunday morning, Lightfoot went looking for him and found him over at the Village Corner club. "He'd been up all night learning everything he could from Reverend Gary Davis, soaking it up like a sponge," says Lightfoot. "That was David."

Lightfoot took Rea with him to New York in December 1964 for his first major recording session. Albert Grossman had been busy trying to land Lightfoot a recording contract. As he'd done with Dylan and his other artists, Grossman wanted Lightfoot to record as many of his own songs as possible so that he could shop them around, and Warner Bros. agreed to finance some demos. Grossman and Court had booked time for him at Columbia's 30th Street Studio in Manhattan. The building was nicknamed the "Church" because it had been an Armenian house of worship. Its two rooms, the large Studio C and the more intimate Studio D, were considered the best-sounding in the business. Miles Davis, Duke Ellington and Billie Holiday all recorded at the Church, as well as two prominent Canadians: Glenn Gould cut his groundbreaking *Goldberg Variations* there in 1955, and in the same location Percy Faith taped his instrumental classic "Theme from a Summer Place," which topped the pop charts in 1960.

Their sessions overseen by Court, Lightfoot and Rea set up in Studio D and were joined by two experienced African-American session players, both in high demand. Bruce Langhorne was a guitarist with a strong, rhythmic style who had graced albums by Dylan and other Greenwich Village folkies and inspired the title character of Dylan's "Mr. Tambourine Man." Bill Lee was a bassist with credits on recordings by Odetta, John Lee Hooker and Ian & Sylvia's self-titled album (he was also the father of future film director Spike Lee). With Rea, Lee and Langhorne, Lightfoot recorded a large number of songs, including "Early Morning Rain" and thirteen others that would eventually appear on his solo debut recording. But first, Grossman had some negotiating to do to find the right record label.

Lightfoot spent much of his time in Toronto on Yonge Street. It seemed like everyone he knew or admired was on the radio or appearing in bigger venues around town. His pal Ronnie Hawkins was getting airplay with "Bluebirds Over the Mountain," his latest single on his own Hawk record label. Hawkins's former backing band was appearing as Levon & the Hawks at Friar's Tavern, while Johnny Cash and Pete Seeger were headlining at Massey Hall on successive nights. Meanwhile, Buffy Sainte-Marie, who'd starred at the 1964 Newport Folk Festival, was giving a concert at Ryerson Theatre. Lightfoot was itching to get in the game.

Grossman arranged Lightfoot's first US appearance with a guest spot at Greenwich Village's Gaslight—the very club in which Lightfoot had seen Dylan perform. From New York, Lightfoot drove west to appear on a multi-artist bill at Detroit's Masonic Temple. It's a wonder he made it there at all: a major winter storm brought the city to a standstill. Still, the so-called Ford CARavan of Music, sponsored by the big automaker, went ahead. The lineup was all over the map. Lightfoot played on the same bill as the Oscar Peterson Trio, political comedian Vaughn Meader, singing poet Steve DePass and folk ensemble the Serendipity Singers. As Lightfoot told writer Barrie Hale in a *Toronto Telegram* feature called "Dig That Country 'n' Lightfoot Beat," "Any way you look at it, we had everything covered—jazz, jazz-pop, pop, pop-folk, folk, folk-country and politics. Everything but rock 'n' roll."

By late 1964, Lightfoot was back at Steele's. From the stage one night, he noticed one particular man watching him intently. Bernie Fiedler was a former salesman who, seeing the value of selling coffee by the cup rather than the pound, had just opened a new coffeehouse in Yorkville. The Riverboat was a nautical-themed joint, with portholes, brass poles and pine-paneled walls. Committed to featuring top folk talent, Fiedler had got wind of Lightfoot and was there to see him perform. "As soon as he came off stage," says Fiedler, "I said, 'Hi, I'm Bernie Fiedler. I own the Riverboat. Whatever this guy is paying you, I'll do double. I want you to come play my club.'" As it turned out, Lightfoot and Fiedler had much in common. Both had been boy sopranos (Fiedler in his native Germany), and both had an eye for pretty blondes. Lightfoot accepted Fiedler's offer to play a weeklong showcase at his club. Immediately, Toronto's media took notice. *The Globe and Mail*'s Marvin Schiff credited Lightfoot with singing in a "guileless manner that is extremely appealing." But, he noted, "There is still a self-consciousness about his stage manner" that "impedes his between-songs banter, making it seem somewhat inane and superfluous."

Lightfoot clearly needed to polish his act, but he had no shortage of supporters around him. Johnny Bassett, a former tennis pro whose father owned the CFTO-TV station and *Toronto Telegram* newspaper, had befriended Lightfoot. Bassett, with Sam Sniderman, the charismatic owner of the Sam the Record Man store, organized a celebration at Steele's Tavern to toast the rising star's new recording, a single on Warner Bros. As parties go, it was a modest affair, with sandwiches paid for by the label and beer donated by Steele Basil, but a large number of media types and members of the folk music community turned up. Ian Tyson (who Lightfoot liked to call "Ned," after Neddie Seagoon, a character on the BBC's *The Goon Show*, a radio comedy they were both fond of) introduced the man of the hour, who delivered strong performances of both sides of his new single: "I'm Not Sayin'" and "For Lovin' Me." Lightfoot explained to one reporter in attendance, "They're 'mistreating' songs about love scenes that just aren't happening." He didn't say how close to home that message might be.

Lightfoot had spent most of his son's first eighteen months on the road, and the constant touring was causing problems at home. The *Toronto Star*'s esteemed critic Nathan Cohen predicted that Lightfoot would be "the next Toronto performer who should move out of the folk song fold into bigger things." But he added that Lightfoot's one complaint about singing was that it kept him up late. "When that happens he spends too much of the day in bed, and when that happens he doesn't concentrate on his songwriting, which, at the moment, is where most of the money is." Clearly, Lightfoot was paying more attention to work than to his wife and infant son, whom they'd now taken to calling Fred.

But, as Cohen made clear, songwriting—and the lucrative royalty payments that came with it—was the priority. Like his father before him, Lightfoot took the responsibility of feeding his family seriously. While other musicians were more relaxed about such things, Lightfoot approached his career in a determined, disciplined way.

"I'm Not Sayin'," Lightfoot's single on Warner, didn't get the expected US airplay. But Grossman successfully shopped it. The singer Nico (later of Velvet Underground fame) recorded a version with guitarist Jimmy Page that was produced by the Rolling Stones' Brian Jones. Meanwhile, Ian & Sylvia's record that spring featured both "For Lovin' Me" and "Early Morning Rain," which gave their album its title. And Peter, Paul and Mary's version of "For Lovin' Me" was getting significant radio play. For Lightfoot, it was a game changer: "When I first heard Peter, Paul and Mary sing my song on Top 40 radio, I nearly jumped out of my skin. I heard it and thought, 'Is this for real?'" Lightfoot didn't have time to celebrate—he had to keep writing.

Every place Lightfoot went in 1965 seemed to spark new songs. In May, he took an eighteen-hour train trip up to Moosonee, a mostly Cree community, on the shores of James Bay. He wanted to see the wilderness and find inspiration in Ontario's remote north or, as he put it, "absorb the whistle stops." There'd be plenty of stops on the 520-mile trip north to Moosonee and back. It proved highly useful, resulting in two brand-new compositions: "Steel Rail Blues" and "Sixteen Miles," each full of poetic longing and honest reflection. His writing was becoming deeper and more expressive. "Sixteen Miles" was the first time he'd written so passionately about Canada's landscape, expressing something of the awe and wonder he felt when walking in the woods in Marchmont with his father and mother. Now he was able to articulate those feelings for the natural beauty around him.

Later that month, Lightfoot performed both new songs at Stan Kain's La Cave (pronounced *kahv*), a small subterranean coffeehouse in Cleveland. Lightfoot didn't know it, but Kain had booked him for the weekend to open for Odetta, the acclaimed spiritual singer. His nervousness was evident when he bumbled his way through the introduction to "Sixteen Miles," as can be heard on a bootleg recording. "If you want to go, you can. I'll probably do a long set," he told the small crowd. "I have this thing: I always like the audience to be interested. Usually, they're not . . . always interested. If you do a long set, you kind of feel that you're . . ." He stopped himself there and let out a nervous laugh before adding, "I put my foot in my mouth there." Once again, Lightfoot proved himself to be eloquent in song but painfully inept in conversation.

Cleveland wasn't a total disaster. During intermissions, Lightfoot would cross the street and catch performances by Stepin Fetchit, the African-American vaudeville comedian played by Lincoln Perry. He later wrote "Minstrel of the Dawn" about the man who'd "make you laugh and bend your ear." Another song came to him while staying at Kain's downtown apartment. "It was hot and humid and I was missing Brita," Lightfoot says. "A storm came up, with thunder, lightning—everything. I had half a bottle of booze, and I started writing a song. For some reason, my mind never moved off the idea of winter the whole time." That became "Song for a Winter's Night," a snowy Canadian classic written on a sultry summer night in Cleveland.

Lightfoot conveyed an intimacy on "Song for a Winter's Night" that would become one of his hallmarks. Its lyrics—simple yet precise and a little old-fashioned—paint a scene of a cabin in the woods, snow falling outside, a fireplace glowing inside and a letter read over and over by lamplight with a drink that needs replenishing. The narrator is alone and longing for a lover. It's a theme as old as the earliest poems and Elizabethan sonnets. When Lightfoot sings

"If I could only have you near, to breathe a sigh or two," he's conjuring up shades of Shelley or Wordsworth. "Song for a Winter's Night" has grown to become a Canadian Christmas favorite, sung by Blue Rodeo, Sarah McLachlan and Mary Margaret O'Hara. But its cozy sentiments have also appealed to non-Canadians, from Harry Belafonte and Tony Rice to Nana Mouskouri, illustrating the universal appeal of Lightfoot's best songs.

Whenever he was in Toronto, Lightfoot was spending more and more time drinking and hanging out with Ian Tyson and Ronnie Hawkins. Bar crawls on Yonge Street weren't always possible, since the three would often be working. But Hawkins, who pretty much had the run of Le Coq d'Or, kept the place open and made sure the club's go-go dancers stuck around so that he and his buddies could trade songs and party with the girls long after closing. Sometimes the carousing continued into the wee hours back at Hawkins's apartment in the city's west end. "My mother had a big house on High Park Avenue with several apartments," says Ronnie's wife, Wanda, "and Ronnie and I moved into one of them after I got pregnant. Our bedroom was in our living room. Some nights, Ron would arrive home with Gord. They'd stagger in and start singing and picking away on guitars. And I was right there, trying to sleep."

Lightfoot's friendship with Fiedler also deepened. Like Hawkins, Fiedler became like family. Fiedler had married Patti Tancock, and the two had opened Yorkville's Mousehole coffeehouse, which Patti ran while Bernie operated the Riverboat. The couple frequently threw summer parties at their house on leafy Roxborough Avenue and would invite Gord and Brita and other artists and their partners to lounge by their backyard pool. One afternoon, Lightfoot did something totally unexpected: he dove fully clothed off Fiedler's roof into the swimming pool. "It was a real stretch, and the pool wasn't that deep," says Fiedler. "Any miscalculation and he could've hit the concrete side. Our hearts all stood still, but that was Gordon." Alcohol was likely involved on that occasion, but at another Fiedler pool party, Lightfoot's quick thinking averted a potential drowning. Says Fiedler, "One of my waitresses, Susan, had brought her baby to the party. We were all around the pool and suddenly the baby fell in. Everyone froze, but Gord leaned over, shot his arm down into the water and pulled the baby out in seconds. It was quite amazing."

In June 1965, Fiedler booked Lightfoot back in at the Riverboat. During his three-week residency, something shifted: Lightfoot began attracting growing numbers of female fans, moon-eyed girls who sighed at his poetry and stayed behind afterward, hoping for an autograph or something more. Lightfoot was becoming a star, and girls were frequently throwing themselves at him—something new for the shy Orillia boy. His fortunes were also changing: where Lightfoot was once covering Marty Robbins, the "El Paso" singer was now covering him. Robbins's recording of "Ribbon of Darkness" had just topped the *Billboard* Country chart and would stay there for seven months, which thrilled its composer. At the Riverboat, Lightfoot sang "Ribbon of Darkness" and debuted a comical song, a number called "Talkin' Silver Cloud Blues" written in honor of the time Hawkins strolled into a Toronto Rolls-Royce dealership and purchased one of the luxury cars—with cold cash. Harry Belafonte, who was making one of his frequent appearances at the O'Keefe Centre, dropped in to check out Lightfoot's songs for his own albums.

While Lightfoot was at the Riverboat, Phil Ochs was performing around the corner at the New Gate of Cleve coffeehouse. One of America's "angry young men of song," and second only to Dylan as a protest singer, Ochs had already become a star of the Greenwich Village scene with songs like "Talkin' Vietnam" and "Here's to the State of Mississippi." Lightfoot heard him sing and was blown away by his "Mississippi" song. But he was even more taken with "Changes," a bittersweet ballad about the fleeting nature of life that Ochs had just written there on the Gate of Cleve's back steps. Lightfoot decided to record it himself.

Ochs was equally impressed with Lightfoot, and the two became fast friends. A former journalism student at Ohio State University, Ochs wrote a nine-hundred-word article about his Canadian chum for *Broadside*, the US folk song magazine, titled "The Ballad of Gordon Lightfoot." The piece opens, "There I was in Canada, stoned out of my mind at 5 in the morning, swapping songs, jokes and bottles with Ronnie Hawkins, the Arkansas rock 'n' roll singer who runs an out of sight bar in Toronto, and Gordon Lightfoot, who is the Canadian Hank Williams. As I listened to Lightfoot sing away that intoxicated morning, I knew he had it." Ochs went on to write that Lightfoot was constantly apologizing for not writing "important" protest songs, yet "he can sing, play, entertain, write, put himself down with a flair that marks an original. Ingrained in the natural Lightfoot is the same spark of human insight that carried Hank Williams, Jimmie Rodgers and Johnny Cash out of show business and into immortality." Then Ochs added, "Now everybody has his faults, and Lightfoot is no exception. He plays golf."

Later that month, Grossman booked Lightfoot at the prestigious Newport Folk Festival, which had previously provided a showcase for Joan Baez, Dylan and Ian & Sylvia. Founded by George Wein, the man behind the well-established Newport Jazz Festival, the folk festival that year featured the biggest names in traditional and popular acoustic music. Baez, Peter, Paul and Mary, Odetta, the New Lost City Ramblers and Ian & Sylvia all appeared in evening concerts. Lightfoot took part in the Sunday afternoon concert, sharing the stage with Patrick Sky and Richard & Mimi Fariña. Interviewed that morning by *The New York Times*'s Robert Shelton, Lightfoot said that he was "aiming at a new thing . . . in the area in between folk and country." Richly melodic and full of small-town yearnings and big-city dreams, his songs were bridging a noticeable gap in the troubadour genre: heartfelt poetry delivered with a sophisticated twang. Helping him forge that new sound were seasoned session players Red Shea and John Stockfish, with whom he had played on the CBC. From that point on, he called on Shea and Stockfish whenever he could afford their backing.

The highlight of Newport '65 was Dylan's appearance, which dramatically altered the musical landscape and signaled the death of folk. His loud, electrified performance on Saturday night, backed by the Paul Butterfield Blues Band, overshadowed everything else at the festival and created a howl heard around the world. Controversy raged. Folk purists screamed "traitor," while rock fans embraced the new sound. In his book *Dylan Goes Electric!*, a colorful and extensive account of the event, Elijah Wald calls it "the night that split the Sixties." It was certainly divisive. Some believed Pete Seeger had an axe and wanted to cut the electrical cables, when in fact he just wanted the volume lowered. There was certainly a lot of booing, over either Dylan's sound or the shortness of his set. Lightfoot watched the whole thing go down from the sidelines.

Pete Seeger and a lot of people were in disagreement about whether to bring the drum kit for Dylan onstage. It would have been the first time anyone had done that at Newport. When Dylan and the band started playing, there was a little booing and some people threw pennies. But most people got into it pretty fast. The best thing I saw was Albert Grossman and [folk scholar] Alan Lomax get into a wrestling match on the ground [during an argument about the volume of Dylan's set]. It was almost like you see on TV. It was a very dry day and the dust was a-flying! That's what I remember.

With Dylan's defiant display at Newport, the genie was out of the bottle. From that point on in 1965, the music charts, as Dylan authority Greil Marcus wrote, "changed every week [and] changed so radically they hijacked memory, to the point that whatever happened the week before could seem to have happened years ago." Dylan was an enormous influence on Lightfoot. "I'd seen him at the Gaslight in New York and thought, 'God, that's good writing. Maybe I can write a great song too.' I was very shy, but Bob always treated me well." There would never have been a Lightfoot song as ambitious as "Early Morning Rain," as confident as "I'm Not Sayin'" or as rooted in tradition as "Ribbon of Darkness" had Dylan not come along.

After Newport, Lightfoot agreed to profile Dylan for the *Toronto Telegram*'s weekly youth supplement "After Four," which was also the name of a local TV show Lightfoot was hosting. Lightfoot arranged to meet Dylan at Grossman's rural retreat in Woodstock, New York. When Dylan arrived, Lightfoot wrote, "he looked as if he had jumped from a passing motorcycle. His glasses, still intact, were horn-rimmed, and he was carrying four volumes of who knows what. . . . After a good meal and a glass of champagne, I questioned him at length about the controversy over his new songbag." Dylan told him, "The stuff I used to write, well there's about a dozen guys writing that stuff now. Right now, I'd like to see someone try to imitate the things I'm doing." Lightfoot noted that Dylan liked a number of his songs, especially "I'm Not Sayin'," while Lightfoot had just recorded Dylan's "Just Like Tom Thumb's Blues." When he and Dylan went to shoot pool, Lightfoot reported that he was "thoroughly put upon for not knowing how to play eight ball."

For all the attention Lightfoot was receiving, he remained deeply frustrated that he still didn't have an album in stores. Since Grossman signed him, Lightfoot had watched as Ian & Sylvia released three albums. The prolific Dylan, against whom he measured himself most, had six out. Timing is everything in the music world, and Lightfoot felt he was missing his moment. Dylan's electric single, "Like a

Rolling Stone," had already topped the charts, signaling the changing tides.

By the fall of 1965, Grossman and Court (a partnership now formalized as Groscourt Productions) finally landed Lightfoot a new record deal. Strangely enough, it was with United Artists, not Warner Bros., which had passed on releasing an album. United Artists was a curious home for a rising singer-songwriter. The label had been formed to distribute records of its movie soundtracks, the biggest of which was the Beatles' *A Hard Day's Night*. Its few recording stars consisted of actors or pop crooners like Steve Lawrence and Diahann Carroll or duo pianists Ferrante and Teicher. Still, the label was promising big things for its new signing. First up was Lightfoot's debut United Artists single, his cover of Dylan's tale of south-of-the-Rio-Grande misadventure "Just Like Tom Thumb's Blues." Lightfoot's version, with its mariachi-style horns, played by jazz trumpeter Clark Terry, has more of a cinematic feel and Mexican border sound than Dylan's original. And Lightfoot sang convincingly of "burgundy," "harder stuff" and "hungry women" who can "really make a mess outta you."

On September 3, Grossman's next move was landing Lightfoot the perfect launching pad: a guest spot on Johnny Carson's *The Tonight Show*. The late-night TV show offered unimaginable exposure, with millions of viewers across North America tuning in from their living rooms and bedrooms. Carson, just three years into the hosting job, already had what the New York *Daily News* called "the most familiar face in America." For the Friday night taping, Grossman and Court were both busy, so shepherding Lightfoot to NBC Studio 6B at 30 Rockefeller Center fell to the Groscourt office manager, Jim Mosby. Lightfoot waited nervously backstage in NBC's greenroom for his call. The other guests were vaudeville veteran George Jessel and pop psychologist Dr. Joyce Brothers. When Lightfoot's turn came, Carson introduced him as "a rising star on the folk scene." Lightfoot performed his new single as well as "Early Morning Rain." Afterward, Carson invited him into his office for a chat over vodka martinis. Lightfoot walked out with an autographed photo of Carson as a gift for Brita, who was at home pregnant with their second child.

Following the taping, Mosby invited Lightfoot to crash at his place in Greenwich Village. He and his wife were expecting a baby themselves, and Lightfoot slept on a couch in the baby's room. The following morning, he was off to his next gig. What Mosby remembers most was how seriously his guest took his work. "Gordon really had his act together, compared to some other artists," he says. "He was very focused on his career and on succeeding. But he was super nice and a real pleasure to work with."

Lightfoot returned home to see Brita and Fred and found that his "Just Like Tom Thumb's Blues" had cracked the Top 10 on Toronto's CHUM radio station. It was only a brief stopover. After a sold-out week at Yorkville's New Gate of Cleve, he was back down to the States for five nights at Boston's Odyssey and a series of appearances at Detroit's Chess Mate and Raven Gallery. Two friends he'd met on the Toronto folk scene gave him a place to crash in the Motor City. Saskatchewan-born Joni Anderson and American Chuck Mitchell had met while performing at Yorkville's Penny Farthing. They married and moved to Detroit, where they shared a fifth-floor walk-up near Wayne State University. Chuck and Joni Mitchell were happy to let Lightfoot stay, and the three would play their latest songs for each other. In fact, on their Wollensak tape recorder, Chuck and Joni made a home recording of themselves singing Lightfoot's "When Spring Was O'er the Land" (he'd provided the lead sheet). Chuck recalls Joni always liking Lightfoot: "She thought he was a good guy, down-to-earth, very creative. They had something in common," he adds. "Both came from modest backgrounds in small Canadian towns, and they shared this survivalist notion to never go back to the restraints of their childhoods. That was one of Joni's main drives and I think Gordon's too."

While in Detroit, Lightfoot heard news that the SS *Yarmouth Castle*, an old US steamship that ran pleasure cruises to Nassau, in the Bahamas, had caught fire and sunk 120 miles east of Miami, taking eighty-five passengers and two members of its crew down with it. He'd always been fascinated by big mechanical things like trains and boats and planes. The sinking of the *Yarmouth* moved Lightfoot to sit and write a lengthy ballad about the disaster. Real events like that inspired him, and it wouldn't be the last time a shipwreck would lead to a song.

In late November, Lightfoot made his proper New York debut at the Town Hall. "A Triple-Decker Musical Treat" read the headline in *Billboard* magazine's review of the show, which featured Lightfoot, the Jim Kweskin Jug Band and the Paul Butterfield Blues Band. It was an eclectic lineup, reflective of the changing sounds of popular music. *The New York Times*'s Robert Shelton singled out the Canadian folk singer's contribution. "Gordon Lightfoot in his local debut," Shelton wrote, "showed a songwriting facility from the poetically introspective to the rural railroad song-tradition of Jimmie Rodgers. Mr. Lightfoot has a rich, warm voice and a dexterous guitar technique." High praise from the man credited with helping to launch Bob Dylan. By year's end, artists from Judy Collins to Johnny Cash to Harry Belafonte had all recorded "Early Morning Rain," and three albums in the Top 50 featured the song. Meanwhile, "Ribbon of Darkness" earned its composer top prize at the American Society of Composers, Authors and Publishers.

On New Year's Eve, Gordon and Brita were greeted with the arrival of a daughter, whom they named Ingrid. It was a happy occasion, but Lightfoot's long days on the road had already put a strain on his marriage. And things weren't going to get any easier with Brita now stuck at home with two kids to look after. With another mouth to feed, Lightfoot had no choice but to keep focused on his career and work even harder.

Lightfoot's debut album finally came out on United Artists in January 1966. The cover photo depicted him as James Dean cool, clad in denim and cowboy boots, with guitar in hand and legs stretched out before him. But with his over-the-shoulder glance, he also looked a little worried about who was behind him on the trail. Although late in coming, Lightfoot's debut, titled simply *Lightfoot!*, was the showcase he'd been waiting for, and with the exclamation mark of its title it boldly announced the arrival of a major talent. Featuring "The Way I Feel," "Ribbon of Darkness," "For Lovin' Me" and "Early Morning Rain"—the latter arguably Lightfoot's finest song and one eventually recorded by his heroes Dylan and Elvis Presley—it was a superbly crafted acoustic folk album. Even those already aware of Lightfoot's work through recorded versions by other artists (Judy Collins was the latest to cover "Early Morning Rain") were impressed by the quality, depth and range of his material. Among the fourteen songs were "Long River," another number rooted in his unabashed love of the Canadian landscape, and the hymnlike "Peaceful Waters," both featuring the work of guitarist Bruce Langhorne. Most unusual was Lightfoot's "Oh, Linda," a stark blues song about a woman who'd done him "wrong," sung with accompaniment only from bassist Bill Lee. The album also included three excellent covers: an urgent rendition of Hamilton Camp's nuclear protest "Pride of Man" and tender readings of Phil Ochs's "Changes" and Ewan MacColl's romantic ballad "The First Time Ever I Saw Your Face."

Lightfoot! earned rave reviews in the US and sold well in Canada, but it didn't deliver anything like the commercial breakthrough Grossman had promised. The album's release was simply too late in coming—and Lightfoot knew it. Dylan had moved on, and Lightfoot's debut had missed the boat. Musical tastes had changed. The boom had gone bust and folk music, which Lightfoot had embraced so artfully, was suddenly passé.

FIVE

Crossroads

L ightfoot wasn't giving up. He understood that the musical tides had turned and a solitary singer with a guitar was not going to cut it anymore. But he also knew his songs were strong enough to carry him. He just had to keep pace with the front-runners.

In early February 1966, *The Canadian*, a magazine supplement published by the *Toronto Star*, ran a cover story on Lightfoot in which he named his rivals. "Dylan and Phil Ochs are the people I want to catch." He added, "They're in a different bag than me, but I expect to write as well as them. I just write songs I think people will dig. Somebody once called my style 'country-and-Lightfoot,' and I guess that's a close enough definition to the way it feels." Meanwhile, Dylan was helping to spread the word about Lightfoot's material. Johnny Cash and June Carter, of country music's legendary Carter Family, visited Dylan at Albert Grossman's place in upstate New York, and Dylan played them several songs by Lightfoot. Carter had never heard of the Canadian artist, but as a result of Dylan's introduction, "For Lovin' Me" would join Cash's "I Walk the Line" as her family's next Columbia single.

The Canadian's cover featured an impressionist portrait of Lightfoot painted by up-and-coming Toronto visual artist Robert Markle. A

Hamilton, Ontario–born Mohawk who refused to be identified as a First Nations artist, Markle had already made a name for himself as a controversial figure in the art world. The provincial courts had deemed his drawings and paintings of female nudes obscene, a charge he challenged on national television, defending them as erotic rather than pornographic. To pose for the portrait, Lightfoot visited Markle's studio on Webster Avenue, in Toronto's Yorkville area, over the course of several days, playing guitar and developing songs while Markle worked. A friendship was forged: "He painted, I wrote songs—we had something in common," Lightfoot told Markle's biographer. The two began hanging out, drinking until closing at the Pilot Tavern and then staggering over to catch bands like Jack London and the Sparrows in nearby Yorkville. Lightfoot learned over beers that Markle's father and brother were skyscraper construction workers. He was fascinated. Lightfoot visited the thirty-eighth floor of the Toronto-Dominion Bank Tower, then in mid-construction, and wrote "Talkin' High Steel," with lyrics about "men perched on the high beams, puttin' rivets in." "I'm disappointed there aren't any Mohawk Indians on the project," he told one reporter. "It would add a twist to the song. I'm told most of the steelworkers are Newfies." The song remains unreleased, but it was another example of Lightfoot's diligent approach to researching compositions, a habit he developed with "Ballad of Yarmouth Castle" a year earlier.

Songwriting sometimes had to wait. Touring was also part of advancing a career, and Lightfoot had to keep his face in front of his fans. He performed for the University of Toronto's Winter Carnival at Varsity Arena, appearing with the Allen-Ward Trio and comedian Rich Little before a crowd of 3,500. He was paid $850 for the gig—excellent money for a single performance. Lightfoot's earning power was growing (Fiedler had paid him $2,000 for six nights at the Riverboat the previous month). His increased income meant that he and Brita could move out of their basement apartment and buy their first property: a triplex at 94 Farnham Avenue, in the city's midtown, where they lived on the main floor and rented out the top two floors to help with the mortgage.

In mid-February, Lightfoot was in England with Ian & Sylvia, performing a nine-city tour billed as the Anglo-American Folk Concert with several local acts, including the Settlers. The head-liners were England's Ian Campbell Folk Group,* while Lightfoot and Ian & Sylvia were billed as "guest stars from America." Also featured was Trevor Lucas, an Australian singer who, Lightfoot says, did rousing renditions of "Waltzing Matilda" that "really got the shows going every time he did it." Travel was all by bus, made neces-sary by a national rail strike. According to Ian Tyson, the food on the tour was terrible and the whole experience bleak. Sylvia remembers pulling into some towns and getting the cold-shoulder treatment at tearooms and pubs. "They weren't used to a busload of rowdies, and they'd actually refuse us service. Gordon would get quite indignant and say things like, 'Oh, so it's "Yankee go home," is it?'" Still, Lightfoot's songs went over well, and the Ian Campbell Folk Group and the Settlers wound up recording "I'm Not Sayin'" and "Early Morning Rain," respectively, while Lucas later covered "The Way I Feel" as a member of British folk-rockers Fotheringay.

Back home, Lightfoot took part in a TV taping of the charity show for Easter Seals at Toronto's Queen Elizabeth Theatre, head-lined by his mother Jessie's favorite, Bing Crosby. After Lightfoot performed two songs, Crosby walked over, shook his hand and said, "Very nice, Gordon, beautiful." Jessie, who was in the audience that night, was delighted. She'd introduced Gordie to Crosby's music when he was just a toddler, and now her son was not only sharing a stage with the legendary crooner but also receiving high praise from

---

* Campbell's sons Ali and Robin later found international fame with reggae hitmakers UB40.

him. After the benefit, Lightfoot took off for dates through the spring in Ottawa, Philadelphia and Detroit, cheered by a positive review of his debut album in *Variety*. In May, *Billboard* reported, "Gordon Lightfoot, whose UA debut LP bowed to unanimous raves last month and sold out in Toronto in two days, holidayed in Nassau recently and found his tune 'I'm Not Sayin',' by [calypsonian-pop group] the Merrymen, at No. 1." Lightfoot had taken Brita to the Bahamas for some sun, hoping that a holiday might help patch things up between them.

Yorkville was jumping, with dozens of clubs and coffeehouses offering blues, jazz, folk-rock and pop artists every night of the week. At the Riverboat, Lightfoot was packing them in, playing as many as four shows a night and drawing lineups down the street. He was backed by guitarist Red Shea and Paul Weidman, a bassist who'd worked with Ian & Sylvia and was filling in for John Stockfish. Along with popular numbers like "Early Morning Rain," he performed "Talkin' High Steel" and a topical one about Gerda Munsinger, an East German prostitute who was in the news for sleeping with two cabinet ministers in John Diefenbaker's government. The Munsinger affair was Canada's first major political sex scandal. In an interview with the *Toronto Star*, Lightfoot admitted to being worried about ruffling feathers. "You never know," he said, "someone might get a bit touchy." In fact, the audience loved it. Fans today can only imagine what the Gerda song sounds like. Like "Talkin' High Steel," it remains buried in Lightfoot's vaults.

One night, Ian Tyson dropped in to catch Lightfoot's last set and another new number caught his attention. At a party afterward at Bernie Fiedler's, Tyson asked Lightfoot about the song: "It's a good one, Gordon, what's it called?" Lightfoot told him it was "Go My Way," and Tyson said, "Why don't you go and get your old guitar and play it for me?" Even though it was four in the morning, Lightfoot obliged and played it for him again; he rarely passed up an opportunity to perform his songs, and, as he'd often done for his aunts back in Orillia, he was used to singing on command. A wistful ballad with a bright, crisp melody of the kind that seemed to come so easily to Lightfoot, "Go My Way" would eventually make it to record, but not for several years.

In July, Lightfoot was booked to play the Cafe au Go Go, in New York's Greenwich Village, on a bill with Jesse Colin Young and Big Joe Williams. The club had become infamous two years earlier when comedian Lenny Bruce and owner Howard Solomon were arrested on obscenity charges. Solomon had a fondness for other controversial stand-up comics like Mort Sahl, George Carlin and Richard Pryor. The Cafe's musical specialty was blues and jazz, but Solomon booked folkies, too: Ian & Sylvia, Richie Havens, Eric Andersen and two artists who had a big influence on Lightfoot: Bob Gibson and Fred Neil. Lightfoot was drawn to the twelve-string guitar techniques of Gibson and Neil and their respective ways with a song. He liked Gibson's entertaining approach and how Neil, who possessed an impossibly deep baritone, could convey honest emotion on bluesy folk songs with a touch of jazz. Lightfoot also shared several personality traits with Neil: both were shy, inhibited, vulnerable performers who were never entirely comfortable in the public eye. Lightfoot became drinking buddies with Neil when they both played the same week at the Gaslight South in Miami. Neil, who wrote memorable songs like "Everybody's Talkin'," the theme from *Midnight Cowboy*, took his Canadian pal out sailing around the sleepy artists' enclave of Coconut Grove, where he lived. Lightfoot never forgot the experience and later developed his own passion for sailing.

———

Lightfoot was soaking up influences everywhere he went. When he was back in Detroit to perform at the Living End, he once again visited Chuck and Joni Mitchell at their apartment. As usual, there'd be gatherings of musicians passing through, including Judy Collins, Tom Rush and Ramblin' Jack Elliott. Joni liked to play everyone her latest songs. "I remember when she sang us a song in her kitchen called 'Clouds,' the one that became 'Both Sides, Now,'" Lightfoot says. "I was really impressed by that." When Joni and Chuck announced they were going on the road, they invited Lightfoot to stay in their apartment. But Joni made one condition. "She left me with the Beatles' *Revolver* album and said, 'Gord, please promise to listen to this while we're gone.' And I did. It was such a damned good album that I got hooked. So Joni got me turned on to the Beatles, which I'd been resisting."

The Beatles visited Toronto in August 1966, playing Maple Leaf Gardens for the third successive year. The Fab Four was still the biggest thing in pop music, but Lightfoot didn't see the band perform at the hockey shrine; he was far too busy trying to figure out what to do about a song he'd been commissioned to write. With Canada's centennial year fast approaching, the CBC decided a TV special was needed to celebrate the country's birthday. Producer Bob Jarvis was aware of Lightfoot's talent, if not his affinity for songs about trains. Besides "Steel Rail Blues," he'd recently composed two other train-themed numbers for a Canadian National Railway promotional film about its freight service. Jarvis told Lightfoot that he was looking for a big folk ballad that captured all the grandeur of Canada's birth and sent the songwriter to the CBC's library to get out a book on William Cornelius Van Horne, the architect of the first Canadian transcontinental railway. Lightfoot went home to his writing room on Farnham Avenue and began reading. Soon, the ideas were flowing.

I started with a ballad, reaching back to an old barbershop tune I used to do called "The Rose of Tralee." I put that to work in the slow part and found this word navvies, which were the railway workers, in the book on Van Horne. I started listening to Bob Gibson's "Civil War Trilogy" and decided to use his format—fast going in, slow in the middle, fast going out. And it came to me. Got into a great key. Open F chord. Same way I'd written "Early Morning Rain," but very few others. I stayed up all night working on it, right up until nine or ten in the morning. Then sleep and pile right back into it. Coffee, cigarettes—nothing else. No booze at that point. The song was done in three days.

With the lead sheet for the song in his guitar case, Lightfoot drove down to Jarvis's office at the corner of Yonge and Gerrard, walked in, sat down at his desk and played him "Canadian Railroad Trilogy," all six minutes of it. "He listened to the whole thing," says Lightfoot, "and when I was done, he said, 'Well, Gordon, I'm impressed.' That's what he said. He told me they'd get Ron Collier to orchestrate it and asked if that would be okay. I said, 'That sounds wonderful.'" It was indeed an impressive achievement. Lightfoot had captured the rugged beauty of the land before European settlement with its "wild majestic mountains" and forests "too silent to be real." And he'd distilled the grinding toil it took to build the "iron road running from the sea to the sea" into a moving musical history lesson.

On New Year's Day, Lightfoot appeared on national television in the CBC special *100 Years Young*, kicking off Canada's centennial. Although there were other performers, including singer Juliette and comedians Wayne and Shuster, Rich Little, and Don Harron playing Charlie Farquharson, it was the "Canadian Railroad Trilogy" that stole the show. Standing tall in a red shirt, black tie and leather vest, Lightfoot sang about "a time in this fair land when the railroad did not run." While actors dressed as navvies swung hammers around him, he pumped out the tune on his twelve-string guitar, picking up steam in the faster sections:

Oh the song of the future has been sung
All the battles have been won
On the mountaintops we stand
All the world at our command
We have opened up the soil
With our teardrops and our toil

It was a stagey recreation of nation-building and the railway's construction; Lightfoot likes to point out that the actors' hammers were actually made of papier-mâché. But he knew he'd struck a nationalistic nerve. Years later, Lightfoot received high praise from historian Pierre Berton, author of *The Last Spike*, who told him, "You did more good with your damn song than I did with my entire book on the same subject."

"Railroad Trilogy" would grow to become a standard and one of the country's most powerful pieces of Canadiana. Lightfoot performed it in early January when he was back filling the Riverboat, playing three shows a night for most of the month with people lining up outside in subzero temperatures. Inside, he, Shea and Stockfish turned up the heat in the packed club, performing old favorites and other new songs like "Rosanna" and "Go Go Round." A lament written for a spurned go-go dancer Lightfoot had met while visiting Ronnie Hawkins at Le Coq d'Or, "Go Go Round" was Lightfoot's latest United Artists single, and it was already racing up the Canadian charts.

The sessions for Lightfoot's second album took place at Columbia's Studio A in Nashville, a legendary facility formerly known as the

Quonset Hut. It had been built in the mid-1950s by producer Owen Bradley, considered one of the architects of the Nashville sound. Out of that studio came hit songs like "Crazy," "El Paso," "Ring of Fire" and "King of the Road." Most significant for Lightfoot, Dylan had recorded parts of his *Blonde on Blonde* album there, as well as his hit "Rainy Day Women #12 & 35." Charlie McCoy, one of Nashville's most in-demand session men, played on those Dylan sessions. "Folk-rock artists would never come to Nashville," McCoy says, "but after Dylan did, man, the floodgates opened. It was like Dylan gave his stamp of approval. Suddenly the Byrds, Leonard Cohen and Peter, Paul and Mary were all coming down."

McCoy, along with drummer Kenny Buttrey, joined Lightfoot, Shea and Stockfish in Studio A for the sessions. John Court is credited with producing, but McCoy can't recall him being present. "Gordie didn't need a producer. He, Red and John played together all the time, and Gordie was really in charge." The atmosphere of the sessions was "typical Nashville," says McCoy, "very relaxed. Kenny and I were digging the songs, Gordie's voice and Red's playing—he was really spectacular. Of course, in Nashville we're around amazing guitar players all the time, and Red was one of them. A funny guy, too, full of energy, laughing and having a great time."

McCoy was a multi-instrumentalist who provided a distinctive harmonica on most tracks, including "Walls" and "Crossroads," another robust song about the working men on whose labor Canada was built. But McCoy was proudest of "Canadian Railroad Trilogy." He contributed some stirring vibrato to the middle section. Did Lightfoot give him specific direction? "Nope, he just said, 'It's a story with a middle part about the workers. Just play what you feel.'"

Lightfoot had an opportunity to really showcase "Canadian Railroad Trilogy" when he made his debut as a singer-songwriter at Toronto's Massey Hall, fifteen years after he'd appeared on that stage as the victorious boy soprano of the Kiwanis Music Festival.

His March 1967 concert was arranged by Johnny Bassett and presented by the *Telegram*'s "After Four" section in association with the
Riverboat's Bernie Fiedler. Tickets got snapped up so quickly that
extra seats had to be placed on the sides and back of the stage. The
concert earned him in the neighborhood of $5,000, a terrific fee for
the time. With his parents, sister and various friends in attendance,
Lightfoot was understandably nervous. But when he walked onto
the stage, dressed in cowboy boots, a light blue blazer, white shirt
and a colorful mod tie, everything fell into place. For the next two
hours, he held his audience spellbound. *The Globe and Mail* called
it a "country-and-Lightfoot parade of Canadiana." The newspaper's critic, Peter Goddard, sighted in Lightfoot a "folky-show-
biz surface hipness." But he applauded the "Indian raga-influenced
'The Way I Feel'" as well as "'Softly,' where Red Shea's guitar and
John Stockfish's bass wove a careful progression of semi-jazz chords
around the melody." He credited Lightfoot as "an unusually gifted
melodist" and called him a "Canadian Charles Aznavour in blue
jeans." From then on, Lightfoot's appearances at Massey Hall became
an annual occurrence—and a yearly ritual for his fans to this day.

Canada's hundredth birthday celebrations continued. Under the
banner of Festival Canada, Expo 67 sponsored national tours by several Canadian artists. Lightfoot went across Canada for the first time,
winding up in Montreal for a week at the world fair's Canadian
Pavilion. His songs expressed all the pride and optimism Canadians
were feeling. Immediately afterward, Lightfoot and his sidemen
played the New Penelope coffeehouse, the city's premier folk and
blues venue and Montreal's equivalent of the Riverboat. With Expo
on, it was packed. Burton Cummings and Randy Bachman, of
Winnipeg's the Guess Who, were in the audience. "Gordon came
out with his sidemen and did an entire sixty-minute set of original
material," says Cummings. "Randy and I kept nudging each other in
the ribs, saying, 'Someday, that will be us. Someday, we'll be able to

do a whole show of our own songs.' We got to meet him afterward, and the whole experience was tremendously inspiring for us, because at that time we were just a cover band." It wouldn't be long before the Guess Who topped the charts with a Bachman and Cummings original, "These Eyes." On the flip side of the single was their tribute song called simply "Lightfoot," featuring the glowing lyric "He is an artist painting Sistine masterpieces of pine and fur and backwoods."* Where Dylan, Ochs and Neil had inspired Lightfoot, the Canadian star was now doing the same to others.

On Canada Day, July 1, Lightfoot wasn't partying—he was in a New York recording studio laying down material for a new single. Yet there were plenty of reasons to celebrate. His second album, *The Way I Feel*, had come out that day, and *Variety* had picked the title track as its single of the week, while *Billboard* called the album "masterful" and predicted that it should establish Lightfoot as "an important contemporary folk artist-composer." *Hit Parader* magazine cited the "timeless appeal" of his music in its review, which appeared alongside a write-up on the Beatles' *Sgt. Pepper's Lonely Hearts Club Band*. With crisp guitars and clear vocals, Lightfoot's warm acoustic tones were resonating all over. Two years later, *Rolling Stone* magazine's Jann Wenner asked Bob Dylan what he was going for with his album *John Wesley Harding*. Replied Dylan, "I heard the sound that Gordon Lightfoot was getting, with Charlie McCoy and Kenny Buttrey and figured if he could get that sound, I could. But we couldn't get it (laughs). It was an attempt to get it, but it didn't come off."

Belafonte had also climbed on the Lightfoot bandwagon. The King of Calypso, a local favorite in Toronto, was back in town for the fifth time in as many years, with another monthlong residency at the O'Keefe Centre. He'd already recorded Lightfoot's "Song for a

---

* Cummings, a talented mimic, later recorded "Maggie May" in Lightfoot's recognizable voice, delivering Rod Stewart's lyrics in a distinctly clipped timbre.

Winter's Night"* and desperately wanted more. Grossman, however, had turned Belafonte down and advised Lightfoot not to let him record his songs before they appeared on his own album. Now Belafonte wanted to meet Lightfoot and make his case in person.

Harry came into the Riverboat and wanted to know why Albert Grossman was running my life, which was a little awkward. I said, "Well, he's my manager." I guess Albert didn't think Harry's records were selling at that point. Harry invited Brita and me to the O'Keefe, where he performed a couple of my songs. He pointed me out in the audience and introduced me, which was a little embarrassing. Then he had us down to the Royal York Hotel, where he was staying, for a party. Mary Travers, Peter Yarrow and a bunch of other people were there. We partied until about four in the morning, and finally somebody had to come and get us all to leave so Harry could go to bed. But he kept bringing up the matter of my material and Albert.

Belafonte had to wait. He eventually recorded another four Lightfoot songs, including "Softly," "The Last Time I Saw Her," "Oh, Linda" and "You'll Still Be Needing Me." But the composer worried that he'd "blown" his relationship with Belafonte. "You don't do that kind of thing to people like Belafonte," he said at the time. "He's like Sammy Davis Jr. or Sinatra—he's powerful." Lightfoot never saw himself as a star of any significant magnitude. Whether it was insecurity or humility, his inherent modesty never allowed him to have too high an opinion of himself.

Dylan didn't take part in that year's Newport Folk Festival. He was holed up near Woodstock, New York, recording what would

---

* Listed on his *Belafonte on Campus* album as "The Hands I Love."

become *The Basement Tapes* with the Toronto musicians who would later call themselves the Band. Instead, Newport's headliners were the old guard of Pete Seeger and Joan Baez, who sang in a trio with Mimi Fariña and Judy Collins. But the highlight of the festival was the Sunday workshop featuring a new guard of performers: Lightfoot, Joni Mitchell and Leonard Cohen—all championed by "Judy Blue Eyes" Collins, folk music's gifted interpreter. She'd already recorded Lightfoot's "Early Morning Rain" and Cohen's "Suzanne" and would soon be releasing her cover of Mitchell's "Both Sides, Now." "I met Gordie in Greenwich Village when I lived there around 1965," says Collins. "We'd have drinks together in the places we were playing in. I heard him sing 'Early Morning Rain' and just knew I had to record it. It's so beautiful and tells such an important story. Like all those great Canadian songs, it's lyrical, musical and timeless."

On August 5, Lightfoot's hometown celebrated Gordon Lightfoot Day for the first time and marked the occasion with a parade followed by two sold-out concerts by the local boy made good. Orillia mayor Isabel Post presented Lightfoot with a centennial medal and told him his name would be added to the town's Hall of Fame. With Gordon Sr., Jessie, Brita, Bev, Fred, Ingrid and other relatives and friends looking on proudly, it was a crowning achievement for the twenty-eight-year-old Lightfoot, who'd been laughed at by townsfolk a decade earlier for even thinking he could make it in music.

Lightfoot had built an enviable reputation. In the United States, he was widely recognized as one of music's bright new lights, with songs eagerly covered by many of his more established contemporaries. But north of the border, he was far more than just another promising denim-clad troubadour. His name was synonymous with a confident Canada caught up in the euphoria of its hundredth birthday celebrations. And his songs, from sweeping historical epics to stirring reflections on the country's natural beauty, had become firmly linked to the strong new sense of identity that swept over Canada that summer. Lightfoot was a star at home, but it wasn't enough.

SIX

Wherefore and Why

Little by little, Lightfoot's profile in America was growing—just not fast enough for his liking. His albums were getting noticed, but they weren't big sellers. His songs were familiar to listeners, but as hits by other artists. Lightfoot could be called critically acclaimed, but not yet a household name. Albert Grossman had more work to do. In the fall of 1967, Grossman's office arranged for Lightfoot to play New York's prestigious Bitter End, in Greenwich Village. Kris Kristofferson called the club a songwriters' "shrine," a place "full of artists, poets, dreamers and drunks where the audiences listened." Since it opened in 1961, the Bitter End had gained renown for its Tuesday night sessions where new singer-songwriters performed against an unadorned red brick backdrop. Paul Colby, who began managing the club in 1968, worked hard to book Lightfoot. "When Gordon played the club, it was something of a coup. My neighbor and nearest competitor, Howie Solomon of the Cafe au Go Go, wanted Gordon very badly. I worked the phones very tenaciously and finally signed Gordon for a gig. Howie was so mad, he ran across the street and yelled at me, 'You're taking the food out of my children's mouths.'"

When Lightfoot pulled open the heavy wooden doors to the Bitter End to do his sound check, inside he met Hank DeVito, a young soundman later famous as Emmylou Harris's pedal steel guitar player. As Lightfoot ran through his songs and DeVito adjusted the audio levels, Jerry Jeff Walker popped into the club. A local singer-songwriter and regular in the Greenwich Village scene, Walker had just recorded a single and wanted to hear it on the Bitter End's sound system. He introduced himself to Lightfoot and asked if he minded. "Go right ahead," Lightfoot told Walker. The two sat listening to the song and Walker asked about the orchestral strings that had replaced the original organ part. "Gord said he thought the change helped a lot and was really encouraging, which was great," says Walker, "because I was feeling pretty down about it." The song was "Mr. Bojangles," Walker's soon-to-be-classic tale of a tap-dancing drifter. As good as the song was, Walker was more impressed by Lightfoot's material, which he heard that night in the club. "I'd already heard Marty Robbins's version of 'Ribbon of Darkness' and loved it. Gord was an earthy songwriter who was really setting the pace for acoustic artists."

Before the year was out, Grossman arranged for Lightfoot to meet John Simon, a bright young staff producer at Columbia Records who had just produced the debut albums of Leonard Cohen and Blood, Sweat & Tears for the label. Simon checked out Lightfoot at Philadelphia's Main Point club and decided then and there to produce his next album. The two later met over dinner in a New York restaurant and talked about ideas for the recording, but they spent much of the night trying not to be distracted by famed Beat poet and On the Road author Jack Kerouac, who was sitting at the table next to them. Plans were made to reconvene in Toronto, where Lightfoot had recently bought a larger house a short distance from the triplex on Farnham, which he and Brita kept as a rental property. Located at 222 Poplar Plains Road, the new house was in a well-to-do area with neighbors that one writer described as "stockbrokers, mining executives, the Bay Street boys"—strange company for a denim-clad musician. At his spacious new home, Lightfoot played his new producer some of his latest songs. Among the romantic ballads, some tinged with pronounced melancholy, one number sprang right out of the day's headlines.

Lightfoot had never written an explicitly political number. Although he'd admired the ability of his friends Dylan and Ochs to tackle social issues, he felt that as a Canadian he shouldn't be adding his voice to the chorus of protest over civil rights and the Vietnam War. Detroit was different. The city was a second home to him. He had friends there, knew the streets and played its clubs many times. On July 23, 1967, a riot broke out when African-American protesters clashed with troops following a police raid on an inner-city bar. The "black day" left many dead, injured and arrested and hundreds of stores looted or burned; losses were estimated at between $40 million and $80 million. The riot hit a raw personal nerve for Lightfoot, who wrote "Black Day in July" in response. When he performed his composition at Detroit's Living End a month after the riot, he introduced it by saying, "This is about your city. I'm sorry it has to be that way."* The song's outrage was palpable.

Black day in July
Motor City madness has touched the countryside
And the people rise in anger
And the streets begin to fill
And there's gunfire from the rooftops
And the blood begins to spill

Simon loved "Black Day in July" and said its power and imme-diacy were "cool." He believed it could be a hit. So, too, did Grossman and executives at United Artists, who released it as a single. The song

* Ochs had earlier written his own song in response to a race riot, "In the Heat of the Summer," sparked by the Harlem uprising of 1964.

soared up the Canadian charts in early 1968. But many US radio stations deemed it too controversial for public consumption and banned
it from airplay. In the song, Lightfoot asked, "Why can't we all be
brothers, why can't we live in peace / But the hands of the have-nots
keep falling out of reach." Too radical? Radio programmers justified
the ban by expressing the fear that playing the song might cause further unrest. For his elusive American breakthrough, it seemed Lightfoot
was going to have to win over audiences from the stage.

Lightfoot was in Los Angeles when he found out about the ban. He
was appearing on Skip Weshner's radio show on KRHM-FM, where
he performed his songs in a refreshingly informal setting. For many
in the LA area, this was their introduction to Lightfoot. Weshner
dutifully plugged the fact that his guest was about to make his debut
at the Troubadour on Santa Monica Boulevard, in West Hollywood.
Owner Doug Weston had run the Troubadour as a folk and country
music venue since 1961, helping launch the careers of Hoyt Axton,
John Denver, Buffy Sainte-Marie and Arlo Guthrie. He also occasionally presented blues artists such as Muddy Waters and stand-up
comedians like the Smothers Brothers. The Troubadour had grown
to become the premier showcase for new talent on the West Coast.
Maybe the radio ban rattled him, or maybe he was overwhelmed by
the prestigious venue, but when Lightfoot entered the club the next
night, he had a serious case of the jitters. Would anyone show up?
And if they did, would they like him?

Chuck Mitchell was living in Los Angeles at the time, now
divorced from Joni. He was there backstage at Lightfoot's show and
witnessed his nerves up close. "Like all of us, Gordon had genuine self-
doubt and wasn't totally secure," says Mitchell. "And the Troubadour
could be an imposing room. But when Gordon walked out on that
stage, he saw that the place was packed. He sang his set and the people

knew his songs. In the end, he got several encores, and when he came offstage, he virtually broke down. It was very emotional." Lightfoot had arrived.

Lightfoot had several brushes with Hollywood while in California. The first was meeting Gale Garnett, a vivacious Canadian actress and singer who'd moved to LA after winning a Grammy for her album *We'll Sing in the Sunshine*, beating out Dylan's *The Times They Are A-Changin'*. At the time, Garnett was fronting a psychedelic folk group called the Gentle Reign and shared a stage with Lightfoot at a folk festival at San Francisco State College, where Lightfoot performed with Shea and Stockfish. Garnett told Dave Bidini, author of *Writing Gordon Lightfoot*—an imagined correspondence—that she and Lightfoot slept together: "Gord was a very straight Scottish Presbyterian guy. It was very sweet, very innocent."

Garnett was right. Lightfoot did have a strong Presbyterian, almost Calvinist, streak in him. He professed not to be religious, but having grown up in a small Ontario town where churches and Protestant thinking dominated, he always held himself to a strict moral code. Throughout his life, Lightfoot faced issues of sin, redemption and repentance—and when reflecting on himself actually thought in those Biblical terms. Guilt, a somewhat strange concept in the decadent world of rock and roll, would weigh heavily on Lightfoot throughout his life as he judged whether he was a good husband, father or son.

The California visit led to Lightfoot's second experience writing for Hollywood movies. He had previously composed several songs for Paul Newman's film *Cool Hand Luke*, although the producers bypassed his contributions in favor of numbers performed in the movie by Harry Dean Stanton.* This time around, Lightfoot was asked to come up with songs for a Burt Reynolds movie called *Fade In*. The producers

---

* One of those unused songs, the first-rate "Too Much to Lose," which likens a love affair to a gambling game, appeared on 1999's *Songbook* box set.

put him up in the historic Hollywood Roosevelt, the hotel where a young Marilyn Monroe was once a resident, and Lightfoot worked hard to come up with songs and recorded demos. Again, nothing of his wound up in the film.

But Hollywood's interest in Lightfoot's songs persisted. A short time later, Lightfoot wrote the title track for *Hail, Hero!*, starring a young Michael Douglas as a hippie who enlists in the army to use love to combat the Viet Cong. The movie's soundtrack also featured an alternative version of "Wherefore and Why." And then, in early 1975, a *Chicago Tribune* columnist, the daughter of the prominent Daley family, reported that Robert Redford wanted Lightfoot to write the theme song for his film *All the President's Men*. The columnist, Maggie Daley, wrote that Lightfoot would be flying to New York to meet with Redford when the first leg of Lightfoot's current tour ended in Milwaukee. A soundtrack deal never materialized, and today Lightfoot denies such a meeting ever took place. "Totally false" is all he will say. Yet there were reports of the two being seen together. Andy Warhol wrote in his published diaries that Lightfoot and Redford were among the celebrity VIPs attending Brazilian star Pelé's last soccer match at Giants Stadium. Lightfoot has no recollection of that Redford encounter either.

The Simon-produced album *Did She Mention My Name* arrived in stores in April 1968, featuring "Black Day in July" as well as the reflective "Pussywillows, Cat-Tails," the lustfulness of "The Mountains and Maryann," songs of longing like "The Last Time I Saw Her" and such string-laden gems as the philosophical "Wherefore and Why." "Pussywillows" drew from his idyllic childhood growing up in bucolic Orillia. But "Maryann" expressed the attraction of "hot blooded mountain love," a reference to a Calgary schoolteacher, whom he'd met while touring Alberta in 1967 on his cross-Canada tour. The album received high praise from the jazz magazine *Downbeat*, the publication that Lightfoot had devoured in his teens and that had led him to Westlake. The review called Lightfoot "one of the most arresting and poetic of the new breed of songwriters, a romantic to be sure, but a clear-eyed realist at the same time." It concluded that his songs were "lyrical, full of tenderness and compassion, but above all real, honest and totally without artifice." Lightfoot didn't know how to be anything else. While some criticized his lack of bravado, others—especially women—found his honesty attractive and his vulnerability appealing.

A new album meant a new American tour to promote it. Typically, six nights in a US club would fetch Lightfoot as much as $600. Lightfoot and his sidemen Red Shea and John Stockfish piled into Lightfoot's 1967 Ford station wagon and set off. It was an efficient operation, with the vehicle just large enough for the trio's instruments, amplifiers and sound equipment (Jack Long, of Toronto's musical instrument rental store Long & McQuade, had designed the PA system specifically to fit the station wagon). The touring pattern was quickly established: Lightfoot did the driving; Shea handled directions. A stickler for tuning, Lightfoot insisted that they arrive early at each venue to tune up at sound check, then make more adjustments immediately before taking the stage. After shows, it was time to greet fans, and Lightfoot would send the gregarious Shea out as the icebreaker. At the backstage gatherings, there'd always be plenty of girls.

It was an intense time to be in the States, with frequent race riots and Vietnam protests. When Lightfoot, Shea and Stockfish arrived in Washington, DC, to perform for a week at the Cellar Door, a transit strike coincided with the Poor People's March, organized by Martin Luther King Jr. Despite the resultant gridlock, the club was filled every night. At one of the parties afterward, where drinks were flowing, Lightfoot met a beautiful German woman. He found out she was a waitress at the Playboy Club in New York and made a mental note of her name with every intention of seeing her again. Alcohol and women were becoming another part of

Lightfoot's touring pattern, although that was hardly unusual for musicians in the late '60s. The more Lightfoot was away from Brita, the more heavily he drank, and the more affairs and one-night stands he had.

After the US tour, Lightfoot needed a new batch of songs for his next album. In June, he flew to England with the sole purpose of overcoming writer's block. The first song came to him in a taxicab on the way from Heathrow to the Stratford Court Hotel. With its lyrics about a woman "waiting for her master to kiss away her tears, waiting through the years," "Bitter Green" was written with Brita in mind. For all of Lightfoot's fooling around, Brita remained his safe harbor—a muse about whom he could romanticize. The question was how long Brita would "wait through the years."

Holed up in his hotel, Lightfoot came up with four other songs: "The Gypsy," "Unsettled Ways," "Don't Beat Me Down" and "Cold Hands from New York," about the alienation he felt on his first trip to that city. For a change of scenery, he took the train up to Edinburgh. There, at a hotel on Princes Street, he met a young French woman named Marie Christine Dupuis. She couldn't speak English, or he French, but they spent what Lightfoot later called "five lovely hours together." His next composition was about a ship that he called "Marie Christine."

Writing songs is about finding the time, because it's an isolated thing. You need to lock yourself in a room to do it, in one shape or another, whether it's an empty house or hotel room. In those days, I was mostly writing songs about nature and love and the refined natural beauty of living.

The songwriting trip was a success. As well as composing new songs, Lightfoot penned forty poems, written in red ink in a lined notebook. He briefly considered compiling the poems and later showed some of them to *Toronto Life*'s Marq de Villiers, who, in the

Jumping a jet plane: Lightfoot at John F. Kennedy Airport, New York, 1966.
© Daniel Kramer.

Bev, Gord Sr., Jessie and Gord Jr. in Orillia. All photos courtesy of Gordon Lightfoot, unless otherwise noted.

The choirboy at St. Paul's United Church, 1947.

The Four Winds recording for Johnny Stark, 1957: Pat LaCroix, Teddy Morris, Lightfoot and an unidentified Westlake College student. Courtesy of Pat LaCroix.

Singin' and swingin' on Country Hoedown: with Tommy Hunter (back row, center) and Lightfoot (right). © CBC Photo Collection.

Have folk will travel: en route to the Algoma Festival, Sault Ste. Marie in 1963: with (from top) Estelle Klein, Bonnie Dobson, Klaas Van Graft, Lightfoot, Beverlie Robertson and Ken Duncan. Courtesy of Beverlie Robertson.

Local boys make good: Lightfoot and Terry Whelan, with bassist Howie Morris, for the Two Tones appearance at Mariposa in Orillia, 1962.

Harry Belafonte, Lightfoot and admiring fan at the Riverboat, July 1967. © York University Libraries, Clara Thomas Archives & Special Collections, Toronto Telegram Fonds, ASC00607.

Backyard boys: with sidemen Red Shea and Rick Haynes, 1968. © Jim Marshall Photography LLC.

A night on the town with wife Brita and Ian and Sylvia Tyson at Steele's Tavern, 1965. © City of Toronto Archives, Fonds 1257, Series 1057, Item 3413.

"If Children Had Wings": at home with son Fred, 1968. © Jim Marshall Photography LLC.

"Fine as Fine Can Be": at home with daughter Ingrid, 1966. © Daniel Kramer.

Chuck Mitchell with his then-wife and musical partner, Joni, recording Lightfoot's "When Spring Was O'er the Land" in Detroit, 1966. © Detroit News.

Family beers: with Jessie, Gord Sr. and Bev in Orillia.

Talkin' Silver Cloud Blues: with Brita and Ronnie Hawkins' Rolls Royce in Mississauga, Ontario, 1968. © Jim Marshall Photography LLC.

Lightfoot with manager Albert Grossman (left), known as the "Floating Buddha," Ronnie Hawkins and Grossman's partner Bert Block, in Woodstock, New York, 1968. © Jim Marshall Photography LLC.

The Man in Black meets the Orillia Kid: with Johnny Cash before taping *The Johnny Cash Show* in Nashville, 1969. © Jim Marshall Photography LLC.

Checking the tapes backstage at Massey Hall, March 1969: with (left) Elliot Mazer, Rick Haynes (standing) and Robert Markle (seated, right). © Jim Marshall Photography LLC.

With Anne Murray and Stompin' Tom Connors at the Juno Awards, 1973.
© Bruce Cole, Plum Communications.

Sound check at Massey Hall, March 1969: with Bernie Fiedler and Rick Haynes.
© Jim Marshall Photography LLC.

Seven Island Suite: navigating
Georgian Bay waters in Sundown,
1970s.

On the Back River in the Northwest Territories, 1978: with fellow paddler Bill Miller.
© Bob Dion.

Slipping away on the Carefree Highway, near Phoenix, Arizona: with Cathy Smith.

Getting in tune, late 1970s: Lightfoot with (from left) Rick Haynes, Terry Clements, and Pee Wee Charles. © Arthur (Art) Usherson.

Sundown sales bonanza, 1974: Lightfoot flanked by Warner executives Mo Ostin and Lenny Waronker, with (from left) Bev, Jessie, Rick Haynes and Terry Clements.

Rolling Thunder Revue, Maple Leaf Gardens, December 1975: with (from left) Roger McGuinn, Joni Mitchell, Terry Clements, Ramblin' Jack Elliot, Lightfoot, Joan Baez, Bob Dylan, Mick Ronson, Ronnie Hawkins, Bob Neuwirth, Ronee Blakley and Rob Stoner. © Arthur (Art) Usherson.

Lightfoot's home at 5 Beaumont Road in Rosedale, Toronto: where Dylan's Rolling Thunder Revue partied and Lightfoot composed classics like "The Wreck of the Edmund Fitzgerald." © Bob Krawczyk.

Sylvia Tyson, Murray McLauchlan, Liona Boyd and Lightfoot in his backyard prior to June 1976 benefit for the Canadian Olympic team. © Bruce Cole, Plum Communications.

With New York City cop in Central Park 1974. © Carl Samrock.

Backstage at Toronto's Nickelodeon, May 1973: Lightfoot, Cathy Smith, Kris Kristofferson, Terry Clements, Rita Coolidge and Ronnie Hawkins. © Arthur (Art) Usherson.

"Eric, try to hold the camera straight": with Cathy Coonley. © Eric Lightfoot, courtesy of Cathy Coonley.

Lightfoot, 1971. © John Reeves.

magazine's June 1968 cover story on Lightfoot, declared him to be "as good a poet as a songwriter." There was even a publisher willing to release a book of his poetry. But Lightfoot, unsure of the merits of his work, never followed through on the idea. Today, he claims he doesn't even have the poems anymore.

Lightfoot didn't return directly home. He flew to New York in the hope of hooking up with the German waitress from the Playboy Club. A taxi took him to Grand Central Station, where he phoned and arranged to meet her after she finished work. What transpired between them in her apartment was captured vividly in Lightfoot's next song, "Affair on 8th Avenue." His lyrics about perfume and long flowing hair coming "softly undone" provided sensuous details of the tryst. And the imagery of "treasures of paper and tin" and a "game only she could win" was distinctly Dylanesque and closer to Leonard Cohen than anything he'd previously written. Lightfoot may have felt bad about the side trip, but that hadn't stopped him writing about it. And the affair gave him one of his best new songs.

Lightfoot's songs were becoming more autobiographical. For anyone looking for clues in his lyrics, "The Circle Is Small" seemed to raise questions about the stability of his marriage.

It's all right to leave but not all right to lie
When you come home and you can't say where you've been
You think it's fine to do things I cannot see
And you're doing it to me, baby, can't you see that I know how it is

The words were sung by Lightfoot, but they could easily have been Brita's. "I use the first person a lot," Lightfoot has admitted, "[but] what I'm really doing is putting myself in someone else's shoes." Whatever the case, he knew his marriage was unraveling.

Lightfoot felt compelled to seek counsel. For a lot of celebrities in the late 1960s, Scientology, the quasi-religious cult formed by L. Ron

Hubbard, seemed to hold some answers. Actresses such as Candice Bergen and Peggy Lipton (the starlet on TV's *The Mod Squad*) and musicians including Cass Elliot and Jim Morrison had all fallen under the spell of Hubbard's Dianetics, the now discredited form of psychotherapy combined with personality assessment. Lightfoot was introduced to Scientology by Dinah Christie, a Canadian actress and former star of TV's *This Hour Has Seven Days*, and agreed to visit the organization's Toronto office.* There, he sat and submitted himself to "processing" on the Scientology E-meter, a device that measured changes in the electrical circuit formed when a participant squeezed the handgrips while answering personal questions. A needle on the meter indicated to the "auditor" when the subject was faced with a repressed memory of past trauma. "Going clear" meant successfully becoming rid of those memories. For Lightfoot, just talking to someone about his marital problems was a useful exercise. "There was so much truth in what I said that I went clear the first time," he maintains. But, like Leonard Cohen, who was also briefly drawn into the cult,** Scientology proved just a flirtation for Lightfoot. "I never stuck with it the way people like Tom Cruise or John Travolta did," he says, "but it was good to have someone to talk to, a bit like seeing a psychiatrist."

At the same time as he was seeking answers and "going clear," Lightfoot was also escaping into the fuzzy comfort of the bottle. Whether it was beer or whiskey, booze became a constant presence in his life for social and professional reasons, serving as an icebreaker at parties and settling his nerves before concerts. The drinking had started innocently enough in Yonge Street bars when he first moved

---

* According to Lightfoot, Canadian jazz guitarist Lenny Breau also tried to get him to join the cult.

** Cohen signaled his familiarity with Scientology in his song "Famous Blue Raincoat," when he asked about going clear.

to Toronto but then grew into a more serious dependency as the decade wore on and he faced bigger audiences, more frequent parties and encounters with women of the sort he sang about in "Early Morning Rain." When things got complicated with Brita, alcohol gave him an easy way to forget his problems—if only for a while. "It made me feel better," he says, "and if I felt better, I could work better."

With Shea and Stockfish, Lightfoot recorded his fourth album, *Back Here on Earth*, over four days in September at Bradley's Barn, Owen Bradley's studio in Nashville. Elliot Mazer handled the production. Mazer was an engineer and understudy to John Simon, who was now busy producing the Band and Janis Joplin for Grossman. Following the sessions, Lightfoot was back in West Hollywood at the Troubadour, this time for a week. The buzz around his shows was strong enough to attract influential critic Robert Hilburn of the *Los Angeles Times*. Hilburn was blown away by Lightfoot, citing his "rich talent" and predicting it would be only a matter of time before "the young Canadian becomes a giant in the industry."

Before Lightfoot returned east, Grossman booked him into San Francisco's hippie ballroom the Fillmore on an unusual bill with the electric blues-rock band Canned Heat. Still, Lightfoot, Shea and Stockfish managed to cook up a robust acoustic sound built around recognizable songs like "Early Morning Rain" and "Steel Rail Blues" and tried out a couple of songs to be released on the new album, "If I Could" and "Long Thin Dawn." Toward the end of his set, he was relaxed enough to crack a couple of jokes about his grandmother before singing "Pussywillows." And for his final song, Lightfoot launched into "Canadian Railroad Trilogy," which, surprisingly, the American audience recognized and applauded on hearing the opening line.

Significant US media coverage continued. *Time* magazine ran a profile titled "Cosmopolitan Hick," based on a self-deprecating remark Lightfoot made about himself. But the article stated that his "assured, straightforward delivery shows him to be that rarity in the folk field—a well-schooled singer." Then *The New York Times* sent Robert Shelton to review Lightfoot's second appearance at New York's Town Hall. Shelton wrote that Lightfoot "looks like a walk-on from *Bonanza*" but credited him with writing "melodies [that are] consistently agreeable" and having a "flawless" guitar technique. He concluded, "If Mr. Lightfoot could project as warm and open a personality as his music does, he could become a sizable talent."

As talented a bassist as John Stockfish was, he had become unreliable: his fondness for amphetamines was causing epileptic seizures. Rick Haynes was working as a technician for the Ontario Research Foundation by day and as a bar-band bassist by night. He heard that Lightfoot was looking for a new sideman and contacted Red Shea to say he was interested. A week or two later, Haynes's phone rang. "Hi," said the caller, "this is Gordon Lightfoot. I heard you'd like to try out for my band. Do you know my stuff?" Haynes didn't really, but he said he did. "Okay, I'll be in touch," said Lightfoot and hung up. Haynes heard nothing for a month or two. Lightfoot was touring, so when the call came, it was from Brita. "Hi, I'm Gordie's wife," she said, in her thick Swedish accent. "We need to make a change. Would you be able to come do an audition?" Haynes, a large man with a cherubic face and a mustache, showed up at Lightfoot's home on Poplar Plains and hauled his bass guitar and heavy Traynor amplifier up to the second-floor music room, where he, Lightfoot and Shea played for several hours. "It seemed to go well," Haynes says. "Red was holding court in the proceedings a little bit, and I realized afterward that they were really just checking out my personality to see if I was a good cultural fit." Lightfoot called Haynes a week later to say he was in and offered him $200 a week whether he played or not. Plus, all his expenses—except cigarettes and booze—would be paid. Haynes accepted. He's still on Lightfoot's payroll nearly fifty years later.

Armed with a new bass player, Lightfoot was now crisscrossing the United States to promote *Back Here on Earth*. In January 1969, he returned to the West Coast for a high-profile gig at UCLA's Royce Hall. His appearance there led to two significant write-ups by Robert Hilburn, who was becoming Lightfoot's biggest booster in the States. Lightfoot was "one of the most exciting new folk-rooted performers in years," wrote Hilburn. He described his performance as "a dazzling display of singing and songwriting artistry that drew long and enthusiastic response from a full house." And he cited several songs from *Back Here on Earth*, including "Bitter Green," "Long Way Back Home" and "Cold Hands from New York," as signs of his "continued growth as a writer." There was no question of Lightfoot's deepening talent: the fresh melodies and impressively poetic lyrics were flowing out of him. Hilburn followed his review with a feature article that also cited Canadian singer-songwriters Ian & Sylvia, Leonard Cohen and Joni Mitchell. "Lightfoot," he noted, "holds the most promise." Then Hilburn zeroed in on why: "Lightfoot's chief weapon, both as a singer and writer, is his strong use of emotion. In an age of the 'super cool,' he digs deep into the warmth of the heart to relate some basic feelings about human longing and desire." Once embarrassed about his unpolished small-town ways, Lightfoot was finding that his lack of artifice had become an asset.

Lightfoot's honest performance style was on full view when he and his sidemen flew to England and appeared on the BBC's *The Rolf Harris Show*. Flanked by Shea and Haynes, both with mustaches, Lightfoot looked straight into the camera and delivered a heartfelt version of "Early Morning Rain." Dressed late-sixties-hip in denim jacket, beads and bell-bottoms, he conveyed an earnest vulnerability as he sang, raising his eyebrows in an expression that suggested pained innocence. Lightfoot's appearance was changing. His hair was showing early signs of a perm provided by his Toronto hairdresser Sandy Bozzo. That perm eventually grew more pronounced and came to define Lightfoot's look through the 1970s. Always big on tradition, Lightfoot has kept Bozzo as his barber ever since.

Adoration for Lightfoot's songs was especially strong in Nashville. The love affair had begun in 1965 with Marty Robbins's hit version of "Ribbon of Darkness" and spilled over to Waylon Jennings, George Hamilton IV, the Carter Family and others. In April 1969, Lightfoot and his band flew down to Nashville to appear on *The Johnny Cash Show*. Cash had been hired by ABC to host a TV show after his two live prison albums, *At Folsom Prison* and *At San Quentin*, proved so popular. Taped at the Ryman Auditorium, home of the Grand Ole Opry, the show's first guests were Bob Dylan and Joni Mitchell. Lightfoot was the headliner on the second episode. After a day of rehearsals, the taping took place on April 28. Cash introduced Lightfoot as "one of the finest entertainers, a singer-songwriter, just a great talent and a friend of mine who came tripping down from the north country fair." Lightfoot performed "Ribbon of Darkness" and "Softly" before Cash joined him on "For Lovin' Me." "I had a real good time with Johnny," Lightfoot says. "He was a very affable, down-to-earth guy, and there was a lot of easygoing chatter backstage and on the show."

While in Nashville, the ever-gregarious Red Shea heard there was a jam session going on in a local hotel room and insisted that he, Haynes and Lightfoot check it out. Elliot Mazer joined them. "Gord's not pushy and would never force his way into a scene like that," says Haynes. "But Red was very outgoing, so he pulled us into the room where Kris Kristofferson, Mickey Newbury and others were playing." Kristofferson, a Rhodes scholar with a master's degree in English literature, was working as a janitor at Nashville's Columbia Records, determined to become a songwriter. Lightfoot was knocked out by a song Kristofferson was singing, something he'd just written called "Me and Bobby McGee." "Elliot turned to me and said, 'You'd better record this before someone else does,'" Lightfoot says. His rendition of Kristofferson's "Me and Bobby McGee" would get recorded later that year, almost a full year before Janis Joplin made a version that became her signature song.*

Lightfoot desperately wanted out of his recording contract with United Artists. He was unhappy with the label's ineffectual promotion of his music. With one album left owing, he came up with the common remedy: deliver a live album, fulfill his contractual obligations and kiss the label goodbye. He asked Mazer to record his next Massey Hall concerts, four sold-out nights at the end of March 1969. Mazer set up a portable studio in the concert hall's dressing room and went to work capturing the magic of his Toronto appearances. "You know, it's really great to be back on this stage," Lightfoot told his audience the first night. "You can wander off around the place, but here in Massey Hall is my home." He wasn't just courting local favor; Lightfoot really did feel most comfortable there, surrounded by family and friends.

The live album, *Sunday Concert*, was released soon after. It included "Ballad of Yarmouth Castle" and four new songs: the philosophical "Apology," the country-flavored "In a Windowpane," the poetic "Leaves of Grass," with its Walt Whitman–inspired title, and "The Lost Children," a moving number about the human cost of war. And the album featured impressionistic liner notes from Lightfoot's painter buddy Robert Markle, who described the singer's followers as "the dollies and the ladies and the buckskinned fringed bandana

---

* Also recorded was Newbury's "33rd of August," although it remains unreleased.

paint-faced boys and the leggy lower pattern swimming silk bright smiled succulent sure little girls with excited love in their eyes." Later that year, Markle crashed his motorcycle on the Don Valley Parkway, suffering internal injuries and breaking both arms. To help out his friend, Lightfoot performed on a bill with the City Muffin Boys and the Downchild Blues Band as part of "The Beautiful Big Bob Benefit Bash" at Toronto's Rock Pile auditorium.

Albert Grossman had his sights firmly set on Reprise Records as the new home for Lightfoot. Reprise was Frank Sinatra's label, a company he formed in 1960 to give himself more creative freedom, earning him the nickname Chairman of the Board. Sinatra sold Reprise to Warner Bros. in 1968, retaining a 20 percent ownership. He'd already hired Mo Ostin, an experienced record executive, to run the label. With Ostin in charge, Reprise had started moving increasingly toward rock and pop music, signing Jimi Hendrix and singer-songwriters like Joni Mitchell and Neil Young. Ostin had also brought in a bright young A&R man, Lenny Waronker, to develop new talent. "Mo had me come into his office one day to talk about possible signings," says Waronker. "He mentioned Gordon Lightfoot and wanted my take on him. I said, 'Enormous potential, both lyrically and melodically. If we could sign him, that would be phenomenal.'" Negotiations with Grossman began in earnest.

In August, Grossman secured his client an enviable recording contract with Warner/Reprise, guaranteeing Lightfoot a million dollars over the next five years. It was the most lucrative recording deal ever signed by a Canadian performer. Lightfoot was now financially secure. More importantly, after years of languishing at United Artists, he was at a label where his music would get the proper treatment. At Warner/Reprise, he was joining some of the best artists in the world. Finally, Lightfoot felt, he was exactly where he belonged.

While in Los Angeles to sign the deal, Lightfoot dropped in to the Troubadour for a drink and to catch comedian Joan Rivers. On the barstool next to him was a dark-haired woman. Drinks, conversation and some serious flirting followed. Her name was Helena Kallianiotes, a Greek-American belly dancer who'd just appeared in *Head*, the Monkees' experimental movie written and produced by Jack Nicholson. In fact, Kallianiotes was living in the guesthouse on Nicholson's Mulholland Drive property in the Hollywood Hills, looking after the estate while he was away filming. She suggested Lightfoot come up to the Hills and see her place. Lightfoot couldn't resist the invitation, and the two spent the night together. The following morning, they heard the grisly news that during the night, just a short drive away, actress Sharon Tate and four others had been horrifically murdered at the home of Tate and her husband, director Roman Polanski. It was part of a shocking killing spree committed by the followers of cult-leader Charles Manson that left a total of nine people dead. Like the violence at the Altamont rock concert east of San Francisco later that year, the Manson murders signaled the end of the innocent '60s.

Landing Lightfoot a new record deal would be one of the last tasks Albert Grossman would perform for his client. In May, Lightfoot announced the formation of Early Morning Productions, named for his signature song. From now on, he would be the boss and control his own bookings, recordings and publishing. He bought a building in Toronto at 350 Davenport Road, opened an office and hired Al Mair. Lightfoot knew Mair well. They'd worked together when Mair was a salesman for the Compo label, Lightfoot's early record distributor. Mair spoke to *Billboard* about how Early Morning Productions would focus on Lightfoot's career to begin with but also branch out to manage other artists. "Initially, we'll just be working on packaging Gordon's own shows across the country, booking halls, supervising promotion, handling all details in the most professional way we can. We'll book concerts in the US as well, especially Gordon Lightfoot concerts. He has never really been properly exposed in the States and it's time he was." By setting up shop in Canada and not moving south of the border as so many of his contemporaries had done, Lightfoot was demonstrating a new way of building a career.

I didn't move to the States, because I wanted to keep my family ties. I liked being near my relatives. I was a bit of a homebody. It wasn't really necessary for me to move lock, stock and barrel. Toronto had a burgeoning music scene and was a great launching pad. It didn't seem necessary to move. So rather than go through that exercise, I was able to stay here and be close to my relatives. I was able to work in the States on the basis of an H-1 visa, which we kept renewing. All you really have to do is get a work permit sorted. Get set up with the IRS down there and pay your taxes. I learned that early on.

It's true that Lightfoot was setting a precedent by staying in Canada, but he could afford to do it. Between his concert earnings, songwriting royalties and record sales, he was earning around $250,000 a year. Mair organized a lavish press conference for December 1 at the Early Morning Productions office to celebrate his new million-dollar deal with Warner/Reprise On orange carpeting, surrounded by Lightfoot's gold records, media and record-company types mingled while knocking back glasses of champagne. But Lightfoot was missing. Mair told the gathering he was absent because he'd only just returned from the Grey Cup football festivities in Montreal, where he'd taken his father to watch the Ottawa Rough Riders defeat the Saskatchewan Roughriders. Truth was, he was nursing a massive hangover. His excessive intake of booze was catching up with him, clouding his judgment and potentially compromising his career.

SEVEN

Between the Lines

Lightfoot now had an album to make for Warner. His first order
of business was to write new songs for it. Wanting more space,
he had bought a large house at 222 Blythwood Road, in a quiet
neighborhood just off Mount Pleasant. In July 1969, while Brita and
the kids were still over on Poplar Plains, Lightfoot moved into the
new house with just a wicker chair and his beloved Quebec table for
furnishings. He went there every day for a month, spending twelve
hours each time, intensely writing, fueled by caffeine, nicotine, booze
and bennies. In his month of solitude, Lightfoot composed thirty-
five songs. Among the standouts were "Sit Down Young Stranger," a
gentle anti-war number about the generational distance between
a son and his parents, "Your Love's Return," a romantic ballad tinged
with melancholy, and "The Pony Man," a dreamy fantasy number
written specially for his children, Fred and Ingrid. But of all Lightfoot's
new compositions, "If You Could Read My Mind" stood out for its
startling honesty. The words had poured out of him onto a shorthand
pad all in one afternoon.

With its visions of wishing-well ghosts, movie queens and paper-
back novels, "If You Could Read My Mind" contained some of
Lightfoot's most vivid imagery. And with lines like "I don't know

where we went wrong, but the feeling's gone and I just can't get it back," Lightfoot was baring his soul like never before. He often drew from personal sources for his songs, but this time there was little doubt he was writing about his broken marriage. The words "heroes often fail" suggest he blamed himself for its demise, but in the phrase "chains upon my feet" is the claim that he was also imprisoned by it. Written from within that emotional cauldron, the song captured the breakdown of a relationship in a bittersweet, poetic way that elevated its composer into a whole new class of songwriters.

Lightfoot couldn't wait to record the new material and spent much of November and December in Los Angeles at Sunwest Recording Studios. Working with producers Lenny Waronker and Joe Wissert, Lightfoot, Shea and Haynes cut a total of twenty songs, with help from some highly notable session players. Ry Cooder provided mandolin on "Me and Bobby McGee" and "Cobwebs and Dust," a gently swaying daydream that also featured Van Dyke Parks on harmonium, while John Sebastian played harmonica on "The Pony Man" and electric guitar on the edgy, rock-tinged "Baby It's Alright." String arrangements on the ballad "Minstrel of the Dawn" and the romantic reverie "Approaching Lavender" came courtesy of Waronker's friend Randy Newman. Lightfoot was pleased with the production. Now he had to decide which of the twenty recorded songs to include on the album.

Before returning to Toronto, Lightfoot taped a performance for the TV show *The Music Scene* in Hollywood. Hosted by Canadian-born comedian David Steinberg, the new series had debuted that fall and been heavily promoted by the ABC network with clips of the Rolling Stones (although the group never appeared). Early episodes featured artists performing the top hits of the day, including Lou Rawls, Tommy Roe, Sérgio Mendes and Sly and the Family Stone. Lightfoot appeared in the Christmas episode, singing "For Lovin' Me" and his newly recorded "Saturday Clothes," joining such varied guests as Chuck Berry, Jerry Butler, Frankie Laine and Davy Jones of the Monkees. After the taping, Lightfoot flew home just in time to spend Christmas with Brita and the kids. Fred was now five, and Ingrid was about to turn four. It was the best of times and the worst of times, as Lightfoot liked to say, quoting one of his favorite lines from Charles Dickens's *A Tale of Two Cities*. Things with Brita were fractious, but for the sake of the family he was determined to keep the peace.

The arrival of the new decade brought much promise but more pressure. Lightfoot's new album, *Sit Down Young Stranger*, came out in May 1970. Canada was eager for its release, and Lightfoot performed several key concerts to get things rolling. First, he played four shows in three nights at Massey Hall before heading off to Ottawa to do another three concerts at the National Arts Centre. While in the nation's capital, Lightfoot learned that he was to be named to the Order of Canada, the government's recognition of "outstanding achievement," joining recipients that year who included media studies guru Marshall McLuhan. He flew up to Ottawa by himself the following March for the investiture ceremony at Rideau Hall.*

Warner decided that Lightfoot's first single off *Sit Down Young Stranger* should be his cover of Kristofferson's "Me and Bobby McGee"—the only song on it he didn't write.** If Lightfoot was ticked, he didn't let on. He was pleased that the album was receiving

---

* Lightfoot was then elevated within the order in 1988. In 2003, he received the top promotion within the order to Companion, Canada's highest honor. Lightfoot wasn't well enough to travel to Ottawa for that investiture, so Governor General Adrienne Clarkson, accompanied by a guard of honor, presented him with the insignia in a private ceremony at his Bridle Path home in Toronto.

** In 2016, Lightfoot teamed up with Kristofferson, Ronnie Hawkins and Willie Nelson to record a new version of the song.

strong reviews, including one from *Rolling Stone*, which called it "some of the nicest folk music on record anywhere." Also heartening: Dylan had just released a version of "Early Morning Rain" on his *Self Portrait* album.

Radio had formidable power during the freewheeling days of the record industry in the early '70s. Station managers, programmers and DJs could make or break an artist based simply on whether they put a record into rotation. Promoting one's album or single was a duty that required visiting radio stations and sitting for on-air interviews. Lightfoot never enjoyed that side of the business but agreed to make the rounds in the United States. "Gord didn't do good interviews; he came off as a small-town guy," says Al Mair, then manager of Early Morning Productions. "If somebody asked him a question, he might say 'yes' or 'no.' People had to pull information out of him. If they started praising him, he'd get embarrassed. It was best to keep him away from radio."

Lightfoot could be more forthcoming if the interview wasn't about him. One issue that got him going was the environment. Awareness of the earth's fragility was growing amid frequent reports of oil spills. The news angered Lightfoot, who'd always felt passionate about the natural world. In an interview with *The Gazette* (Montreal), he vented his frustrations. Although not inclined to political protest, Lightfoot even pointed fingers. "American mining companies are strip-mining in the Rockies and all that natural beauty is being destroyed," he told journalist Dane Lanken. "In the Arctic, they're giving away thousands of acres for oil drilling, and there's no way that the polar bears and the reindeer and the Eskimos are going to survive that." Lightfoot concluded by saying, "People just don't realize that the air they're breathing is actually killing them. Pollution has completely killed Lake Erie, and Lake Ontario will be dead in ten years. The American atomic tests in the Aleutians are killing all the wildlife up there: whales take one breath of radiation and they've had it." Lightfoot's ecological passion took him to Ann Arbor, Michigan, that April to perform at the first Earth Day event. More than fourteen thousand crowded into Crisler Arena to hear him, along with the Chicago cast of *Hair* and activist Ralph Nader.

Lightfoot's social concerns led him to an unusual venue that same month. Following the lead of his friend Johnny Cash, who'd performed at Folsom and San Quentin prisons, Lightfoot took his songs into the maximum-security Kingston Penitentiary, in eastern Ontario. Unlike Cash's concerts, it wasn't taped, and there were no film or TV cameras. In fact, there was no advance publicity at all about the appearance, which had been organized at Lightfoot's request by the *Toronto Telegram*. It was simply the man, his music and four hundred inmates dressed in prison gray, who roared their approval to songs about women ("Bitter Green") and those that questioned authority ("Boss Man"). The *Telegram*'s Fraser Kelly was there and noted that the inmates—"rapists, murderers, junkies, con artists"—were only mildly enthusiastic about "Canadian Railroad Trilogy" but got wildly worked up over "Black Day in July." After performing two forty-five-minute sets, Lightfoot was taken on a tour of the penitentiary, which he found deeply moving, especially watching the convicts parade single file from their cellblocks to pick up their trays of food. Lightfoot told Fraser, "Man, they were people, people with faces and feelings. That's when [the emotion] hit me—not when I was singing."

That summer, Lightfoot broke his right hand and had to cancel performances at the Stratford Festival, in southwestern Ontario, and with Blood, Sweat & Tears at the Hollywood Bowl. He was wearing a cast when he showed up on the Toronto Islands for the Mariposa Folk Festival. He'd gone with a female friend to see his pals David Rea, Joni Mitchell and Ramblin' Jack Elliott perform. And when Lightfoot was promoting his album in the United States that summer, the injury was mentioned in several news reports. The *Los Angeles*

Times attributed his broken hand to a car accident in Toronto, while *Billboard* said it was caused by "an ill-fated karate demonstration." In fact, Lightfoot had lost his temper with Brita at home. During one of their frequent fights, he had put his fist through a door.

Lightfoot's broken hand was an ugly metaphor for the dissolution of his marriage. Beyond their initial attraction, Brita had been hugely supportive of his career, and with her level head and mathematical skills she had remained a sounding board and financial adviser. But there was no longer any way to bridge the gap. Lightfoot moved out of the family home and into a high-rise building behind Maple Leaf Gardens at 50 Alexander Street, where Bernie Fiedler was living. Lightfoot rented a large, twenty-eighth-floor apartment, as well as a studio apartment across the hall, which he left empty strictly to work in. Then he hired a professional designer to decorate and furnish his living space with red flocked wallpaper, gold velvet couches and deep-pile burgundy carpeting throughout. Around the apartment stood Tiffany lamps and Inuit sculptures, with fine art on the walls, including Markle's portrait of him, in shiny gilt frames. He even had a pool table and a specially made pop-up coffee table with a slate top that concealed a bar. It was a plush bachelor pad befitting a single man of considerable wealth.

The cast was still on Lightfoot's hand in late August, when he flew out to California for a meeting with Warner. Los Angeles was abuzz with news about the arrival of a talented English artist with a hot new album who was making his US debut at the Troubadour. The Troubadour had grown to become a landmark music venue, with artists like James Taylor, Laura Nyro and Linda Ronstadt all making their debuts there. Tom Waits would be discovered at one of its open-mike nights the following year. "During the golden era of folk-flavored singer-songwriters," noted Robert Hilburn, "the Troubadour in West Hollywood was the most important club in America for showcasing talent. No one in the record industry wanted to miss the opening night of a potential star. Whole tours were built around when—or even if—artists could get Troubadour bookings."

The English sensation was named Elton John, and Lightfoot wasn't going to miss his opening night. When Lightfoot walked into the Troubadour, the place was jammed. Also in the audience were Leon Russell, David Crosby, Graham Nash, Quincy Jones, Henry Mancini, Mike Love of the Beach Boys and Neil Diamond, who introduced the twenty-six-year-old Englishman from the stage. Said Diamond, clearly starstruck, "Folks, I've never done this before, so please be kind to me. I'm here because [I've] listened to Elton John's album. So I'm going to take my seat with you now and enjoy the show." Lightfoot was blown away by John's performance. "It was just three guys: Elton with a great big grand piano, a bass player and a drummer with huge set of drums," he says. "And boy, you knew right there you were hearing a professional sound." He was particularly struck by the songwriting of Elton John and Bernie Taupin, who composed the songs' lyrics. When Lightfoot next appeared on Skip Weshner's LA radio show, he performed a cover of the John and Taupin composition "Your Song." A recording can be found on YouTube, but Lightfoot, perhaps embarrassed by its rough quality, questions whether it's actually him.

Lightfoot's hand healed in time for his fall tour, which took him to Boston, Hartford, Chicago and Detroit. On October 3, 1970, he made his debut at New York's Carnegie Hall. Despite a driving rainstorm that night, he performed to an over-capacity audience, singing songs that ranged from "For Lovin' Me" to "The Doomsday Song," a brand-new humorous epic, twenty-two verses long, about pollution and war that he'd written to perform at US environmental teach-ins. *The New York Times* reported that Lightfoot shone before a "devoted audience," while *Record World*'s Gregg Geller noted that he "cast a magical spell over Carnegie Hall, transporting the full house back to a day when audiences hung on a performer's every word." Lightfoot's songs, Geller added, "speak to matters of universal concern in a soft-spoken, understated manner." That was becoming Lightfoot's hallmark: meaningful, melodic songs that connected with people, crafted to stand the test of time.

Two weeks later, Lightfoot was back in Los Angeles for a week-long engagement of his own at the Troubadour. Although he'd already played there several times, with Warner's promotional muscle now behind him it was a much bigger deal. On opening night, the club was packed, with late arrivals perched on folding chairs in the balcony and others forced to sit on the steps leading to the club's upper level. Lightfoot sang a mix of early songs like "Steel Rail Blues," recent ballads such as "Saturday Clothes" as well as covers of Kristofferson's "Me and Bobby McGee" and Dylan's "Love Minus Zero / No Limit." There were some familiar faces in the crowd, including Bernie Fiedler and Helena Kallianiotes, Lightfoot's LA girlfriend. Kallianiotes's star was on the rise after her memorable role in Jack Nicholson's *Five Easy Pieces* as a lesbian hitchhiker who swears like a sailor. On this visit, Kallianiotes tried to convince Lightfoot to buy the mansion across the street from Nicholson's property on Mulholland Drive, which belonged to comedian Dan Rowan of *Rowan & Martin's Laugh-In*. It was up for sale for a mere $250,000. Lightfoot actually considered it, but he passed. Nicholson himself stopped by the Troubadour and invited Lightfoot, whom he'd nicknamed "Footsie," to an afternoon party at his place in the Hollywood Hills.

Opening for Lightfoot that week was Dee Higgins, a Toronto folk singer who Lightfoot signed to a publishing deal with Early Morning Productions on Fiedler's and Al Mair's recommendation. Looking back, Higgins says the entire week was a thrill. She says that at one point during the weekend gathering at Nicholson's, "Gord nodded toward someone singing with a guitar and said to me, 'Listen to this guy, because he's going to be very big.' It was Kris Kristofferson."

When Lightfoot's tour took him to Vancouver for several sold-out shows at the Queen Elizabeth Theatre, Nicholson and Art Garfunkel were there in the audience. They were in town shooting *Carnal Knowledge*. Lightfoot's growing fame was attracting some high-powered company.

Although Lightfoot's world increasingly included celebrities, he was unimpressed by the trappings of fame; his main social circle still consisted of old friends from the folk circuit.

While in California, Lightfoot decided to drop in on Ramblin' Jack Elliott, who lived in the town of Fort Bragg, north of San Francisco. He called up Brian and Bruce Good, bluegrass musicians from the Toronto area who were in San Francisco with James Ackroyd to record their album *James and the Good Brothers* with members of Jefferson Airplane and the Grateful Dead. "Wanna do a road trip?" said Lightfoot. The Goods were game—especially since they had friends living in a hippie commune near Fort Bragg. Lightfoot rode with Brian and two friends, Mike Watson and Tim Lown, while Bruce and James traveled in another car with their manager, Gail Hellund. Brian remembers passing a hitchhiker on the side of the road with a guitar and one sign that had "Boulder" on it and another that simply read "Mother." Says Brian, "Right away, Gord started working on a song about it." That song became "10 Degrees and Getting Colder." Lightfoot's "Redwood Hill" also came out of that trip, which Lightfoot documented in a handwritten journal entry that wound up in Bruce's possession:

Recently I went up into the Redwood Hills in Northern California with James and the Good Brothers, a startling troupe of songwriters from Richmond Hill, accompanied by Michael and Tim from Toronto and Gail. There were seven of us in the musical safari, traveling in two automobiles armed with three acoustic guitars, one electric bass and an amplifier. The rain had been falling for two days and we encountered flash floods, several hundred wandering sheep and about 16,000 discarded aluminum beer cans. After what seemed like an endless journey, we arrived at a place called Elk. There we found one bus, one farmhouse, two naked children, three women, five giant redwoods, one chainsaw, five loaves of fresh bread, two musicians and not one single can of beer. And so it was that from there we covered the remaining thirty-seven miles to Fort Bragg in about 32 minutes flat. Two jays en route, we drove up Highway One til we had reached a decent motor hotel where we took out crash insurance on units thirty-eight and forty of Building A. Shortly after we arrived in Fort Bragg, we found Cat Mother, owner and custodian of the house we had visited earlier, setting up at the community hall for a benefit dance called the "January Stomp," an evening of full-ass folk-rock entertainment. Readers should understand that James and the Good Brothers are not a full-ass rock combo; they are merely a very strong trio of performing musicians dealing in acoustic commodities.

Lightfoot and Ramblin' Jack were both in the audience at the January Stomp—which featured James & the Good Brothers and Cat Mother & the All Night Newsboys—until thick clouds of marijuana in the hall brought an early end to the show. "In the middle of the concert the smoke alarm went off," says Brian Good, "and the fire trucks came, forcing everyone to evacuate the hall." He adds with a grin, "It turned out to be a false alarm caused by the amount and kind of smoke in the building that night."

Pot smoking was all good fun. But harder drugs had begun taking their toll among musicians. Jimi Hendrix died that September from a barbiturate overdose, followed the next month by Janis Joplin, who overdosed on heroin. Both tragedies shook the music world, but the loss of Joplin, Grossman's star client and friend, hit Lightfoot's circle especially hard. On New Year's Eve 1970, Lightfoot was in Woodstock, New York, at Grossman's for a party. There was no singing of "Auld Lang Syne" that night. Instead, Grossman proposed a toast to Joplin. Lightfoot remembers how the memory of her cast a spell on the room.

At about ten to twelve, a silence fell over the entire place. Everyone suddenly stopped talking. It was as if they were afraid to speak or maybe they were expecting Albert to say something more. But he never said a word. I almost spoke a couple of times, but I'm glad I didn't. It went on like that for about half an hour, just everyone sitting in silence. Then it gradually dissolved and people eventually relaxed again.

Emperor Smith was a disc jockey at Seattle's highly influential KJR radio station, which had a reputation as a tastemaker in the United States. DJ Smith discovered "If You Could Read My Mind" on *Sit Down Young Stranger* and started playing it instead of the single "Me and Bobby McGee." Soon, other radio stations jumped on board, and Lightfoot's song started getting airplay across the country. Prompted by the strong listener response, Warner/Reprise released "If You Could Read My Mind" as the follow-up single to "Me and Bobby McGee." "It's a highly sophisticated, beautiful song, but it didn't have a conventional structure, so I assumed radio wasn't going to accept it," says Warner producer Lenny Waronker. "But it became our unexpected hit, and a very pleasant surprise." Almost immediately, the song reached *Billboard*'s Top 40.

In February 1971, thanks to snowballing radio play, "If You Could Read My Mind" hit number 5 on the *Billboard* Hot 100 singles chart and number 1 on the magazine's Easy Listening chart. Not surprisingly, Warner/Reprise wanted to rename *Sit Down Young Stranger* after the new hit. Lightfoot was strongly opposed and flew down to Los Angeles to tell the label folks so. Mo Ostin and Lenny Waronker sent him to see Stan Cornyn, head of merchandising. Lightfoot wasted no time getting to the point: "Why are you changing the title of my album?" Cornyn replied with a question: "Gord, did you take algebra?" Lightfoot said, "I took it, but I sure as hell never passed it." "Well, Gord," said Cornyn, "changing the name of the album is the difference between x and $8x$." Lightfoot understood. "Go ahead and change it," he said, and flew straight back to Toronto. Up to that point, *Sit Down Young Stranger* had sold about 80,000 copies. The title was changed and within six weeks it had sold 650,000 copies. And it kept on selling. Lightfoot finally had his long-awaited US breakthrough.

Riding high on a hit, Lightfoot took his show into New York's Fillmore East, promoter Bill Graham's companion venue to his San Francisco hippie hall. Music was changing, with heavier, more adventurous sounds reflecting the times. Lightfoot's concert was scheduled the day after appearances by Fleetwood Mac and Van Morrison and just a few days before Quicksilver Messenger Service and Eric Burdon & War. Although Grossman was no longer officially managing Lightfoot, he was there with him in the wings, offering support before his former client took the stage. Lightfoot was nervous about how he was going to go down in the rock auditorium and told Grossman so. "Albert didn't tend to say much," Lightfoot says, "but when he said something, you'd hear it." That night, Grossman gave him some advice that has stayed with him to this day: "'Just remember, Gordon,' he said, 'never give the audience less than they expect.'"

Lightfoot took that advice to heart when he played to two packed houses at California's Santa Monica Civic Auditorium in May, promoting his new album, *Summer Side of Life*. The country-flavored album had been recorded during the winter at Nashville's Woodland Studios. Several of its songs were rooted in Lightfoot's California adventure with the Good Brothers, including "10 Degrees and Getting Colder," "Cabaret," which included lyrics about hitchhiking north to Mendocino, and "Redwood Hill," where the influence of the Good Brothers' bluegrass music was most apparent. Lightfoot, Shea and Haynes were joined by top Nashville players, including fiddler Vassar Clements, pianist Hargus "Pig" Robbins and the Jordanaires, Elvis Presley's backup singers of choice.

Lightfoot's vivid storytelling made *Summer Side of Life* a superb album. Standout songs included the Latin-tinged "Miguel," a tale of separated lovers whose romance ends tragically, and the stirring title track, which explores a young man's emotions before he goes off to fight in a war. Lightfoot sang the lyrics of each song with such conviction that their message rang instantly true. And the musical accompaniment—simple, gentle and unobtrusive—helped give both songs an appealing, timeless quality. The album also featured "Cotton Jenny," a jaunty country tune that Lightfoot would call a "toe-tapper" and that Anne Murray made popular, and "Talking in Your Sleep," an intimate number that sensitively deals with a female partner's infidelity. In his review of the album in the *Los Angeles Times*, Robert Hilburn wrote, "Because it is such a warm, personal album, it may do this year for Lightfoot what *Sweet Baby James* did last year for James Taylor." Label mates on Reprise, Lightfoot and Taylor were running neck and neck as the pop world's most sensitive male troubadours, with songs as emotionally honest as those of Joni Mitchell or Carole King.

Hilburn had become Lightfoot's biggest supporter in the United States. In Lightfoot's hotel room on the Sunset Strip, the singer-songwriter opened up to him: "There are all sorts of temptations—the social life, the drinking and the chicks—that always face you. But it's self-destructive. You have to treat your talent with respect." Then, perhaps with Janis Joplin in mind, he added, "There are so many people who have ruined their talent because of drugs and other things. There are a lot of times when I stay out too late, when I drink too much. I'm still learning about discipline. I'm still guilty of misusing my talent. But as long as you remain conscious of it, as long as you don't let it get the best of you, it's probably all right."

It was a stunningly honest confession, not at all in keeping with rock-star posturing. But that was Lightfoot. Whenever he let his guard down—which was rarely—out of his mouth would come the most extraordinary things. On the surface, he was a celebrated, sought-after troubadour, one with a somewhat rugged, road-hardened image. But deep down, he was still a small-town guy of surprising sensitivity. As Lightfoot's star continued to rise, that attractive duality of toughness and vulnerability would face increasing challenges.

EIGHT

Tilting at Windmills

Cathy Smith was a beautiful twenty-four-year-old brunette who had worked as a waitress at the Riverboat. She'd already had a baby from an affair with Levon Helm and had put the child up for adoption. Smith was on her way up to see Bernie Fiedler in his apartment on a May evening when Lightfoot, who lived in the same building, stepped into the elevator. Lightfoot, she recounts in her memoir, *Chasing the Dragon*, "was wearing jeans and a denim vest, with expensive cowboy boots. The sleeves of his striped shirt were rolled up to the elbows, and he wore wire-rimmed glasses. Dark blond curly hair, long sideburns and a round country-boy face." They recognized each other immediately; they'd had a one-night stand eighteen months earlier, after Lightfoot and Ian Tyson had met Smith and her girlfriend Joyce Ivall at Yonge Street's Edison Hotel. Sparks rekindled, she and Lightfoot began seeing each other again. Almost immediately, after just a few evenings together, Smith moved into Lightfoot's apartment and his most tumultuous love affair began.

Their first date took place downtown at Winston's, one of Toronto's most high-end restaurants, where Lightfoot ordered a $300 bottle of Château Lafite Rothschild to toast their romance and his US success. But their regular dining spot was Harry's, a restaurant owned by Harry Barberian, just a short walk from the Alexander Street apartment. Lightfoot loved Harry's steaks, and his favorite maître d', George Bigliardi, always took care of him, ensuring that he and Smith got a quiet table in the back. The wine was always flowing. According to Smith, she and Lightfoot "drank so much Châteauneuf-du-Pape we should have bought an interest in the vineyard." It was not uncommon for the two to down two or three bottles a night, followed by green Chartreuse in long-stemmed glasses. Some nights, they took in hockey games. Maple Leaf Gardens was right on their doorstep, and Smith joined Lightfoot in cheering on the hometown Leafs. Afterward, they'd head up to the Gardens' Hot Stove Lounge or back to Harry's for more drinks. Then they'd stagger home, according to Smith, "drunk and madly in love."

The popularity of "If You Could Read My Mind" landed Lightfoot a return trip to England in June 1971. Invited to the Royal Albert Hall, he performed his best ballads, early hits and such distinctly Canadian numbers as the Maritime classic "Farewell to Nova Scotia" and his own "Canadian Railroad Trilogy" before a full house. He also played a new song from the *Summer Side of Life* whose message was totally lost on his English audience. Sung partly in Lightfoot's stilted French, "Nous Vivons Ensemble" was his earnest attempt to address the subject of Canadian unity. With a separatist movement calling for Quebec to leave Canada, Lightfoot felt compelled to express the need for his country to stay together.

While in London, Lightfoot appeared on the BBC's *Top of the Pops*, where he, Shea and Haynes performed "If You Could Read My Mind." The trio also taped an hour-long special for the BBC's *In Concert* TV series, standing on a small stage surrounded by an intimate studio audience. Under the glare of spotlights, Lightfoot looked every inch the folk darling as he sang early and current hits. While lights illuminated his blond curls, multiple camera angles showed the colorful rainbow, sun and birds patches sewn on the front and back of his denim jacket, the sleeves of which had been stylishly cut off. With a medallion around his neck, Lightfoot was in full troubadour mode, performing his train songs, highway ballads and tales of moving on. The audience loved his impassioned "Summer Side of Life" and the introspective "Talking in Your Sleep," but saved its heartiest applause for "Early Morning Rain," a song long familiar to folk devotees in England.

The BBC's *In Concert* special remains Lightfoot's best filmed performance, capturing him at the peak of his creative powers. It was also Red Shea's last regular appearance as Lightfoot's lead guitarist. A peerless finger-picker, Shea had been with him for six years, contributing quicksilver solos and filigree fretwork that helped to define the Lightfoot sound. His guitar work enhanced so many songs, nowhere more prominently than on "Canadian Railroad Trilogy" and "If You Could Read My Mind." Shea had also been an engaging road companion for Lightfoot, a drinking buddy as adept with thoughtful conversation as he was with hilarious jokes. But having found God and become a Jehovah's Witness, he wanted to leave the touring lifestyle behind and spend more time with his family. When touring resumed in September, Terry Clements would become Lightfoot's new guitar man. Lightfoot had met him in Los Angeles while working on music for *Cool Hand Luke*. With shoulder-length hair and dressed head to toe in denim, Clements was an easygoing guy who would become a close friend, someone with whom Lightfoot could share a song and a drink.

Lightfoot spent part of the summer holed up in his writing apartment—sometimes until sunrise—working on new songs, while Smith, according to her memoir, was busy "embroidering his jackets or adding various beads and baubles to the clothes he wore onstage." This would become Lightfoot's pattern: writing to deadline to meet his recording contract with Warner Bros. Another pattern was established that summer: after meeting his writing deadline, Lightfoot took August off, telling Smith he was going on a monthlong canoe trip up northern Quebec's Rupert River, responding to a challenge from Ottawa high school teacher Michael Landry. Joining them on that trip was Toronto canoe-tripping enthusiast Bob Dion and several of Landry's students. For the next decade, canoeing became a summer habit for Lightfoot, who found much-needed solitude in the wilderness. He also used the trips to dry out and get himself ready for recording and touring.

I was working so efficiently back then. I'd write all the songs I needed leading up to the canoe trip with the plan that as soon as I got back, I'd start getting them ready to record. The trips were hard work, really hard. Like boot camp. But they helped get me in shape and looking human again, because when you drink you certainly aren't fit. It became a form of therapy.

Maybe he was having doubts about his relationship with Smith, or perhaps he developed some romantic notion about his marriage, but when Lightfoot returned from his trip he moved back in with Brita and the kids. The reunion lasted only a few days before they both realized it was a mistake. The feeling was gone and neither of them could get it back. The marriage was over. He returned to his high-rise apartment, and Smith moved back in a short while later.

Lightfoot rounded out the year with two nights at Carnegie Hall. One of the new songs he performed spoke volumes about his ambition, the pressure to create, the lure of the road and the toll all of it took on his marriage. It was a stark confessional called "Ordinary Man." In an interview in New York with England's *Melody Maker*, he was asked to explain the origin of the song. "I've been through some of life's pitfalls, like I wasn't able to stick it out on the domestic scene," Lightfoot admitted to the female reporter. "I guess the song is written to my wife."

Try to see my side

It's not your ordinary pride that keeps driving me on

It's that lonesome, restless feeling that you feel under the gun

And it leads me to the highway but it keeps my body warm

And as I wander to the cities and the towns

I get so lonesome knowing you could be around

And when the show is over, there's a holiday motel

Another empty bottle and another tale to tell

Try to understand

I'm not your ordinary man, still I can't deny

You go with me everywhere

Like a shadow in the gloom

I remember all the good times

There's a ghost in every room

Brita, Fred and Ingrid haunted his next album. *Don Quixote* was recorded in Los Angeles in late 1971 and early 1972. Along with "Ordinary Man" and the title track, inspired by Cervantes's tilting-at-windmills hero, it included the bittersweet "Looking at the Rain," which expressed the wish that "this was all a dream" and the hope that he'd find his love beside him when he awoke. Guilt weighed heavily in songs like "Second Cup of Coffee," in which "sleep was filled with dreaming of the wrongs that I had done / And the gentle sweet reminder of a daughter and a son." Ever the romantic, Lightfoot had also written one glowing love song, "Beautiful," as a parting gift to Brita. It would become his next single and eventually one of his most popular songs, the kind of dreamy ballad that would figure prominently in his live shows for decades to come.

The cover of *Don Quixote* featured a determined-looking Lightfoot, guitar in hand, looking straight at the camera. He was sporting a beard and a brown leather jacket that originally belonged to Jerry Jeff Walker. Lightfoot had admired it while Walker was in Toronto performing at the Riverboat; the burnished leather had the look of autumn leaves. Walker threw Lightfoot the jacket as he was stepping off the elevator in his hotel and it became a hot potato, getting tossed back and forth. When the elevator doors finally closed, it was in Lightfoot's possession. "I loved that jacket, so I guess that's how much I loved Gordon," says Walker, who adds with a laugh, "I thought he needed it for his image."

The jacket, along with his new beard, did help give Lightfoot a cool mystique. Somehow, his mellow sound continued to coexist comfortably with his tough persona. That paradoxical blend had begun on *Summer Side of Life*, took hold with *Don Quixote* and would continue on his next recording. These became the albums that defined Lightfoot most strongly.

As well as songs of love and regret, *Don Quixote* featured several compositions that reflected Lightfoot's consuming interests. "Ode to Big Blue," about a legendary great whale that lost its family to hunters, was in keeping with Lightfoot's ecological concerns, while "Christian Island (Georgian Bay)" was about the joys of sailing, something he'd taken up in earnest after being introduced to it by Fred Neil in Coconut Grove several years earlier. "Brave Mountaineers" is Lightfoot's simple reverie about growing up in the country without any concern for time. "I need to be there," he sings, "when the world gets too heavy and the shadows cross my mind." Reading between the lines, it's easy to see the attraction of getting back to Orillia and away from big-city pressures.

While finishing the album in Los Angeles, Lightfoot returned to the Troubadour. He'd long since outgrown the three-hundred-seat nightclub but maintained ties with its owner, Doug Weston, and played the intimate venue to try out new material on audiences. In its review of his opening night, *Billboard* called Lightfoot a "strong, gutsy, masculine, erudite singer, whose material carries the weight of his conscience." The reviewer added, "Lightfoot's stern face, augmented by his newly grown beard, creates an image of a hard disciplinarian. This is partially true in his music, because his voice maintains a stolid level of intensity. I find nothing wrong with that because there is a complete excitement being generated with every song, and one does not get bored with the same tempo and intensity." It's true: there's a similarity in much of Lightfoot's material because he often relies on the same keys and rhythms. But it was the consistently high quality of his compositions that enabled Lightfoot to stand out from so many of his contemporaries—and attract other artists to his songs.

Frank Sinatra was the latest to come calling. The legendary singer, who'd scored number 1 hits in the 1960s with "Strangers in the Night" and "Somethin' Stupid," was looking for songs for his next album and telephoned Lightfoot. "He said he was doing an album of what he called 'saloon songs' and wondered if I could write something for him," Lightfoot says. "I had to tell him I wasn't in a writing mode at that time but would send him a couple of songs." One of them was "If You Could Read My Mind." Recording engineer Lee Hirschberg was mixing *Don Quixote* by day and working with Sinatra by night, both at Amigo Studios. Hirschberg says that Lightfoot dropped in on the Sinatra session the evening that Ol' Blue Eyes was considering recording "If You Could Read My Mind." "Don Costa had written a great arrangement, a kind of semi-swing thing, not too fast," Hirschberg recalls. "But as the orchestra started playing it, Sinatra suddenly threw down the lead sheets and said, 'Forget it. I can't sing this. There's too many words.' I don't know if it had anything to do with Sinatra's love life, but he was having difficulty with women at the time."

In March 1972, "If You Could Read My Mind" was nominated for a Grammy Award for Best Male Pop Vocal Performance. Lightfoot was invited to perform the song at the televised award show in New York City, but the producers wanted him to keep his performance to under two minutes, effectively cutting the song in half. Lightfoot had clear ideas about how his music should be presented. One reason he'd formed Early Morning Productions was to take control of all areas of his career. He was calling the shots now. Lightfoot thought about the Grammy request for about a second and refused, missing out on a chance to shine on music's biggest night on television. He simply wasn't going to let his song be chopped up to fit some producer's format.

Lightfoot took charge again when unwanted recordings began reappearing in stores. He was peeved that United Artists was trying to cash in on his new fame by reissuing his early work under the title *Classic Lightfoot*. The reissue, he felt, would compete with his new recordings. But he was furious when the American Metropolitan Enterprises label reissued all of his Chateau recordings in a compilation called *Early Lightfoot*. He promptly instructed Al Mair to buy up every copy he could find, and Lightfoot personally took an axe to them in the yard behind the Early Morning Productions office. "It pissed me off," he says, "because people would hear those recordings and be confused or misled into thinking I was still doing a Jim Reeves or Pat Boone kind of thing. Axing them sounds violent, but it was the best way of ensuring people wouldn't hear them. Strike them once on each side and throw them into the dumpster." He adds, "We could've poured gasoline on them, but that would've just brought the fire department around."

On the eve of another multiple-night stand at Massey Hall, by now an annual ritual, Lightfoot granted an interview to another woman, this time the *Toronto Star*'s Marci McDonald. The lengthy profile caught Lightfoot in a defensive mood: defensive about the money he was making ("it always comes down to an accusation—that you're just in it for the money"), defensive about the bachelor-pad apartment he lived in ("I won't be here long cause it's ruinin' my image") and even defensive about being so defensive ("there I go, defendin' myself again"). McDonald, who interviewed Lightfoot both in his apartment and later over dinner in a Yonge Street steak-house, contrasted his sensitive songs with a man who can be "brusque to the point of boorishness in company, so socially inept he is uncomfortable to be with." And she concluded that he was like Cervantes's Don Quixote, "always manning his battlements." Lightfoot explained to McDonald that no one in his hometown ever thought he would make it and that it was only through perseverance, "goddam will" and "a lot of drive" that he had succeeded: "I was clumsy, square, awkward, shy, insecure—couldn't talk to people."

Always his own toughest critic, Lightfoot then told McDonald he was happiest on the road—a simple statement that spoke volumes: "There's an excitement about bein' in motion. I love it. I love the electricity of havin' real people there, live people." But Lightfoot's long absences on the road—not to mention his infidelities—had ruined his marriage and put a distance between him and his kids. "Have you ever had your son look at you with an accusation that you walked out on him?' he asked McDonald rhetorically. Thrilling though it was, being in constant motion took a toll that Lightfoot would have to live with all his life.

The following night, midway through his first Massey Hall set, the left side of Lightfoot's face suddenly went numb. Shaken, he somehow was able to finish the concert. As luck would have it, Dr. Bill Goodman, the Toronto folk community's ear, nose and throat specialist, was in the house and came backstage, where he immediately diagnosed Lightfoot's affliction as Bell's palsy, a form of temporary facial paralysis usually caused by nerve damage. Goodman ordered a prescription of cortisone, which enabled Lightfoot to complete his string of concerts. The doctor also sent him to Mount Sinai Hospital for three electric shock treatments to stimulate the motor nerve functions back to life. Bassist Haynes remembers that Lightfoot lost the ability to whistle. "He used to whistle on a couple of tunes," he says, "so that changed things." The affliction also prevented him from smiling. "It was bad," confirms Lightfoot, who admitted to one reporter that he cried himself to sleep wondering if he'd ever get better. "I was still able to sing, but it affected my speech on one side. And one of my eyes wouldn't close, so to keep the air off [it] I had to wear a patch for a month or two. That was disturbing. But we had a tour overseas coming up and another album due, so I just willed myself right into it." His "goddam will" and the sturdy Lightfoot stock led to a remarkable recovery.

Lightfoot's fame and bank account continued to grow as some of the pop world's biggest stars covered his songs. First, Barbra Streisand included an emotional "If You Could Read My Mind" on her pop-rock album *Stoney End*. Then, Elvis Presley cut a brisk reading of "Early Morning Rain" that he later included on *Elvis Now*. Lightfoot was thrilled; as a boy, he'd once done Elvis imitations in front of a mirror, and now the King of Rock and Roll was covering one of his songs. He immediately got Mair to buy tickets to Presley's spring concert in Buffalo and make arrangements to meet Elvis after the show. Come the day of the concert, Lightfoot and Mair drove down in a limousine and saw Presley perform a twenty-one-song set list that included all of his biggest hits and a few recent covers, but not "Early Morning Rain." Still, at the end of the concert they started to make their way toward the backstage area. Slowed by the crush of the crowd, they hadn't yet reached backstage when the familiar announcement came over the auditorium's sound system: "Ladies and gentlemen, Elvis has left the building." Lightfoot never got to meet the King. More than forty years later, in March 2016, he and his band visited Graceland, in Memphis, for the first time, and Lightfoot was cheered to learn from one of Presley's associates that Elvis had wanted to record his "The Last Time I Saw Her."

Anne Murray scored a major hit that year with her rendition of Lightfoot's "Cotton Jenny." The song's down-home charm suited Murray, who'd soared to fame by pairing up with Glen Campbell, appearing first as a regular on his TV show and then recording a popular duets album with him. Many in the industry thought Lightfoot and Murray, the top solo stars in Canada, would make the perfect pop couple, something the two resisted.*

Anne and I never sang together. People always wanted us to team up, but we never would. It was too obvious, almost too Canadian. We talked about it on the phone one day. She wanted to be her own entity too. So I said, "Well that's what we'll tell them: we're not going to do duets on TV or recordings together. We'll just continue to do our own things." And that's how we've done it.

Still not fully recovered from Bell's palsy, Lightfoot played two dates in June, at London's Albert Hall and Dublin's National Stadium, then returned to Toronto for a prescribed break from performing. He holed up with Cathy Smith in his apartment and spent long hours in his studio across the hall, working on songs for his next album. Sitting alone in a big room with windows facing west, no rugs and just his desk and chair, Lightfoot would often start working at sundown, watching the setting sun as he composed, and continue until dawn. More than drugs, alcohol was Lightfoot's mainstay, and his capacity for wine and whiskey was astounding. According to

---

* Murray did try to get Lightfoot to sing a duet with her on her 1993 album, *Croonin'*, and was miffed when he said no.

Smith, he "lived up to every inch of the image of the hard-drinking, hard-playing cowboy singer." Lightfoot, she added, "drank a lot— more than any man I'd ever known," and Smith drank to keep up with him. Some of the songs Lightfoot came up with that summer, including the melancholic "Can't Depend on Love," reflected a con- tinuing despondency over his split with Brita. But others, like the jaunty "You Are What I Am," reveled in a giddy joy over his love affair with Smith.

The Mariposa Folk Festival had become wildly popular since returning to Toronto in 1968 and settling on Centre Island. Big- name headliners were overshadowing workshop performers. To shift the focus back to its roots, Mariposa's organizers by 1972 had ended their practice of closing each day with a major concert. But plans for a lower-key festival that July soon went awry. First, Murray McLauchlan shared his Saturday set with Joni Mitchell. Then, Bruce Cockburn turned part of his slot over to Neil Young. Neither Mitchell nor Young had been scheduled, and their surprise appear- ances drew massive crowds. Bob Dylan was wandering around the island with his wife, Sara, trying to look inconspicuous in jeans, white shirt, red bandanna and rimless glasses. Dylan watched perfor- mances by bluesmen Taj Mahal, Bukka White and Roosevelt Sykes. Lightfoot, wearing rose-colored glasses, was there too and caught a set by newcomer John Prine before sauntering off. When he sat down on a picnic table someone handed him a guitar, and Lightfoot began to strum and sing. Soon, several other guitarists joined him, and a crowd of about 150 gathered around. Lightfoot and Dylan later bumped into each other and were instantly surrounded by fans and autograph hounds. Dylan beat a hasty retreat and took a private boat back to the mainland, but not before arranging to meet Lightfoot at his apartment that night.

Lightfoot and Dylan had been mutual admirers, covering each other's songs and following each other's career ever since that first meeting over a pool table at Grossman's Woodstock retreat. Yet Lightfoot was nervous at the prospect of Dylan visiting—and getting shown up again at pool was only part of it. Dylan was aloof and inscrutable, a difficult guy to get a handle on, and he had a way with words that Lightfoot found intimidating. Plus, as much as Lightfoot could crank out songs when he put his nose to the grindstone, there was no keeping up with Dylan. The encounter at Lightfoot's apartment was awkward in the extreme, according to Cathy Smith and confirmed by Bernie Fiedler. Bob and Sara Dylan arrived and plunked themselves down together in Lightfoot's favorite leather chair. Lightfoot asked Dylan if he'd like something to eat. A cheese sandwich, Dylan replied, which Smith dutifully went off to make. Lightfoot, thinking it should be something more substantial, raced into the kitchen and told Smith to make it ham and cheese—which Dylan then refused because of his recent adherence to Judaism. The rest of the evening had long periods of silence with a few mumbled exchanges, and Dylan and Lightfoot mostly just eyeballed each other. Dylan later joked on his *Theme Time Radio Hour* in 2006 that he and Lightfoot had a "fierce musical feud" similar to the intense early '60s battle between Jamaican singers Derrick Morgan and Prince Buster.

Murray McLauchlan, who also lived at 50 Alexander Street, moved in the same social circles, and was often at Lightfoot's parties, understood better than most the nature of the Dylan–Lightfoot relationship. "Dylan was very respectful of what Gord was doing," says McLauchlan. "They both had fans that wanted a piece of them and sensed in each other that they faced a different set of circumstances than most people. It's like belonging to an exclusive club. You've suddenly got a pass to the penthouse. Gord and Dylan were a part of that club. They're both reclusive and eccentric, so to some degree they're kindred spirits. Except Gord's life is not a fabrication.

He is who he is. Bob Dylan is a complete myth." It's possible that these kindred spirits—one down-to-earth, the other wrapped in mystery—each wished they could be a little more like the other. But Lightfoot could never really change who he was. It was so inbred in him, he simply couldn't escape it. Maybe he never wanted to.

NINE

Sundown

B y 1972, Lightfoot's star had risen high enough that he could call the shots. He didn't have to leave Toronto to make a record if he didn't want to; people would come to him. When it came time to record his fourth Warner album in two years, Waronker, engineer Lee Hirschberg and arranger Nick DeCaro flew up from Los Angeles for the September sessions at RCA Studios at 225 Mutual Street. In addition to guitarist Clements and bassist Haynes, Lightfoot brought back Red Shea for extra guitar. Lightfoot already had a new batch of songs. He planned to use strings, provided by members of the Toronto Symphony Orchestra, on three of them: "That Same Old Obsession," "Can't Depend on Love" and "Hi'way Songs." But mostly he was aiming for more of a country sound with a hint of bluegrass, so he booked Bruce and Larry Good of the Good Brothers to provide autoharp and banjo, Ollie Strong for pedal steel and American picker David Bromberg for slide dobro.

Lightfoot had rarely used a drummer in the studio, and never one on tour. A recording engineer at RCA Studios introduced him to Barry Keane, a tall, thin studio drummer with a gentle face. Keane remembers a bizarre introduction to the recording star: "We were listening to 'You Are What I Am,' which I hadn't played on yet, and

Gord said, 'We need to put some leg on it.' I had no idea what he was talking about. He set up a couple of chairs. The song starts, and Gord starts playing hand drums on his legs. So I follow suit. Lee [Hirschberg], the engineer, says, 'It's good, but not quite the right sound.' Gord looked at me and said, 'Drop your drawers.' He stood up, undid his pants, and they fell to his ankles. He didn't seem like a practical joker. So I dropped my pants, and there's Gord and I sitting side by side playing drums on our bare thighs. Lee yells, 'That's it!' And that's how we recorded it."

Lightfoot called the new album *Old Dan's Records*. It was a title he and Smith had come up with, a play on the words "old dance records." When the album was released in November, it quickly topped the Canadian charts. Lightfoot's instinct to go country had paid off. But in the United States, the album peaked at number 95. Reviewers criticized the use of orchestral sweeteners. Stephen Holden's review in *Rolling Stone* said the strings "serve to make perfectly decent songs sound like schlock." Lightfoot, he added, "clearly wants to be all things to all people—rustic folkie, cosmopolite, social commentator, and above all, the apostle of romantic love." Compared to the warm, stripped-down acoustic sound of *Summer Side of Life* and *Don Quixote*, the strings seemed out of place on *Old Dan's Records*. But Lightfoot was on a roll. He was forging his own distinct sound, one that would become more fully realized on his next album.

Seeking quality time with Smith and some inspiration for songwriting, Lightfoot rented a farmhouse on a fifty-acre property on the outskirts of the city, which served both as a love nest and a creative retreat. "It was way up in King Township, near Aurora," he says. "I had a great writing room there, a really good space. Wrote quite a few songs there. And Cathy was around when I was doing them. She wanted to get married, but we both knew that I wasn't going to get married. I'd just gotten out of a marriage." The King farmhouse, the first property on the west side of Bathurst Street, north of the 16th Sideroad, was also conveniently located close to where Red Shea and the Good Brothers were living, if Lightfoot ever wanted to play music.

Life with Smith was in fact becoming increasingly fractious. Smith looked after Lightfoot, acted as a creative sounding board and boosted his confidence. But they also pushed each other's buttons, and alcohol was often a factor. Lightfoot could be impossible to read, which frustrated Smith, and she got him mad. Her brazen flirting with other men drove him crazy with jealousy. Smith had already had an affair with Lightfoot's friend Brian Good, which Smith herself admitted couldn't have been a more hurtful choice.

It was his jealousy of Smith that eventually gave Lightfoot his biggest hit. One night in 1973, he was alone at the farmhouse writing songs, fueled as usual by coffee, booze and cigarettes. Smith had driven into Toronto to party with some friends. The whole time she was gone, Lightfoot fretted about who she was with and what she might be doing. "I was hoping that no one else would get their hands on her," he once said, "because she was pretty good-looking." It led Lightfoot to write his sexiest song, one that expressed exactly how he felt about Smith "lying back in her satin dress" or "looking fast in her faded jeans." But "Sundown" also had a paranoid and menacing tone, as a threatening Lightfoot vented his mistrust of someone who might be creeping around his back stairs, looking to move in on his woman. One of the song's clever refrains reflected his growing dependency on alcohol: "Sometimes I think it's a shame / When I get feeling better when I'm feeling no pain." Overall, it expressed the trap Lightfoot found himself in, knowing the object of his desire was no good for him yet being unable to resist her. And the torture of it all was driving him to drink more than ever—sometimes as much as a bottle of Canadian Club a day.

As great a capacity for liquor as Lightfoot had, drinking was starting to get the better of him. In early 1973, he performed in Honolulu and later boasted to an English reporter that he "spent eight days there getting drunk." The Honolulu concert was marred by Lightfoot yelling and swearing throughout the show at the light and sound crew, resulting in boos from the audience. It wasn't the first or last time Lightfoot's frustration at poor lighting and sound sent him into a rage, but the alcohol was clearly fueling the fire. Back in Toronto, during his record five sold-out shows at Massey Hall in March, he was so badly behaved that one woman sent a letter to the *Toronto Star* complaining that his language was offensive to her and her fourteen-year-old daughter. Wrote Eunice Mouckley: "When [Lightfoot] came on stage he told the audience that he was stoned, had been to too many parties and had gotten to bed at eight o'clock that morning. All during the concert he proceeded to utter a string of obscenities interspersed with musical selections. He had a young audience and it should have deterred him from advertising the fact that he was high. The language he used all evening was inexcusable." Lightfoot, usually a perfectionist about his concert presentation, was oblivious.

Booze alone hadn't brought down Lightfoot's marriage, but liquor, combined with an increasingly reckless lifestyle, certainly contributed to its demise. Lightfoot's divorce from Brita was front-page news across the country. Divorce in Canada in 1973 was still a big deal. Until just five years earlier, adultery was the only legal grounds on which a couple could be divorced. And the Divorce Act still required a three-year separation first. Newspaper reports spelled out the details of the Lightfoots' court proceeding. Brita had returned to their Blythwood Road home after a trip to Sweden in 1970 and found another woman in the house. In the courtroom, Lightfoot admitted adultery, and Justice Frank Donnelly awarded Brita custody of Fred and Ingrid and $4,500 a month for support. She was also given a lump payment of $150,000 for a new home. *The Globe and Mail* reported that Lightfoot had earned more than $1 million the previous year. His divorce settlement, newspapers claimed, was the largest of its kind in Canadian history. Legend has it that Brita's lawyer walked out of the courtroom after the trial singing "That's what you get for lovin' me," although Al Mair, who was called in to testify, doesn't remember that. "I didn't want to get involved," says Mair. "Her lawyer was arguing that Gord was as big as Harry Belafonte, and I was having to argue that he wasn't. It was one of the most uncomfortable things I had to do." It was more uncomfortable still for Lightfoot. For a man so intensely private, it was excruciating to have his dirty laundry aired in public.

A couple of years earlier, Lightfoot had written and recorded the humorous "Divorce Country Style," with sardonic lyrics like "Now I've told the lawyer that I think the house should be mine / You take the car and the kids and I'll take the wine." Lightfoot never released it, but he performed the song for the next several years, maybe trying to take the sting out of a painful subject. The truth was, he felt he'd badly mishandled his relationship with Brita, as he later reflected.

When did I know the marriage was over? Probably from the day it began. Maybe even before. I knew I didn't want to marry, but I promised. I wouldn't be talked out of it. Infidelity finally ended the marriage. Unavoidable. I was not well behaved enough to expect the relationship to last. It reached the point where it had to terminate. I had to move out. Then the last few years I started drinking a lot. There was one thing that took place that really knocked the shit out of everybody: Fred got hit by a car in that dip in the road on Blythwood. He was very young, just seven years old, and was badly bruised and shaken up. It was the day after I moved out, and I'd slept on a couch in my office. Had to go right back up there to tend to the situation. He was down. It made me feel really small at the end of that relationship.

———

As bad as Lightfoot felt about the breakup of his family, he had no time to wallow. He had plenty of tour dates booked and TV appearances scheduled and his record label was readying his new album for release. There was no question "Sundown" was going to be the album's key track and Lightfoot's next single. According to Lenny Waronker, his producer, "It only took forty-five minutes to record, and the way Gordon played it on his twelve-string was so powerful it just filled up the room. It was a dark song with some real tension in it. As soon as it was finished, everyone knew it was going to be a hit. Gordon knew it too. The song was incredibly cool." The *Sundown* album arrived in record stores in January 1974, with a cover of a denim-clad, sandal-wearing Lightfoot sitting cross-legged in the hay-filled barn on his rented farmhouse property.* The reviews were uniformly positive. New York's *Village Voice* declared that the album "maintains all the strengths of his early work. But it adds to them an extraordinary sensitivity to pain—his own and others—and to joy. The Ramblin' Man who roamed untouched through strangers' lives has been replaced by, well, a grown-up. By someone who understands that his actions have consequences."

That view of the thirty-five-year-old singer-songwriter was echoed by *Rolling Stone*'s Stephen Holden, who this time wrote, "Lightfoot's reflections are those of a mature man, capable of strong, romantic and political emotions, tempered by a suave sexuality and an elegiac mysticism." It was true. There was a deepening maturity in the songwriting on *Sundown*, from the sensitive portrait of an inner-city Christmas on "Circle of Steel" to the philosophical

---

* Photo taken by acclaimed Toronto photographer John Reeves, who also shot the covers of *Don Quixote*, *Old Dan's Records*, and *Gord's Gold*. His portrait of Lightfoot appears on the cover of this book. Reeves died in 2016.

freight-hopper's tale in "The Watchman's Gone." Lightfoot was pushing himself to dig deeper.

One of *Sundown*'s most ambitious songs, "Seven Island Suite," is also one of Lightfoot's best. Inspired by his sailing experiences on Georgian Bay, it captures the awe and wonder of witnessing natural beauty—something Lightfoot had felt since his childhood on the shores of Lake Couchiching. The rhythm of the song ebbs and flows as he observes that "anybody with a wish to wander could not fail to be aroused." But "Seven Island Suite" also serves as a cautionary tale, as Lightfoot contrasts the idyllic setting with materialistic pursuits: "Living high in the city, guess you think it's a pretty good way. . . . You seem to think because you got chicken to go you're in luck." The song concludes with him singing, "It's time you tried living on the high side of the bay, you need a rest / Any man or a woman with a wish to fade away could be so blessed."

Lightfoot's wish to wander is also reflected on "Carefree Highway." The title occurred to him after seeing it on a road sign between Flagstaff and Phoenix while touring Arizona. Struck by the words, he wrote them down and saved them for his next writing session. The recorded song, full of feelings of loss and longing over an "old flame," became Lightfoot's next hit after "Sundown," climbing into the North American Top 10 and buying him more time to complete his follow-up album. Mostly, "Carefree Highway" captured the wanderlust common in Lightfoot's work. As he told one writer that year, "I've always had this desire to keep moving. That's why a lot of my songs are about travel. It's a rebellion, I guess, against staying in one place too long, against getting bogged down. I've always felt this need to keep moving. It's inside me."

Despite that restlessness, Lightfoot still seemed to feel the need to have a home base. Living in the farmhouse north of the city had lost its allure, so Lightfoot bought a new property in Toronto, at 98 Binscarth Road, on the eastern fringe of the exclusive Rosedale neighborhood. As with his previous home on Blythwood, it was on a secluded street near a ravine and provided the privacy suitable for someone of Lightfoot's level of fame. He was still with Smith and gave her the run of the third floor. But their relationship was becoming increasingly toxic. Smith claimed in her memoir that Lightfoot's temper had led him to hit her, something he denied. "A lot of our problems must have been due to drink," she wrote. Lightfoot was not a violent man, but he did, like his father, tend to bottle up his emotions. And his temper could sometimes uncork those emotions, with explosive results.

While Lightwood was recording *Sundown*, Gordon Lightfoot Sr. had been diagnosed with stomach cancer and hospitalized. Gordon Jr. stayed as close to his dad as a taciturn man like him would allow. His father could never show the warmth of a loving parent the way his mother did, but the younger Gordon certainly respected his steady, hardworking elder. And he naturally wanted his dad's approval for his latest album. So when Gordon Sr. was back home from the hospital following treatment, his son drove up to Orillia with a recording of *Sundown*. "He heard the album as he was laid up in his bedroom," says Lightfoot. "I brought a tape machine and played it for him." Although his father didn't say much, he did tell his son that he thought it sounded "very professional."

My dad was very young when he died, just sixty-three. Four other guys he worked with also died young. Some people said it was because of the chemical that they used in the dry cleaning. It poisoned the air. My dad ran that business nearly until he died. He was so hardworking. Very highly thought of too. He loved to play golf and loved to curl, and he did both with great enthusiasm. He was sick for such a long time that it was almost a relief when he died.

Gordon Sr. died in Orillia's Soldiers' Memorial Hospital on March 5, 1974, just as *Sundown* was beginning its climb to the top of the charts. Sadly, he missed out on seeing his son achieve the pinnacle of pop success. Before he passed away, Gordon Sr. told his son that he'd really like to see him hire Bev, his sister. She was smart, organized, good with numbers, he told him, and could really help around the office. Lightfoot followed his father's wishes and offered his sister a job. Bev, whose marriage had just ended, was happy to make a fresh start. She moved to Toronto and began working at Early Morning Productions.

Lightfoot set about touring to promote his new album and took a high-profile US gig hosting the popular late-night TV series *The Midnight Special.* He then returned to Canada from LA for multiple shows in Ottawa, Montreal and Toronto. He taped all of his Massey Hall shows with the intention of producing a live album. But, typical of Lightfoot's perfectionism, he scrapped the planned live recording when he heard the difference a broken fingernail made to his guitar playing. That summer, another UK tour took Lightfoot to Belfast and Dublin and once again to London's Royal Albert Hall. He also made his debut at LA's Universal Amphitheatre for three dates.

"Sundown" was one of the songs Lightfoot took with him on his six-concert tour of England. While "Sundown" was steeped in sexuality, others, such as "Somewhere U.S.A." and "Carefree Highway," expressed the joy of being on the road. But a more thoughtful Lightfoot emerged in the protest strains of "Circle of Steel," the spiritual lament "Too Late for Prayin'" and the epic "Seven Island Suite," a six-minute paean to the healing power of nature. In interviews he gave to English magazines like *Melody Maker*, Lightfoot sounded more excited about getting back to nature on his upcoming five-week canoe trip in northern Quebec than he was about recording his next album. Going into the wilderness, he said, was both thrilling and therapeutic. "It's hard work. You paddle fifteen or twenty miles a day and do away with the amenities of life. The expedition is a revitalization of the mind processes, stripping you down to basics." Canoeing demanded organization and orderliness, two things Lightfoot excelled at. And with his disciplined approach to work, he thrived on the challenges of wilderness trips.

In June, *Sundown* hit the number 1 spot on the *Billboard* and *Cashbox* album charts, while the title track simultaneously topped the singles charts. It was a rare double-pinnacle feat, one that catapulted Lightfoot into superstardom, boosting every aspect of his career, from record and ticket sales to media coverage and venue size—even the number of groupies waiting for him backstage. "Sundown" eclipsed Paul McCartney & Wings' "Band on the Run" and Lightfoot relished beating one of the ex-Beatles. "I remember we knocked McCartney out of first place. That's as close as I got to catching up to those guys, because they were always there, and you always had to compete against them."

Was Lightfoot equipped to cope with the changes? Yes and no. As the consummate professional, he adapted well to performing in bigger and better venues. But as the innately shy, small-town guy, he had difficulty adjusting to big-time fame and the glare of journalistic scrutiny. Two major magazine articles captured that duality.

In a cover story in *Saturday Night*, writer Jack Batten focused on Lightfoot's "vulnerability" and how he "looks at the world through eyes full of questions and doubts." Lightfoot admitted to Batten that, being self-managed, he took a greater interest in the business side of things than most artists. He explained that he'd let his contract with Albert Grossman expire three years earlier, although they were still on very amicable terms. But looking after his own affairs had its risks. "I talk business and you'll write that," he told Batten, "and then people'll say, 'Look, he doesn't care about the art, only the business.' That's why I'm not hot on interviews. I don't want to look wrong or stupid."

Meanwhile, in a piece titled "A Heavy New Star Named Lightfoot," *People* magazine described him as a recluse who tried to stay out of the media so that he could "walk down the street without being recognized."

It also mentioned Lightfoot's fondness for Canadian whiskey in coffee before concerts and how he was now "lonely and womanless."

Lightfoot and Smith had finally split up that summer, after three tempestuous years. Lightfoot had allowed her to sing backup on *Sundown*'s "High and Dry" and had taken her on tour, including to a show at West Point military academy. "We were playing in a big concert hall to a roomful of cadets, all in uniform," recalls Lightfoot. "[I] brought her out to sing harmony on that song and when she left the stage all the guys in front were yelling, 'Bring back the girl.'" But the last straw came when Smith sang backup on Murray McLauchlan's *Day to Day Dust* album, on a song ironically called "Do You Dream of Being Somebody." "What the hell are you doing?" Lightfoot screamed at her. "Living in my house and working for the competition?"

"Gordon saw it as a big betrayal," confirms McLauchlan, who knew Smith as a neighbor at 50 Alexander Street but never had sexual designs on her. "I wasn't at all surprised that they broke up," he adds. "Cathy would come down to my place because 'Gordie was in a mood' or a 'rage.' There was a lot of jealousy, a lot of drinking. They weren't a good match. Gord's not that complicated; he's very down-to-earth. Cathy was extremely complicated, smart and ambitious. I suspect that she probably saw Gordon as a means to an end, an opportunity. Not a gold digger, that wasn't her game. But she was attracted to fame. She wanted to be around famous people, maybe perceiving that as a shortcut to being famous. Gord was in love with her, but she was looking to fly the coop."

Now on his own, Lightfoot spent the month of August pursuing his two summertime passions: sailing and canoeing. Sailing on Lake Huron was the perfect escape from the pressures of songwriting, recording and touring, and Lightfoot loved to be out on the water, sipping from his cup in the summer wind, with whiskers on his chin, as he sang on *Don Quixote*'s carefree "Christian Island (Georgian Bay)." His canoe trip that summer was on the Dumoine River, in western Quebec. Where sailing was a pleasurable escape, canoeing was brutally hard work. But Lightfoot knew he needed the enforced exercise and abstinence from booze to get himself in shape for another season of touring and recording.

Sundown's sales surpassed the two-million mark, and Lightfoot and his band embarked on the next three months of touring. First up was an exhausting ten-day tour of Australia, which began in Melbourne and included Sydney, Adelaide and Brisbane and then took them all the way west to Perth. In between was an unusual stop in exotic Hobart, Tasmania, where the venue was situated next to a casino filled with Saudi Arabians in long white robes. Outside were luxurious yachts docked in a big semicircle. "I'll never forget that," says Lightfoot. "We played a good show that night and then went gambling until quite late. During our stay, our hosts took us to a natural zoo with all the wonderful marsupial animals of Australia— every kind of species you could imagine. Duck-billed platypuses, Tasmanian devils, the whole bit."

The same tour included seven successful weeks of concerts throughout the American Midwest and Eastern Seaboard. But negative reviews greeted Lightfoot's last concerts of 1974. After his performance at the world-famous Grand Ole Opry in Nashville's Ryman Auditorium, *The Tennessean* newspaper panned Lightfoot's failed attempts at humor during the show and his admitted "rotten mood" about audience requests for songs he no longer plays. He was also angry about the recent *People* magazine article, which he called "baloney" for focusing on his divorce and making it sound recent. "Lightfoot on Wrong Track," *The Tennessean* headline read.

His mood was no different during one of four sold-out appearances before twelve thousand people at the Lincoln Center's Avery Fisher Hall. Lightfoot stalked off stage, fuming about his own sound system. *The New York Times* critic John Rockwell wrote, "The whole thing—the walkout had been preceded by curses between verses of his songs and sour remarks about 'a bummer in the Big Apple'—was simply self-indulgent on Mr. Lightfoot's part. Perhaps he would prefer obscurity to fame, but there must be more civilized ways of obtaining it." The negative reviews deeply upset Lightfoot, as all criticism did. "Gord was having issues with how we were being mixed onstage, with outside sound gear and personnel to run it," recalls Haynes. "But it was also party central time for him, so things got looser. He didn't have management, and that's when a tough manager would come in and say, 'Listen, you've gotta straighten out and fly right.'" Flying high and ever more recklessly, Lightfoot was getting all the warning signs that he was in trouble.

TEN

All the Lovely Ladies

L ightfoot kicked off 1975 with *Cold on the Shoulder*—remarkably, his eleventh album in just ten years. It was easily Lightfoot's most personal album to date. "All of the songs about relationships are out of my own experiences, either directly or indirectly," he told a Chicago reporter. "You know, you just take a specific situation and then let your imagination flow. And believe me, I've been through all kinds of relationships. Sometimes I've been burned and wound up on the losing end and sometimes I've won." Then, paraphrasing one of the refrains in "Sundown," he added, "Of course, sometimes when you win, you end up losing."

Where the *Sundown* album had been forged out of a torrid sexual affair, *Cold on the Shoulder* was the chilly aftermath of the breakup. Cathy Smith's influence was apparent throughout, including on the title track, which Lightfoot has said deals with "loneliness and remorse." "Now and Then" describes how a relationship on its last legs continues to exert its power to attract and repel. "A Tree Too Weak to Stand" is a cascading folk song of startling confession that details "the price of lust" over a chiming twelve-string guitar. Smith could well be the woman in the long dress on the bluesy "Slide on Over," a song that comes closest to expressing the sexual ache of

"Sundown." And she's long been rumored to be at the heart of "Rainy Day People," a wistful number about a lover who could listen well and share darker moods. The song became Lightfoot's next hit single, topping *Billboard*'s Easy Listening chart and reaching the Top 30 of its Hot 100 chart.

Cold on the Shoulder explores other themes of love. Lightfoot had made arrangements with Brita to see his children regularly. The bond with his kids had already inspired "The Pony Man." Now he'd written a tribute to his daughter; the string-laden "Fine as Fine Can Be" was Lightfoot's song for Ingrid. And "All the Lovely Ladies" is another tribute of sorts, an old-fashioned celebration mostly of women, including maybe even Lightfoot's mother, Jessie, who sat in his audience each night dressed in all their "finery."

One song was not the least bit personal. "Cherokee Bend" tells the story of a First Nations boy who fled a life of mistreatment to join the rodeo. It's loosely based on Hal Borland's 1963 young adult novel *When the Legends Die*. Lightfoot had read an adaptation of the novel in *Reader's Digest*. It remains one of his few story songs inspired by fiction rather than historical fact.

The album did include one obvious clunker. With a dull melody and such mawkish, simplistic lines as "In the name of love she came / This foolish winsome girl / She was all decked out like a rainbow trout / Swimmin' up stream in the world," "Rainbow Trout" was a rare example of Lightfoot at his worst: lazy and uninspired.

As much as *Cold on the Shoulder* explored matters close to home, Lightfoot remained "paranoically cautious" about opening up in interviews. He occasionally made exceptions. In a five-thousand-word cover story in the influential US music magazine *Crawdaddy*, Lightfoot told Nancy Naglin, "I find it real difficult to come to terms with the idea of settling down with one person for the rest of my life. I don't think I'm ever going to get married again, and if I was to do it, I'd wait until I was forty. When you're away from the woman, continually confronted by other women, you suddenly find yourself in a weak moment. Then you've gone and stepped over the traces and you gotta go home and confront your old lady. It's a two-way street. You're going to have to offer her the same deal. You can't ask a woman to be faithful if you're not going to be faithful to her. That's where it's broken down for me twice." Lightfoot's candor about his failed relationships was shocking, coming from someone usually so guarded.

The new album's cover showed a bearded, denim-shirted Lightfoot with his guitar. He was seated at his writing desk, its surface strewn with sheets of paper, and to one side was a pencil and a Chianti wine bottle. An almost ghostly figure of a dark-haired woman was standing in the shadows, just over his right shoulder. Many have assumed that woman to be Cathy Smith, but it was another woman. "She was a fan and we went out for a while," is all Lightfoot will say about her now. Private as ever, Lightfoot has never understood why people need to know details about his life.

Cold on the Shoulder was racing up the charts, selling more than 470,000 copies worldwide in the first three weeks. Lightfoot toured extensively throughout the year with his band, which now also included Red Shea, who had rejoined for the year, and Ed Ringwald, a pedal steel player from Waterloo, Ontario, who quickly earned the nickname Pee Wee Charles. At the Miami Beach Auditorium, an attractive blond woman in the front row was getting hassled by venue security for photographing Lightfoot. Seeing this, Lightfoot came to her rescue and arranged to have her admitted backstage. She was a fan, who also happened to be named Cathy. Over drinks backstage, she and Lightfoot hit it off. They talked about seeing each other again, and a few weeks later Cathy Coonley flew to Toronto.

Meanwhile, Lightfoot was upset about another record label capitalizing on his fame. This time, it was United Artists reissuing his early recordings. Instead of taking an axe to destroy the unwanted albums as he'd done last time, Lightfoot battled the competition by going into the studio and recording new versions of his songs from the United Artists days. That fall, Reprise released *Gord's Gold*, a twenty-two-track collection featuring new takes on Lightfoot favorites like "Early Morning Rain," "I'm Not Sayin'" and "Canadian Railroad Trilogy" as well as his Warner Bros. hits. Another example of Lightfoot taking charge of his career, *Gord's Gold* became a bestseller, the greatest-hits package every fan, old and new, wanted to own.

That summer, Lightfoot bought another Rosedale mansion, at 5 Beaumont Road. Like his Binscarth property a short distance away, it was on a quiet street by the ravine and had equally rich and famous neighbors, like the Bassett broadcasting family, the Eatons and Cardinal Emmett Carter. Cathy Coonley joined Lightfoot in the sprawling, 7,500-foot home, with its spacious rooms and high ceilings. It was a little surprising, so soon after the departure of the other Cathy in his life, but Lightfoot didn't really like living on his own. In fact, Coonley was with him almost everywhere he went: on tour and sailing on Georgian Bay. Lightfoot had purchased his own yacht in Los Angeles and had it driven on a rig all the way up to Georgian Bay. It seemed natural to christen the thirty-nine-foot boat *Sundown* after his chart-topping hit. Although it was a large vessel, Lightfoot found he was able to sail it himself and would take Coonley and friends, most often his guitarist buddy Terry Clements, on trips.

We had many a pleasurable ride on Sundown. *We'd go as far as the west coast or the east coast of Georgian Bay, around the Bruce Peninsula and up to Lion's Head, which was an all-day or all-night sail. Sometimes we'd sail out to Hope Island, stay overnight to make the crossing the next morning to Lion's Head. There were places where you could go and dock among the islands, places like Bone Island, up in those areas, the northwest section of Honey Harbour. We'd spend the night, build a fire and then set off again the next morning.*

Lightfoot and Coonley shared one canoeing experience. She'd joined him, Bob Dion and three others on a twenty-five-day canoe trip along the Churchill River, which flows for a thousand miles across Alberta, Saskatchewan and Manitoba into Hudson Bay. Coonley could keep up with the paddling and portaging challenges, which Lightfoot admired, but the heat, mosquitoes and wasps ultimately forced them to cut the trip short by a day. "We were getting near Flin Flon," Lightfoot says, "and decided to bypass it and keep going down and come out at Amisk Lake, where there's a place called Denare Beach. That's where we called it quits. We stopped at a bridge, got picked up by a truck and eventually made our way back home."

They were good traveling companions. On another occasion, Lightfoot and Coonley took a thirteen-hour train journey to the Ontario town of Hornepayne, north of Lake Superior, just to check the Canadian National Railway's claim about its train's punctuality. Lightfoot was writing a new song and had come up with the line "Was it up in Hornepayne where the trains run on time?" He wanted to see for himself if it was true.

It was a fun trip—took a bottle of booze and away we went. We got to Hornepayne and went and checked out the CN rail yards. Afterwards, at a restaurant, some people came in and recognized me. Nice folks. We went out and bought a bunch of beer and had a big jam session with them that lasted all day long. Those same people came and visited me in Rosedale about three years later.

Lightfoot's first European tour took him to Amsterdam, Hamburg, Munich and Frankfurt. He was scheduled to travel on to London to perform at the Royal Albert Hall, but his flight was badly delayed. By the time he arrived at London's Westbury Hotel, he was in a lousy mood. Allan Jones, then a music writer for *Melody Maker*, was there to interview Lightfoot and remembers him as "cantankerous." Lightfoot, Jones later recalled, burst into the hotel room where Jones was waiting, flung his shoulder bag forcefully against the wall and bellowed, "Someone get me a drink. Man flies all the way from Frankfurt, the least he expects of his record company is that they get him a goddamn beer." During the course of their hour together, Jones criticized the music of Lightfoot and some of his folk contemporaries as being "sentimental." Lightfoot ended the interview and kicked him out of his hotel room. Jones would remember Lightfoot as a "bully." It couldn't have gone worse.

Lightfoot fared better when he appeared again at New York's Avery Fisher Hall. Opening for him was Mimi Fariña, the spirited folk-singing sister of Joan Baez. This time around, Lightfoot didn't curse his sound system or storm offstage, and the same *New York Times* critic applauded his performance: "Mr. Lightfoot has a husky baritone with an evocative quick vibrato, and he phrases with a light, precise rhythmicality. He has a blond-bearded, outdoorsy sex appeal that demonstrably pleased a number of women in the crowd. It's a neatly attractive package, even if Mr. Lightfoot is still unable to disguise completely a shyness or arrogance that translates into coldness onstage. And it was nice to see him in a comeback from the sourness he engendered last time."

Work often took Lightfoot to Los Angeles. That fall, while there for a meeting at Warner, he stayed with Joanne Magee, a waitress from the Troubadour whom he'd been seeing. When he woke the next morning, there was a four-month-old baby lying next to him. "He's yours," Lightfoot says Magee told him. "I said, 'Okay, he's mine. I'll come see him next time I'm in town.' Which I did. And that's what I did from that point on. Every time I went to LA, before recording, performing or going to parties, that was the first place I went." Everyone in Lightfoot's circle back in Toronto insisted he have a paternity test, but Lightfoot refused, believing the boy was his. His sister, Bev, was convinced Magee was taking advantage of her brother. Lightfoot remembers getting into a major standoff with her about it one night. It says a lot about Lightfoot's character—his trusting nature and sense of loyalty—that he never questioned Magee nor shirked support duty. Lightfoot continued seeing his son, whose name was Galen, whenever he was in LA. He recalls a time when the boy was seriously ill with an ear infection.

I walked in the house, and there was this miserable child, crying in pain from his earache. Joanne tells me, "We can't get rid of it and I don't know what to do. I can't afford to go to a doctor." And I remember taking him in my arms and walking him around the house, looking at his poor little face, the tears and the mucous running down his nose. And I said to him, "I think I'm going to be looking after you from this point on." I came back to Toronto and told Bev, "Set it up so she gets child support by the month. Pay the health insurance and tell her to get a doctor and arrange it all directly through my office." I did that for the next twenty-two years—until Galen turned twenty-five. I've stayed in touch with him. He works for a restaurant, purchasing wines for the operation, and is now married. I attended the wedding and danced with Galen's mother and Emily, the bride.

In the late fall, Lightfoot was busy working on his next album. He liked to rehearse new songs with his band in the sunroom of his Beaumont Road home. Rehearsals usually went from noon until six. Drummer Barry Keane, by then a full-time band member, remembers that at the end of the first day Lightfoot started playing something no one recognized. "What's that?" Haynes asked. "It's a song I'm working on about a shipwreck I just read about," Lightfoot said.

The week before, Lightfoot had been writing on the third floor of his house and came down to the kitchen for more coffee. A report on the 11 P.M. CBC news told of the sinking of a giant freighter, the SS *Edmund Fitzgerald*, in a fierce storm. "I remember it so well," says Lightfoot. "The wind was howling even in Toronto that night, and I went back up to the attic thinking, 'I wonder what it's like up on Lake Superior.' It must've been awful. I didn't think about it again for another week, but I already had a melody, like the drone of an old Irish chantey. No story, just the chords."

Lightfoot played the tune again at the next rehearsal, and by the third day he and Clements had worked out guitar parts. For the next two days it was the same thing: music but no lyrics. The following Monday, Lightfoot and the band headed into Eastern Sound Studios, on Yorkville Avenue in Toronto. "First day in the studio, Gord's doing live vocals with the band on four or five songs," says Keane. "It's going really well. At the end of the day he starts playing this mystery tune again. I don't think Rick has even played a note on it yet. On Tuesday, we record another three or four more songs, and then Gord plays that tune again. The engineer asks about it. The third day, it's the exact same thing. By the fourth day, we've recorded all of the songs and it's three in the afternoon on Thursday. We'd finished. The engineer suggests we use the remaining time to work on the shipwreck song. Gord says, no, it's not ready. But the engineer convinced him to put it on tape. I was in the drum booth, across the room from Gord, and I asked him when he wanted me to come in. He said, 'I'll give you a nod.' Gord starts playing, the guys are doing their thing. Gord starts singing, then gives me the nod. I do my drum fill and we finish playing it. And that was the record. Not only was it a first take, but it was the first time we'd played the entire song and the first time we'd even heard the lyrics."

Tom Treece, a Michigan musician, was in Eastern Sound on the same night, making plans to record there with his rock band Brussel Sprout. The group's producer had invited him to come check out the studio. To Treece's delight, he was allowed to sit in a side room and watch as Lightfoot and his band recorded the shipwreck song. It was a magical moment Treece would recount in his memoir, *But What Do I Know?* "I remember the haunting sound that [Lightfoot's] guitarist produced by playing through a new device called a synthesizer," writes Treece, "and how—when he recorded the vocal— Lightfoot cleared the studio and killed all the lights save the one illuminating his parchment of scribbled words. For a fledgling singer-songwriter, I was in heaven."

Lightfoot had come up with the lyrics after finding an article titled "The Cruelest Month" in the November 24 issue of *Newsweek* magazine. He read the opening line and was instantly captivated: "According to the legend of the Chippewa tribe, the lake they once called Gitche Gumee 'never gives up her dead.'" As he'd done with "Canadian Railroad Trilogy" and other factually based songs, Lightfoot set about thoroughly researching his subject, taking a documentarian's approach to the task, detailing the ship's 26,000-ton load, the hellish winds and monstrous waves and the fate of captain and crew—even recounting how the church bell in Detroit's "Maritime Sailors' Cathedral" "chimed til it rang twenty-nine times for each man."

Lightfoot had been fascinated by ships his whole life; he witnessed one being launched when he was just seven years old. "It slid sideways in the water, creating a great, powerful wave," he told Michael Schumacher in his book *Mighty Fitz: The Sinking of the Edmund Fitzgerald.* Lightfoot added, "When the *Edmund Fitzgerald* went down I owned a sailboat. I imagined what that wave might have been." For Lightfoot, there was something mystical about a sinking ship that touched him deeply. He'd previously written a sea tragedy song with "Ballad of Yarmouth Castle," about the 1965 sinking of a cruise ship. As he told Schumacher, "Shipwrecks are different than your coal mine or railroad disasters. They have a different quality, a mystique and mysteriousness. Witnesses usually don't live to tell the tale." It was unorthodox subject matter for a pop song, but "The Wreck of the Edmund Fitzgerald" became Lightfoot's next single and a surprise hit.

On November 17, Lightfoot turned thirty-seven. Bev decided to throw her brother a surprise party at his Rosedale mansion. She invited sixty or so friends and business buddies, who gathered quietly around the pool table under the Tiffany shade. Lightfoot was busy writing upstairs, and they waited while Bev went to call him. When he came down and everyone yelled birthday greetings, he burst into tears. He walked past them and sat down at his Steinway piano in the living room. Looking out the window with tears still in his eyes, he softly played some instrumental tunes from the 1940s, songs his parents loved. Out of respect for his privacy, the guests listened only briefly before moving to other parts of the house, leaving Lightfoot alone to play out his melancholy with just a bottle of wine for company. It's possible that the birthday surprise had made him think how much he missed his kids and his dad, for whom he hadn't truly grieved.

Another year, another seven months of travel. In 1974, Lightfoot had scaled back his touring to seventy-one dates from eighty-six the previous year. But there was no letup in 1976, with seventy-two planned concerts. Success meant that Lightfoot could now afford to dispense with commercial airlines and fly around North America strictly on privately leased planes. Lightfoot calculated that the flexibility of traveling by smaller Lear jets, although costly to rent, saved him about twenty nights a year on the road. The first stop on the tour that year was a strange one for a bearded folk singer in faded denim and turquoise bracelets: the luxurious Sahara Tahoe Hotel in Lake Tahoe, Nevada. But playing in the popular ski resort and casino town showed just how high Lightfoot's star had risen. He was getting an estimated

$40,000 for six shows in three nights. Frank Sinatra was performing the same weekend across the street at Harrah's. "I've never played a club like this before," Lightfoot admitted to the *Toronto Star*'s Peter Goddard, who flew down to cover the unusual event, "but I was in Vegas a while back and saw Wayne Newton and Gladys Knight and the Pips and figured if they could play places like that, we could too."

Drummer Barry Keane was making his touring debut at the Sahara Tahoe. Lightfoot with drums was not as revolutionary as Dylan going electric, but it was unquestionably a good move. Combined with the rich textures of Pee Wee Charles's pedal steel, Keane's drums gave Lightfoot's music added depth, drama and dynamism. Keane remembers being really uptight in Lake Tahoe—and not just because it was his first gig with Lightfoot. "Gord likes to be in his comfort zone, and there were a lot of things outside his comfort zone," says Keane. "He'd never played a casino or a hotel and he'd never played with a drummer. The hotel had hired an orchestra of twelve strings and horns to back him up. Gord had got his arranger Nick DeCaro to come with his charts and conduct. The rehearsals were a nightmare. There was no set list. Back then, Gord didn't like to be held to an order. I had asked him beforehand what songs I should learn, and he'd simply said don't worry about it. So all through rehearsal I had to guess what to play or was frantically asking Rick. And I've got Nick set up behind me with the orchestra asking *me* which song is which. Gord got angry, fired the orchestra and sent Nick home. It was an exercise in pure frustration." But the shows went ahead, with just Lightfoot and his band, and were hugely successful, with encores every night. The hotel management was so thrilled they asked him back—twice in 1977—for much bigger money.

After the stress at the casino, Lightfoot wasn't pleased about having to immediately fly to Los Angeles to appear again on *The Midnight Special* for an episode hosted by Wolfman Jack and Helen

Reddy. Although the TV series was a big deal, Lightfoot hated television appearances. They always made him anxious—too many things
outside of his control. When he and the band arrived at the NBC
Studios in Burbank, Lightfoot was already grumpy. As the rehearsal
for the taping dragged on, with constant stops and starts, it became
clear Lightfoot just wanted to get the hell out. At one point, someone at the foot of the stage kept calling up to Lightfoot. "I'm looking
at this guy who's trying to get Gord's attention and thinking he
looks really familiar," says Keane. "Gord knew he was there but was
ignoring him. The guy was like a little kid and starts pulling on
Gord's pant leg. Finally, Gord looks down and says, 'John, for
Christ's sake, I'll be with you in a moment.' It was John Denver."[*]

At the taping itself, Lightfoot was equally impatient with the floor
director, who kept breaking in and having him start over as the crew
struggled to get sound levels. It became a battle of wills, says Keane.
"Gord says to the director, 'Get your cameras rolling, 'cuz we ain't
stoppin'.' We were playing the first song, and the floor director walks
up and yells cut, and Gord's not stopping. We played five songs all
the way through, but they didn't have the cameras rolling for the first
one. They got what they got ["Don Quixote" and three songs from
the new album: "Race Among the Ruins," "Spanish Moss" and "I'm
Not Supposed to Care"]. Gord says, 'Thanks, see ya,' and we were
out of there. He was definitely in charge."

The new recording, *Summertime Dream*, came out that May. It
was Lightfoot's twelfth studio album, the sixth to feature Waronker's
production and the first under a second negotiated deal with Warner/
Reprise. Positive reviews greeted its release. The *Toronto Star*'s Peter
Goddard called it Lightfoot's best and most important album to date,
citing a new complexity of meaning in the songs: "It's a sophisticated

---

[*] A major star himself, Denver had credited Lightfoot's "Early Morning Rain" with inspiring
his hit "Leaving on a Jet Plane." The two would soon share stages together.

work but one, because of Lightfoot's discipline and love of melody, that seems simple on the surface." In particular, Goddard singled out "The Wreck of the Edmund Fitzgerald" as a sign of musical growth and the hit potential of "Spanish Moss" and the title track. *Rolling Stone*'s Billy Altman also applauded Lightfoot's melodic strengths and how his "meticulously constructed tunes and arrangements never fail to lift you from the doldrums." Altman noted that the album contained just two compositions with messages: the folk narrative of "The Wreck of the Edmund Fitzgerald" and the anti-war "Protocol." "Songs like these are now more exceptions than rule for Lightfoot, but that matters little," he wrote. "It's hard to argue and hum at the same time." Goddard and Altman were right. *Summertime Dream* was another high-water mark for Lightfoot, whose songwriting gifts and recording skills were indisputable.

On May 22, Lightfoot and his band appeared on the first season of *Saturday Night Live*. Created by Toronto-born Lorne Michaels, *SNL* catered to hip young viewers with a mix of comedy sketches and musical performances. Michaels featured top Canadian talent, including comedians like Dan Aykroyd and later Martin Short, Mike Myers and others. Lightfoot was just the second Canadian musician, after Anne Murray, to appear on the show. He and the band flew into New York by Lear jet and drove over to the same NBC studio he'd been in eleven years earlier when he appeared on *The Tonight Show*. Following an afternoon of rehearsals, the episode went live and Lightfoot, wearing a polka-dot shirt and suspenders, and his band, all decked out in denim, performed "Summertime Dream" and "Spanish Moss." Lightfoot then became part of a comedy skit in which he attempted to play a third song, "Sundown." Actor-writer-director Buck Henry, the episode's host, interrupted: "Excuse me, I'm sorry, Gordon, but I thought I explained that you're only gonna do two songs." Lightfoot protests, "But look, we came all the way from Toronto." At that, Henry says, "Now you're beginning to irritate me," snaps his fingers and nods at someone off-camera. In steps gonzo comedian John Belushi, dressed as his samurai character, Futaba, who proceeds to snap Lightfoot's guitar strings with wire cutters. End of song. "John was really intense," recalls Lightfoot, "but it was a fun experience." Six years later, Lightfoot wasn't so pleased to be associated with Belushi. Their names were all over the media in connection with Cathy Smith, who had given the comedian a fatal heroin overdose.

Lightfoot and Smith had never got into hard drugs; she started using heroin after their relationship ended. Smith first met Belushi through Levon Helm when the Band appeared on *SNL* in the fall of 1976. She had gravitated next to the glittery lights of Los Angeles, where she hooked up with country singer Hoyt Axton and, according to Bob Woodward's book *Wired*, became involved in dealing cocaine and heroin to stars like the Rolling Stones' Keith Richards and Ron Wood. Smith met Belushi again through Richards and Wood and later admitted in court that on the night of March 5, 1982, she injected Belushi with eleven speedballs—combined doses of cocaine and heroin—in Bungalow 3 at Hollywood's Chateau Marmont. She served fifteen months in the California state prison for her role in Belushi's death and went on to live a peripatetic life under an assumed name. Lightfoot could easily have shut her out of his life at that point. Instead, he helped her out financially—even setting up a book deal for her memoir. "I felt sorry for her and wanted her to make some money of her own," says Lightfoot, who showed a compassion for Smith that few others would. "We'd had a good time, and I did care for her, but she was just too hot to handle."

Three days after his *SNL* appearance, the normally reclusive Lightfoot did something unprecedented: he invited the media into his Toronto mansion for a press conference. Sunburned from sailing on Georgian Bay with Cathy Coonley and sporting his polka-dot shirt with blue jeans and suspenders, Lightfoot announced to forty TV and newspaper reporters that he would perform a benefit concert the following month at Maple Leaf Gardens to raise money for the 1976 Canadian Olympic team. The games were taking place that summer in Montreal and immediate action was needed. "Some of our track and field people are in rags," Lightfoot told the gathering. Ken Twigg, executive director of the Canadian Track and Field Association, stood up to say the situation wasn't quite that dire. But the radiator Twigg was sitting on caught his pants and ripped them, giving Lightfoot the best punch line of the afternoon. Joining Lightfoot at the press conference were fellow performers Sylvia Tyson, Murray McLauchlan and classical guitarist Liona Boyd. Some newspaper accounts couldn't resist noting that Lightfoot was showing a paunch, the result of heavy drinking, and derisively describing the opulent decor of Lightfoot's home, with its flocked wallpaper, Tiffany lamps, pool table and Steinway piano.

The concert took place on June 11. Lightfoot opened and closed the show, receiving ovations and prolonged applause when he and his band performed "Summertime Dream" and "Sundown." He seemed pleased to act as host, introducing Boyd, McLauchlan and Tyson in turn. But he couldn't have been thrilled with the headline the following day: "McLauchlan Steals Show at the Olympics Benefit." Yet it was true. Wearing the jersey of Maple Leafs star Darryl Sittler, which he'd grabbed from the team's dressing room before hitting the stage, McLauchlan scored the biggest applause with his performance. Backed by his group the Silver Tractors, he also delivered the loudest set of the night. "Gord was the draw, but I had a great band and a few hits of my own," says McLauchlan. "We just kicked ass, which I think caught Gord a little by surprise." Still, Lightfoot stands by his choices for the lineup: "I wanted Murray because he's such a brilliant performer. I wanted Liona because I knew how great she was, doing her classical thing in her long dress. And I wanted a thrush, so I got Sylvia on board." Ultimately, Lightfoot met his fundraising goal of $200,000, to be shared between the Canadian Olympic Association and Twigg's allegedly raggedy organization. He was doing his part for Canada, but his own career kept calling, pulling him back onto the road.

ELEVEN

Flying High

Touring in 1976 left Lightfoot exhausted and exasperated. He'd performed dates all over the United States, including a four-night stand at LA's Universal Amphitheatre. A trip to Europe with stops in Germany and the Montreux Jazz Festival had been nerve-racking: engine troubles on separate jetliners had caused two emergency landings before band and crew finally arrived, late, in Frankfurt.

The European trip had taken a toll, although Lightfoot did get to hang out in a Swiss hotel bar with Leonard Cohen and was highly amused by the Montreal troubadour's smooth ways with the waitress, ordering drinks and flirting in his impeccable French. Ultimately, the tour left Lightfoot in desperate need of the restorative benefits of another canoe trip. But another career breakthrough was about to test his integrity—and his ability to cope with even greater fame. At one of the stops on the canoeing route, his sister, Bev, contacted him. "The Wreck of the Edmund Fitzgerald" was getting radio play, despite its somber subject matter and six-and-a-half-minute running time, and Warner wanted to release it as his next single. But to make it more radio friendly the label wanted to shorten the track. Lightfoot agreed, but only if the verses were left alone, and thirty-five seconds were shaved off the song's instrumental sections instead.

Six weeks after its release, "The Wreck" became a massive hit. Warner promotion manager Mike Stone was astonished. "I see an awful lot of records," he said, "and I have never seen one take off like this." The song had clearly struck a nerve with a wide range of listeners, including the families of the *Edmund Fitzgerald*'s victims. Added Stone, "Wives and children of the crew have written very touching letters to Lightfoot since the album came out and he has made a point of replying to every one."

Ian Tyson remembers being in Oklahoma, "doing some cowboy work, riding horses," when he heard his buddy's shipwreck song on a country music radio station. "There I was, out on the windy plains, and couldn't believe what I was hearing," Tyson says. "It sounded amazing. Gord's melodies have always been great—he doesn't have to work at those. But his words on that, the clarity of the lyrics, just blew me away. It has the mark of some serious research, like he really wanted to get the story right. But I found it very weird to be hearing that kind of song getting any radio play at all. That wouldn't happen now. They wouldn't even put out something like that today."

By November—almost a year to the day from when Lightfoot first heard about the ship going down—"The Wreck" hit number 1 on Canada's *RPM* charts and number 1 and number 2 on the US *Cashbox* and *Billboard* charts, respectively, making it his most successful single after "Sundown."

New success brought new demands. Warner Bros. chief Mo Ostin was pushing Lightfoot to sign with high-powered management. Since parting ways with Albert Grossman, Lightfoot had kept things close to home. Al Mair had been running Early Morning Productions for him but had left earlier in 1976 to concentrate on Attic Records, the label he'd started. Lightfoot always insisted on loyalty within his inner circle and may have been unhappy that Mair's focus was split between Lightfoot's affairs and Attic's. For his part, Mair had grown tired of having to deal with the complications in

Lightfoot's personal life. "I would be on the road with him," he says, "and my wife would get calls at 3 A.M. from a jealous Cathy Smith, saying, 'Where is Gord? I've called his hotel room and he's not there.' Dragging my family into his personal affairs was the beginning of the end."

That summer, Bev had taken over the running of Early Morning Productions for her brother. "I taught Bev about the publishing side of things," says Mair. "It wasn't rocket science with Gord. He'd compose a new song, write out the lead sheet to copyright it and file it away with the Library of Congress in Washington. I'd been trained in New York by Gord's lawyer and learned how to set up files for a publishing company. Each song would have a separate file. In the back of it would be the copyright notice, and in front you have the various mechanical licenses. Most of it was just handling the licenses when all of the cover versions flew in."

Meanwhile, Ostin kept pressing. One day, Lightfoot got a directive: go see Jerry Weintraub. The son of a gem salesman, Weintraub was a self-made entertainment mogul with the gift of the gab. He'd started modestly as a talent agent representing clients like Jack Paar and singer Jane Morgan, who became his second wife, and ran both Management Three and the Concerts West booking agency. In 1970, he took on John Denver, then an unknown, and soon turned him into a major star, through concerts, TV specials and film roles. With his now legendary chutzpah, Weintraub convinced Elvis Presley and his manager, Colonel Tom Parker, to let him produce Presley's national tour. He took Frank Sinatra from "saloon singer to stadium singer," according to Sinatra's biographer.

Lightfoot met with Weintraub and his partner, Ken Kragen, in Los Angeles, but he wasn't sure about the plans they had in mind for him.

So I went to see Jerry at his home in Beverley Hills. Mo sent me. I had just been out in the bush before flying to LA for the interview. My sister, Bev, was there too. I drank Jerry's champagne with him and his wife, Jane Morgan. Jerry had just injured himself playing tennis with George Bush Sr. and was walking around with a cast. They wanted to put me in the studio with a producer for a Kenny Rogers type of sound. Take me to another level and make me a big star, they said. Focus on the vocal and not necessarily do all my own stuff. Get me in with an orchestra and make a really commercial record. I could've put my guitar away! They were doing it already with John Denver. I wasn't sure I could go through with it. I thought, I'm only good at what I do. Plus, I was drinking pretty heavily and afraid that I'd make a horse's ass of myself overnight.

For whatever reason, Lightfoot signed the contract. On December 11, 1976, *Billboard* magazine reported that Weintraub was Lightfoot's new personal manager and that Lightfoot's sister, Beverley, would act as liaison between the two.

Almost immediately, Lightfoot regretted it. Lenny Waronker had a bad feeling about the deal as soon as he heard. "In those days, managers were control guys," says Waronker. "When Gord mentioned Weintraub, I thought, oh, no. I wasn't even sure if Weintraub understood Gord. But Gord decided to make that move, which went against his instincts. He couldn't get out of bed for a week because he felt he made a huge mistake and was selling out. He called me and said, 'I can't do it.' This was an artist who didn't behave like an artist. He was a no bullshit guy and felt that what he'd done was bullshit. Being Gord, he felt he needed to fly back down to LA himself and speak to Jerry face to face rather than have a lawyer or Bev handle it. And he asked me to come along.

"We're sitting in Weintraub's office," Waronker continues, "and Weintraub comes in. Gord is looking down at the floor and says, 'I know I committed to you, but I'm sorry, I just can't do it.' Weintraub could see how upset Lightfoot was and started talking very calmly about all the things he could do for him. Gord is still looking down and finally looks up at Weintraub and says, 'Jerry, I can't stand the hype.' And that was it. It was the most amazing thing to witness, to see an artist, who is absolutely true to who he is and what he does, have the courage to own up to a mistake and deal with it. It was so real. You felt for him the whole time. You could feel the pressure and the pain he was going through, because he knew he'd made a commitment, and to not follow through went against everything he stood for. This is a guy who takes his responsibilities very seriously. I already thought highly of Gord, but my respect for him went way up after that."

Weintraub, seeing Lightfoot's resolve, reluctantly canceled the contract. Some might view it as a missed opportunity for Lightfoot—a chance for him to enter the pop stratosphere inhabited by Denver, Rogers and Sinatra. But that wasn't Lightfoot. He couldn't bear the narcissists and fast-talking denizens of the celebrity world. Nor did he want greater success if it was going to force him to be a phony. He knew he'd be happier if he just continued doing it his own way.

Sometimes, it seemed, doing it his own way had its costs. On November 25, Robbie Robertson invited Lightfoot to attend The Last Waltz, the Band's farewell concert at San Francisco's Winterland Ballroom. Robertson wanted to quit touring, and he was organizing one grand final performance featuring more than a dozen special guests in a concert to be filmed by Martin Scorsese. Lightfoot flew to California with Cathy Coonley and was looking forward to seeing many of his performing buddies, including Bob Dylan, Ronnie Hawkins, Joni Mitchell and Neil Young. He also knew promoter Bill Graham from his Fillmore appearances and producer John Simon, who was serving as music director for the concert. With Albert Grossman there as well, it was like Old Home Week, a gathering in which Lightfoot certainly belonged. As Robertson later told this author, "Over the years with the Band, we'd run into Gordon every once in a while and always admired him. He was the one we knew more than anybody else from the folk scene and he wasn't fearful of crossing over the tracks to our side because his songwriting straddled both popular music and the folk tradition."

When he arrived at the Winterland, Lightfoot was expecting nothing more than a special evening with friends.

We walk in, Cathy and I, and Robbie comes up to me and the first thing he says is, "Gord, do you want to sing?" I said, "I don't have anything prepared; I don't have my guitar, and I'm supposed to be sitting with Mo and Lenny from Warners." If I thought I was going to be called upon, I would have gotten ready. Because that's the way I am. I need a little bit of notice. So I declined, and Cathy and I went and sat with my people. Ron Wood was at our table too, and everyone had a helluva lotta fun. Really enjoyed the show. Ronnie Hawkins wore his wife's fur coat onstage. The guy that really blew me away was Van Morrison. Jesus, he really lit the place up. And Dylan played "Forever Young." It was a great time.

Lightfoot would have made a perfect addition to the show, but since spontaneity wasn't his strong suit, he never appeared onstage. *The Last Waltz* went on to become one of the most revered concert movies of all time.

Lightfoot remained focused on his increasingly busy schedule, heading back south of the border early in 1977. After three dates in Lake Tahoe, he flew to Los Angeles for the nineteenth annual Grammy Awards at the Hollywood Palladium. "The Wreck of the Edmund Fitzgerald" was nominated for two awards. Dressed in his "penguin suit" tuxedo and wearing tinted aviator shades, an overweight Lightfoot sat in the audience with Cathy Coonley, watching performances by Natalie Cole, Sarah Vaughan and the duet of Chet Atkins and Les Paul. Stevie Wonder won four awards that night, beating

Lightfoot for Best Male Pop Vocal Performance. Host Andy Williams, who'd recorded Lightfoot's "The Last Time I Saw Her" and "If You Could Read My Mind," joked that it was good of the Grammys to throw a get-together for Stevie. Then the 5th Dimension's Billy Davis Jr. and Marilyn McCoo sang portions of all the compositions nominated for Song of the Year, with Davis offering the first two lines of "The Wreck of the Edmund Fitzgerald." Never have the words "Gitche Gumee" sounded more soulful. In the end, Lightfoot lost out to Barry Manilow's "I Write the Songs," written by Beach Boy Bruce Johnston. Lightfoot claims it was a good thing he didn't win that night at the Grammys.

I got very drunk, quite plastered. It was during a period when I was starting to do irrational things. I actually don't know what I would've said if I'd won and had to go up there. I was worried about that, because I knew how far gone I was. I would've said something, and everyone would've said, "That was fine, that was good," but I would've thought it was just terrible. I've always been that way: very self-critical. Worried about my performance. Worried about the way I look.

Lightfoot's behavior could certainly be attributed to his heavy drinking. The excessive intake wreaked havoc on his system, making him irritable as well as irrational. It seemed that he was caught in a vicious circle: the more success he experienced, the more he abused alcohol and suffered, personally and professionally, as a result.

TWELVE

Sailing On

Lightfoot's reticence was well known among interviewers. Many journalists tried to get the intensely private man to open up, but few succeeded. Lightfoot did, however, speak candidly about drinking, songwriting and other subjects with his friend Robert Markle in an insightful 4,200-word article titled "Knowing Lightfoot." Markle was planning a book about his famous musician buddy, although it was never completed. The article was written during and after Lightfoot's sold-out seven-night stand at Massey Hall in March 1977. Markle interviewed Lightfoot over beers at Toronto's Brunswick House tavern, and backstage at Massey Hall. Markle's description of the faithful throng at the Church of Gord was particularly revealing: "Outrageously beautiful girls dressed outrageously, laughing as they snuggled into their seats. Factory-sealed records on their flowered laps, behind their excited eyes lay the hope of an autograph. Some carried flowers, gifts. Parcels carefully wrapped. And Instamatics. Flashbars. Boys in jeans and hand-stitched shirts from Mexico or shops up the street. Men in suits from smart downtown. Sensible looking boys and girls out spending their precious time together. Grey suits, executives. Boppers, dopers. Dreamers, aspiring virgin talent. Fans. Fanatics. Old and young, hip and square, nice and easy, neat and street chic—all waiting for Gordon Lightfoot to take over their lives for a moment, all waiting to get lost in his . . . just for a little while."

After the concert, Lightfoot whispered to Markle, "I love this place. Playing Massey Hall is like Christmas to me. I'm home, I get to see my family, all my friends." That has remained true every time Lightfoot has played Massey Hall. It has always been a special night, for him and for his fans, even as recently as his sold-out 2016 concerts and at the after-show gatherings in Massey Hall's lower level, where family, friends and the most devoted Lightfoot followers, or Lightheads, gathered. The only differences: much of the audience is older and autographs have been replaced by selfies, for which Lightfoot dutifully poses with his lucky fans.

Back in the 1970s, the after-concert parties at Lightfoot's Rosedale mansion were legendary. Markle noted that Lightfoot threw an excellent gathering, with lots of food and free-flowing drinks and tunes coming from his Seeburg jukebox. At the 1977 party, Lightfoot's family and friends all appeared keen to meet his guests as he made his way with them through the large gathering, "shaking hands, exchanging pleasantries, accepting compliments." The host introduced Liona Boyd, who played some classical guitar pieces. Then Murray McLauchlan, well into his cups according to Markle, picked up a guitar and sang a humorous ditty written especially for his friend, after which he and Lightfoot went off to shoot a game of pool "for big bucks." When all the guests had left, Lightfoot, alone with Markle, spoke with remarkable candor about fears, writing blocks and the distraction of booze.

> The next ten years is going to be music, and sailing. I'm just now getting interested in this business. I get tired of it sometimes, sometimes it really gets to you. If I dry up, that's the time I'll start thinking about other things. Right now, it's no

problem. I don't find writing to be a frightening experience. I mean, I've actually made enough money at it that I can at least get along if I don't write. But I don't know. I guess there's going to come a time when the valve's gonna shut off, like anything else. So it's a matter of discipline. Sometimes I drink too much and I . . . waste a lot of time. You know, drinking. . . . If I didn't drink I'd probably get a lot more done, but I wouldn't have any fun. And I wouldn't have anything to write about. You've got to do something. You've got to have relaxation. And drinking is my relaxation. If I have people around the house, shooting the baloney, I like to have a drink in my hand. But nevertheless, they say it's bad for your health and, well, I just don't know. I'm a very simple human being. Sometimes life looks a little bleak to me, like the only thing you have to look forward to is getting old. I don't know if that's too groovy or not. But I'll tell you one thing, it's nicer to get old and have something than to get old and have nothing. So I'm one up there, too, probably. Life's been pretty good to me, basically, up until now. The way I've been plotting my course I don't see any end in sight, right now.

There was no letup for Lightfoot. In July of 1977, he became the first pop star hired by the MGM Grand Hotel in Las Vegas. Venues in Vegas were more accustomed to glitz 'n' glamor, wisecracking entertainers or seasoned lounge lizards like Paul Anka or Wayne Newton. When Lightfoot took the stage for the first night of a weeklong stand at the two-thousand-seat supper club, there was no schtick, schmaltz or snappy dialogue, just, as *Variety* noted, "the original rugged article, dressed in jeans and a blue shirt with only a sparse amount of reflecting sparkles." The entertainment trade weekly added that Lightfoot sang "in his clenched-teeth, deep drone style standing center with no errant moves within an interior setting embellished by polished wood paneling and furniture, Tiffany glass panels, a stairway leading up to a door that nobody uses and some potted palms stashed about among his four support musicians." Lightfoot was unapologetic about his just-give-them-the-songs per-formance, telling one columnist, "If the audience doesn't like what they hear, it probably means I wasn't ready for Las Vegas."

When Lightfoot returned to LA's Universal Amphitheatre in August for the first of five shows, critic Robert Hilburn noted he was more relaxed than at his Las Vegas opening. In his otherwise positive concert review, Hilburn lamented two things: the brevity of Lightfoot's set due to his opening act (once again Mimi Fariña) and his "usual supply of corny jokes." Offstage, he could entertain with his dry wit, but onstage he was guilty of horrible groaners. While deadpanning to the Amphitheatre audience during band introductions, Lightfoot said, when he came to Ed Ringwald, that Pee Wee was only the pedal steel player's nickname and that his real name was Rusty Nails. Terry Clements, Lightfoot explained, had once been cited for heroism for stopping a runaway horse. "He bet on it," said Lightfoot, using a shopworn Henny Youngman line. Worse, he told the audience that Rick Haynes had six children because his wife, Marilyn, was hard of hearing. "When Rick would get into bed next to Marilyn, he'd say to her, 'Do you want to go to sleep or what?' And she'd say, 'What?'" It was the same feeble joke he used to tell about his grandparents back in the days of the Two Tones. In many ways, a part of Lightfoot never left the "Pav" in Orillia.

While he was in LA, Lightfoot learned that the Troubadour, the 170-seat club that had given him and so many others their start, had fallen on hard times. Industry heavyweights Elliot Roberts, David Geffen and Lou Adler had cornered top talent and booked them into the Roxy, a former strip club they'd converted into a music venue more than three times the Troubadour's size. Determined to keep his door open, owner Doug Weston pulled out all the stops and invited back many of the Troubadour's original stars. Lightfoot didn't hesitate to help out his old friend. Lightfoot, Tom Waits, Warren Zevon and Johnny Rivers all played at the club's twentieth anniversary celebration. Paul Body, who worked as the Troubadour's doorman throughout the '70s, remembers Lightfoot's appearance well. "Lightfoot was a major star by that time, so it was pretty classy for him to be playing there," says Body. "Some artists probably had their arms twisted to play, but I don't think he did. He and his band came in, totally professional, and did their thing, really tight and on the money." Whenever Lightfoot played the club, there were always beautiful women, all dressed up, who came out to see him, Body says. "He looked like a movie star, all blond hair and square jawed, and the women couldn't get enough of him. He and Leonard Cohen both had that effect on women."

Lightfoot may have enjoyed the company of female fans on the road, but his deeper relationships at home were troubled. Lightfoot's children, Fred and Ingrid, were far away. Brita had taken them to the south of France, because she believed that French immersion and a European-style education was best. Lightfoot had agreed, but he missed them badly. He flew over once expressly to see them in their village near Montpellier, only to get into a fight with Brita, turn around and fly straight home. The pain of separation from his kids gnawed at him, and he closed the letters he wrote to them with "Stay in touch . . ." One of Lightfoot's saddest songs is "If Children Had Wings," which he wrote that year and planned to include on his next album. "If children had wings I would sing them their song / With a smile on my lips and a tear in my eye," Lightfoot wrote, insisting his "love still goes on."

Nor were things harmonious between Lightfoot and Cathy Coonley. His heavy drinking bothered Coonley, and they were now often apart when he was on the road. The temptations of female companionship were everywhere. According to Liona Boyd, who toured frequently with Lightfoot and the band between 1976 and 1978, there was never any shortage of women. Boyd wrote in her memoir that while she and Lightfoot "avoided any romantic entanglements, he was routinely approached by beautiful women with stars in their eyes—from eighteen-year-old groupies and poetry-loving college students to older married women. Sometimes one of his female conquests would accompany us in the plane." One girlfriend who tagged along in the Lear jet, says Boyd, was a dancer from Chicago's Joffrey Ballet.

Lightfoot had plenty of other distractions too. Although not a flashy spender, he was becoming "looser with the purse strings," as he puts it. Along with his 1890 Rosedale mansion and his sailboat *Sundown*, he owned a brand-new Cadillac convertible and a Buick that Coonley drove. He had a membership at the Cambridge Club, the exclusive men's athletic facility at Toronto's then-posh Sheraton Centre. Most of all, he liked sailing. Sometimes, when navigating Georgian Bay while inebriated, he suffered the indignity of running his boat aground, requiring the harbor police to tow *Sundown* free. Lightfoot fell in love with the beauty of all-wood vessels after meeting Vic Carpenter, a master builder from Port McNicoll, Ontario, who owned a natural mahogany boat. Carpenter showed Lightfoot his plans for a luxurious forty-five-foot cruising sloop that he'd never developed beyond the drawing board. It took one day for Lightfoot to talk himself into ordering the boat. It came to be called *Golden Goose*.

With increased wealth came Lightfoot's greater sense of social responsibility. Benefit concerts would become a regular part of his schedule not only in 1977 but for years to come. In October, he joined Harry Chapin, John Denver and James Taylor in "Four Together,"

Chapin's charity concert for World Hunger Year at Detroit's Olympia Stadium. Folk stars with hits were now filling massive arenas just as easily as the biggest rock bands. More than seventeen thousand people watched four of the world's top solo artists take turns performing on Denver's own revolving stage. Lightfoot's versatile guitarist Terry Clements backed each of them. It was quite a show. Chapin, the Brooklyn-born humanitarian, sang his number 1 hit "Cat's in the Cradle," while Taylor sang his popular "Fire and Rain." Denver, who'd pestered Lightfoot at *The Midnight Special* taping, offered his chart-toppers "Annie's Song" and "Sunshine on My Shoulders." Lightfoot chose "The Wreck of the Edmund Fitzgerald," "If You Could Read My Mind" and two new songs, including "If Children Had Wings." At his suggestion, he and Denver also teamed up to harmonize on "Irish Lullaby," a favorite of Lightfoot's parents that Gord had recorded at school as a boy. They dedicated it to Bing Crosby, who'd died the previous week. Crosby had once sung the song himself.

In the book *The Electric Muse: The Story of Folk into Rock*, co-author Dave Laing investigated the post-Woodstock singer-songwriter phenomenon and the rise of artists like Lightfoot and Jim Croce. "The immense popularity of [such performers beginning] in the early 1970s can probably be traced to their studied casualness and the anti–show business approach they took to their music," wrote Laing, "a 'no-frills' policy which entered the pop mainstream via the folk scene." Lightfoot, he added, was among the very best craftsmen working on the border between folk and rock. "The smoothness of his voice and the ease of his melodies make him seem deceptively like another of the Denver/Croce breed of acoustic songsters. Yet beneath the immaculate surface of his music, Lightfoot has developed a personal synthesis of all the things a traveling troubadour in North America should think about: highway and hitchhiking songs which capture the mixture of despair and exhilaration of that condition [and] love songs [that] can take situations of loss or unhappiness and keep the feeling this side of sentimentality." Lightfoot's tales of the road and ballads of the heart all had the unmistakable ring of truth. There was no doubting his voice or emotions. The man behind those songs had risen all the way to the top of the music world.

Lightfoot donated all the proceeds of his December 1977 concerts at New York's Avery Fisher Hall to the American Cerebral Palsy Association. It was only five years earlier that he had been stricken with facial paralysis while onstage at Massey Hall. In the Avery Fisher's lobby before the concert, Lightfoot was cheered by a group of young girls who were singing Christmas songs and serenaded him personally with "Rudolph the Red-Nosed Reindeer." A buoyancy was evident in his performance that night, later broadcast by New York's WNEW-FM. The songs that made it onto the broadcast include some of Lightfoot's biggest hits, along with several from his next album, whose release was just a month away. Perhaps thinking of the children singing in the lobby, Lightfoot included two songs written with his own kids in mind: "The Pony Man" and "If Children Had Wings." Today, bootleg tapings of the concert are revered by Lightfoot fans, or Lightheads, who consider it one of their hero's best live recordings.

At the start of 1978, Lightfoot's new album, *Endless Wire*, was released. Its cover photo, taken by Coonley in Las Vegas, showed a determined Lightfoot looking out from behind rose-tinted aviator glasses in a hotel room with the Las Vegas skyline in the background. The album was Lightfoot's attempt at more of a rock sound, and it was greeted with largely positive reviews. The *Toronto Star* credited Lightfoot for branching out with the "most radically different [album] he's ever made," cited "Daylight Katy" for its hit potential and called the title track "quite possibly the best-crafted piece he's ever written." *Circus*, the US rock magazine, likewise applauded Lightfoot's new direction: "More pulsing than his earlier records, it uses a stronger back beat and heavier guitar sound on songs like 'The Circle Is Small' and 'Songs the Minstrel Sang.' The title track nearly approaches rock & rolling with a moderately fast tempo and wiry guitar. Even the arrangements, lushly done by Lightfoot himself (except for session man Doug Riley's string parts), are elaborately foreign to the folk atmosphere of his older songs."

Similarly, England's *Melody Maker* detected "more aggression and bite here than the man's ever displayed on record before" and singled out "If There's a Reason" as "an outstanding song with an unexpectedly bluesy feel." Lightfoot estimated that he'd spent more than five hundred hours on the album, including the writing and refining, "making it better, fuller and more satisfying." He'd rerecorded "The Circle Is Small," from his *Back Here on Earth* album, believing he could do a better job this time around. It became the album's first single. And one song, the lusty rocker "Sometimes I Don't Mind" was quite up to date with his romantic life, expressing desires for his Joffrey dancer girlfriend in the line "When I'm thinking of you ballerina alone / There's a fever around, I don't know what to do." The extra effort paid off. *Endless Wire* reached number 22 on *Billboard*'s pop chart, and its second single, "Daylight Katy," a song he'd written about Coonley, hit number 3 on the Adult Contemporary chart. Once again, Lightfoot was riding high.

But the good times came to a screeching halt when Lightfoot's drinking caught up with him. On February 16, at 2:18 A.M., he was driving his black Cadillac on Dixon Road near Highway 27 in Toronto's Etobicoke suburb. He'd left his high beams on, drawing the attention of a cop, who pulled him over for a breathalyzer test. Lightfoot blew well over the legal limit of 80 mg of alcohol per 100 mg of blood: 110 mg. He was taken to the station and tested again, where he registered an even higher reading of 120. Lightfoot was released and driven home, and three days later he was charged with impaired driving. A court date was set for August. His drinking problem was now a news story splashed all over the papers. For someone so intensely private, it was deeply humiliating.

Lightfoot was acquitted that fall on a technicality, but it was only a temporary reprieve. His case would be in and out of the courts for the next three years. He was finally found guilty in October 1981 of driving while intoxicated. Surprisingly, he was fined only $200—a pittance for a wealthy man. The real punishment was his renewed embarrassment, as his conviction was once again front-page news.

With a new album to promote and seventy-five tour dates to perform throughout 1978, Lightfoot had no choice but to "press on," as he liked to say. March was once again Lightfoot season in Toronto. The annual lovefest at Massey Hall was so dominant in the concert hall's schedule that the Toronto Symphony now booked its vacation around those dates. This time, Lightfoot performed nine sold-out shows, breaking a record he established the previous year. There seemed to be an insatiable appetite for the man. In the audience at Massey for at least one of the nights was Lynne Ackerman, a thirty-four-year-old office worker who was easily Lightfoot's biggest fan—not a groupie but a devotee. She'd first seen him at Steele's Tavern back in 1965, followed him to the Riverboat the next year and caught him pretty much everywhere since, staking out his hotels and waiting patiently for him at stage doors around the continent and beyond, once even flying to Amsterdam to greet him at the airport and waiting twelve hours when the flight was delayed. Ackerman received the ultimate reward when a photo of her standing next to the object of her obsession appeared in the gatefold of 1969's *Sunday Concert* album. Although Ackerman loved other celebrity musicians, including Cat Stevens, George Harrison and Bob Dylan, she really only had eyes for one. "No one ever measures up in comparison with

Gordon," she told journalist Ron Base, who billed her as the "Ultimate Fan." "Lynne is mad about Gordon Lightfoot, obsessed with him," wrote Base. "In her shabby little west end apartment, a huge poster of a short-haired, leather-vested Lightfoot adorns the hall. Pictures of him overflow from trunks, his name is constantly on her lips."

Ray Conlogue, writing in *The Globe and Mail*, summed up the Lightfoot phenomenon at Massey Hall: "Gordon Lightfoot isn't so much a musician as a mascot. Up he goes, centre-stage at Massey, that squared jaw and distant manner telling us that it's cool he's here to give the converted everything they want." And give he did, performing some of his earliest songs, all the big hits and more recent numbers like his newest album's title track. Just after intermission, Lightfoot came back onstage to a pile of notes and presents left by his microphone stand. One note was a request. "We haven't done this in a long time," he said, after reading it, "but okay." The song was the Maritime seafaring ballad "Farewell to Nova Scotia." Lightfoot could always relate to a folk song about a departing seaman and his wooden sailing ship: his stage that night was adorned with a framed photo proudly displaying *Golden Goose*, his newly completed mahogany sloop.

Despite his popularity with fans, a backlash in the Canadian media began that year, criticizing Lightfoot's lifestyle and personality traits. He was by far Canadian music's biggest star, rolling in royalties and a perennial winner at the Junos, Canada's premier music awards. It made him an easy target. Two magazine cover stories simultaneously depicted him as a troubled man who liked to play it safe. Larry LeBlanc, writing in Toronto magazine *The City*, cited his "outrageous egotism," "immense ambition" and "sizable insecurity" while insisting he was "extraordinarily sensitive to criticism." The last claim was certainly true. Journalist Tom Hopkins was frustrated by his failure to get Lightfoot to open up for a profile in *Maclean's* magazine. Turning to those who knew him, Hopkins quoted Al Mair in the article calling Lightfoot "one of your bigger male chauvinists and a leading exponent of the double standard." It was a criticism that stung—especially coming from a former associate. Among Lightfoot's most deeply embedded small-town values was his code of loyalty, which he expected from those around him and which he returned. He never forgot the knock. Whenever someone mentioned anything negative about him, Lightfoot would snap back, "You read that *Maclean's* article, didn't you?"*

But there were many sides to the man. An article in the *Arizona Republic* revealed one of those sides. In May, before his two shows in the Phoenix area, Lightfoot got a call in his hotel room from a twenty-five-year-old woman, Sun Davis. Her friend Tricia Kirlin was a Lightfoot fan, and Tricia was in hospital following a car accident that had left her with a broken back and massive brain injury. Would he be willing to visit her? Lightfoot had had only two hours' sleep the previous night, but he agreed and spent half an hour with Kirlin and other patients in the hospital's rehab unit. Davis told the *Arizona Republic* that Lightfoot's visit "made a world of difference to her friend's outlook."

Bernie Fiedler had also been a beneficiary of Lightfoot's generosity. In October 1973, Fiedler ran afoul of the government and was facing eighteen months in jail for failure to pay tax on admission charges at the Riverboat. When Fiedler revealed he had no means of paying the government the $36,000 he owed, Lightfoot told Al Mair to write the check, something Mair strongly advised against. Write the check, Lightfoot insisted. What about the interest? Mair asked. No interest, said Lightfoot. What about the term? No term. Just write the check. Problem was, it turned out that Fiedler actually

---

* Oddly enough, Lightfoot attended the *Maclean's* hundredth anniversary bash in 2005, along with four hundred of Toronto's A-list set, but made a quick exit. Some speculated he was miffed that performers at the event covered famous songs by Dylan, John Lennon and Gilles Vigneault but not him. Lightfoot's office claimed he left early to be with his kids.

owed the government closer to $90,000 (the equivalent of half a million dollars today) and had to go back to Lightfoot twice more, cap in hand. To Lightfoot's credit, he bailed his friend out on all three occasions—typical of the loyalty he demanded of others and always gave back in return.

In June 1978, Lightfoot performed four shows in two days at San Francisco's War Memorial Opera House and turned over all the proceeds to Greenpeace, the environmental watchdog organization. "They need the money," he said, "and that's a good place to generate some publicity for them." Lightfoot was careful not to overbook himself with benefits, but his concern for the planet would lead him to devote more time to environmental causes than to any other issue.

Lightfoot took his bluegrass buddies the Good Brothers touring with him in the United States in 1978, introducing them to US audiences, beginning in Wheeling, West Virginia. "They could really crack that market," he told the *Toronto Sun*, "and if they did, the rest of the States would follow." Lightfoot had already written liner notes for the Goods' 1977 album, *Pretty Ain't Good Enuff*, and given his blessing for the trio to record his "Alberta Bound," which quickly became a staple of their live shows. For the next two years, the bluegrass boys opened for Lightfoot in venues all over America, none bigger than Los Angeles's Universal Amphitheatre. "He was so generous with his stage," says Bruce Good. "At the end of each show, Gord would invite us back up onstage to take what he'd call 'zee bow,' and we'd all do a big group bow to the audience. All kinds of famous artists would come backstage afterward to see Gord, people like Jack Nicholson, Emmylou Harris, some of the Byrds—we were star struck." Twin brother Brian adds, "Gord liked hanging with us. We were a good buffer for him in those after-show situations, because he's really a pretty shy guy." As one tour segment came to an end, Lightfoot asked Bruce, "Can we play golf tomorrow, man?" That night, Lightfoot and the Good Brothers flew home in the Lear, landing at 7 A.M. in Toronto, where a waiting limousine whisked them up to the Uplands Golf and Country Club in Thornhill, north of the city, where the Goods were members. "We changed into some golf clothes," Bruce says, "and were on the course by nine—the first to tee off that day."

Was Lightfoot a good golfer? "Not bad, but he was better at shooting pool than playing golf," says Bruce. He recalls an incident that speaks volumes about Lightfoot's competitive nature and how much of a stickler he was for the terms of any deal. "I remember once we were playing pool for a buck a game and I lost. So Gord asks, 'Where's my dollar?' And I'm looking at a millionaire, and for a split second I'm thinking, You're not serious, are you? Today, I look back on it and think, Of course he was serious—he wanted his dollar because he'd won it fair and square and that was the deal. That's Gord. Always playing by the rules."

During his touring hiatus that summer, Lightfoot did a little sailing in *Golden Goose* with Vic Carpenter, its builder ("I never sailed her without Vic—too big"). Then, in July, he undertook a physically challenging 673-mile canoe trip on the Back River in Canada's Northwest Territories. It is the country's twentieth longest river and was the most demanding of the eleven wilderness trips he did. Lightfoot continued to rely on these marathon outings to work off what he called his "spare tire" from heavy drinking. He and his five canoeing partners—including Bob Dion and Bill Miller—found the Back River trip especially grueling because of the large number of portages they had to make with their two canoes.

We were icebound on the Back River, at a place called Beechey Lake. We weren't able to travel through certain lakes because they'd be plugged with ice. We carried the canoes ten miles one day, after which there was another three-mile portage. So we ended up portaging thirteen miles—the longest I ever did. We figured we'd stop at the ten-mile point, camp and continue in the morning. But we got such a head of steam that we did the whole thing. It only got dark about one hour each night, so we just kept going. It was really, really hard work. Some of the portages on that trip were filled with mud and mire and mush and we had to lift the canoes sideways in order to get through some of that stuff. We got involved in some stretches of river where we traveled eight miles but only wound up going one mile. It was like a maze where you'd go in one way, come around and then go the other. It's called a serpentine. We had two tents for camping, and we'd cook with small mountaineering gas stoves. There wasn't much firewood up in the tundra. We did some fishing, but mostly we took all our own food in with us. Saw all kinds of wildlife, including a grizzly bear with her cubs. I enjoyed watching the muskox. They loved to play on the sides of the slopes, run back and forth in groups. They're huge animals. I stood about twenty feet away from one; he looked at me, I looked at him and then he just ambled off. I got inspired to write some songs on those trips, which are some of the most glorious experiences I ever had.

While Coonley was the subject of Lightfoot's latest single, "Daylight Katy," the other Cathy he'd shared his life with was clearly still on his mind. His next song from *Endless Wire* to make the charts was "Dreamland," a country-flavored number rooted in the jealous nature of Lightfoot's love for Cathy Smith. "Sometimes I remember when / We were all dressed up in style," he sang over the bittersweet strains of Pee Wee Charles's pedal steel, "I don't recall the gist of it all / But you drove the young men wild." The lyrics further reveal the pain she caused: "You could wrap me around your finger / 'Til it caused my heart to break / There was too much toil in dreamland / And too much love to take." Lightfoot was still trying to get Smith out of his system. Meanwhile, rumors were circulating that he and Coonley would marry. The couple planned a six-week vacation together in Honolulu, where Lightfoot's 1978 tour finished in November. The break would also give him a chance to write some songs for his next album and play a little golf.

Coonley had more traditional values than Smith and had even convinced Lightfoot to attend church in their neighborhood at Rosedale United. He began singing there that Christmas Eve after members of the congregation came to his door and asked if he'd take part in the holiday services. It became a tradition that continues to this day. When Lightfoot appeared on Christmas Eve 2016, he told the congregation that it was his thirty-second time performing at the church. After singing his "Sit Down Young Stranger" solo, Lightfoot joined the other churchgoers in a round of carols.

In fall 1978, Dylan once again came calling. According to *Toronto Sun* columnist Gary Dunford, Dylan dropped in at a party at the Beaumont Road house after his October 12 appearance at Maple Leaf Gardens. He and Lightfoot shot a game of pool—only this time Lightfoot beat Dylan. Dunford dubbed Lightfoot the "Orillia Hustler" and wrote that "Our Gordie whups that little millionaire's tail. [Dylan] wasn't feelin' too fine after that big game. You ever seen a millionaire with his tail between his legs?" Dunford's hyperbole stuck in Lightfoot's craw for a long time. When he called the columnist a year later over another exaggeration, he took him to task, which Dunford duly reported: "You had him leaving with his tail between his legs," he quoted Lightfoot as saying. "How do you think he feels when his clipping service sends that to him?" Lightfoot might well have been feeling just a little smug, though, after suffering that pool table humiliation in Woodstock years earlier.

————

With fewer than fifty concert dates scheduled for 1979—the lowest number in years—Lightfoot had time to focus on writing for his next album. He could also spend some time competitively sailing *Golden Goose*. The previous year, the forty-five-footer competed on the Georgian Bay Yacht Racing Union circuit, winning three of five races. She'd also competed in the Port Huron to Mackinac Island sailboat race, with Lightfoot going up against cable TV mogul Ted Turner's yacht *Tenacious*. Running the 290-mile length of Lake Huron, it ranked as one of the longest freshwater races in the world and, having debuted in 1925, was one of the oldest and richest in tradition.* In 1979, *Golden Goose* sailed in the other "Mack" race: the 333-mile Chicago to Mackinac course, which ran the length of Lake Michigan. As usual, Lightfoot skippered his boat and led his crew in tacking, jibbing and trimming, all highly demanding tasks. Exercise has remained a part of Lightfoot's routine. Even in his late seventies, he takes a highly disciplined approach to daily workouts at his Cambridge Club, as if the cardio exercises were a physical—maybe even a spiritual—cleansing.

With his fortieth birthday coming up in November, Lightfoot was reflecting on the more than half of his life that had been spent in the music business. Writing in *Chatelaine* magazine, Peter Goddard took stock of what he'd achieved: "Like a good craftsman, [Lightfoot] has never wavered from what he set out to do: to write popular music with good singable melodies. It's music that never strays too far from the popular sound of any particular period, but remains unalterably his own creation. There is greatness in his achievement, not just through what he has written but through the loneliness it has cost him to write it." Goddard knew better than most about Lightfoot's loneliness. He'd been writing about him since the

---

* Racers who compete in twenty-five races earn the soubriquet Old Goat, while anyone who reaches the fifty-race number becomes known as a Grand Ram.

mid-1960s. Lightfoot was a solitary figure out of necessity; he wasn't just another celebrity looking to keep his private life away from the media. He removed himself from everyone and everything in order to work without distraction. Songwriting, for him, had to be wholly focused and all consuming.

For his 1978 stint at Massey Hall—another record-breaking nine concerts—Lightfoot broke with tradition and hired an opening act, Colleen Peterson, a blond songstress born in Peterborough, Ontario, who would tour with him for much of the year. Peterson had been voted Canada's most promising female vocalist in 1967 and, strangely, was awarded the same prize again a decade later. At Massey Hall, she provided what one critic called a "flashy" opening set, full of octave-jumping vocals and jazzy chording. By contrast, Lightfoot stuck to his tried-and-true performance style. "Few people in popular music are allowed to remain so consistent and still grow in popularity," wrote *The Globe and Mail*'s Paul McGrath, "but there is something about Lightfoot's personable style that continues to gain admirers. Admirers is perhaps not strong enough— the people who go to see him seem to genuinely adore the man." By coincidence, that same night, Nico—the model-actress-singer who once covered Lightfoot's "I'm Not Sayin'" before becoming a darling of New York's art scene with the Velvet Underground—was performing at the Edge, a small club just up the street from the Church of Gord.*

Lightfoot did only one benefit that year, teaming up again with Harry Chapin and joined by Waylon Jennings and Dave Mason.

---

* Nico, born Christa Päffgen in Cologne, never met Lightfoot, although it's intriguing to speculate about what might have transpired if they had, given Lightfoot's fondness for European blondes. Nico did meet Canada's other poetic folk star, Leonard Cohen. "Paralyzed by her beauty," Cohen followed the German ice queen around Greenwich Village and various Manhattan haunts at exactly the same time Lightfoot was having his affair with the German waitress at New York's Playboy Club. While Lightfoot's muse became the source of "Affair on 8th Avenue," Nico inspired Cohen's "Take This Longing."

They performed at the Nassau Coliseum in Long Island, New York, to raise money for a ballet company and two local symphony orchestras. Lightfoot, still overweight from excessive drinking, was not in his best voice—something that *Billboard* magazine observed in its review of the concert, commenting that he was "occasionally short-winded as he attempted notes that were not in his repertoire." However, the reviewer did feel that Lightfoot's songs "outweighed any vocal snags and his four-piece band provided sensitive support for the rich imagery of the lyrics."

Lightfoot's singing was better later in the year when he appeared in the opening show of the highly rated PBS television series *Soundstage*. Taped before a studio audience in Chicago, the hour-long concert was something of a rarity, as Lightfoot admitted on screen that he wasn't entirely comfortable in the confined space of a TV studio. During the concert, he sang two newly written songs: a sea chantey called "Ghosts of Cape Horn," which had been commissioned for a documentary, and "On the TV," his song about Hornepayne, "where the trains run on time," which would be renamed "On the High Seas." But the year ended on a distinctly sour note. While in Los Angeles recording his next album, Lightfoot and Coonley were robbed at gunpoint in their hotel room at the Continental Hyatt on Sunset Strip.

There was a knock at the door and Cathy and I assumed it was room service or somebody that we knew. Two guys, very smooth and well dressed, burst into our room and one of them pushed me face-first against a wall and stuck a gun right under my jaw. Scared the hell out of us. While he had me pinned to the wall, I heard Cathy yell, "Take your hands off me." I thought the guy was going to rape her. They ended up stealing everything they could find: $3,000 in cash, all my credit cards, watches, my tape deck, my phonebook and my briefcase, which had a lot of Cathy's jewelery in it as well as five tapes of the basic tracks we were going to work on in the *studio. I had bought Cathy a $27,000 diamond engagement ring, but they didn't get that—Cathy had stuffed it under a cushion. We were in a suite, and they pulled out all the phone lines except one, which they missed. As soon as they were gone, we called down to the front desk and reported it. The funny thing was, Rick [Haynes] had got on the elevator at the same time as they were going down and noticed my briefcase. He was going to stop them, but something told him not to say anything, which was a good thing, because at least one of them was armed. We didn't get to sleep until three in the morning, because the cops came and we had to fill out reports. About a month later, I got a call. They wound up catching not the thieves but a black kid trying to use one of my credit cards some place. The girl at the cash register knew the kid wasn't Gordon Lightfoot.*

Getting robbed at gunpoint wasn't the worst of it. Relations between Lightfoot and Coonley had become highly strained. His bottle-a-day habit was at the root of their problems. At times, things between them were more volatile than they'd ever been with the other Cathy in his life. Fights followed by separations became a pattern. Although he and Coonley were engaged and had shared many adventures together, tensions between them had grown into a stubborn wound that wouldn't heal. By decade's end, a second marriage for Lightfoot seemed unlikely.

THIRTEEN

On the High Seas

L ightfoot entered the 1980s racked by uncertainty. For one thing, he was unsure where his relationship with Coonley was headed. Although engaged, they still had difficulty staying together. Coonley couldn't tolerate Lightfoot's drinking—especially the moodiness and bad temper it brought on. And he still wasn't fully committed to the idea of marriage. The bonds of matrimony felt too much like the proverbial chains of love. The harsh words they'd exchanged so frequently had soured things. As he'd put it in a recent song, "The wine has grown bitter."

Lightfoot was also unclear where he now fit in the music world. *Endless Wire's* commercial performance had been disappointing, selling only half a million copies in the United States, compared to one million for *Summertime Dream*. Listening tastes had also shifted; singer-songwriters and their albums, no matter how well produced, were no longer commanding the attention they once did. Audiences preferred the glittery, hedonistic, dance-oriented songs of funk and electropop or the leaner, twitchier, do-it-yourself recordings of punk and new wave. Rather than continue experimenting with rhythms and dynamics as he'd done on his last album, Lightfoot reverted to his tried-and-true acoustic sound.

His next album came out just in time for his annual March stand at Massey Hall. Although *Dream Street Rose* was one of the first digitally recorded albums ever, there was not much else about it that could be called modern. At a time when an edgy, dance-rock number by Blondie topped the charts and even Paul McCartney was dabbling in synthesizers, *Dream Street Rose* was completely out of step with the times. The album title was taken from a 1932 Damon Runyon short story. And the romantic ballad of the same name was every bit as old-fashioned. Lightfoot had written it for Cathy Coonley during one of their earlier separations. Over chiming acoustic guitars, he sings earnestly of how she'd been in all his dreams since she'd been gone. "I'm gonna love you / From now on," he promises.

The rest of *Dream Street Rose* was either steeped in the past or followed typical Lightfoot song patterns. His cover of Leroy Van Dyke's tongue twister "The Auctioneer" was a throwback, something he'd been performing in concert as early as the mid-1960s. Two of the best tracks revisited familiar themes. The wilderness-loving "Sea of Tranquility" was inspired by Lightfoot's childhood memories of woodland creatures and such aquatic life as frogs, otters and rainbow trout. And the sea chantey "Ghosts of Cape Horn," like "Canadian Railroad Trilogy," was a historical number commissioned for another medium, in this case a documentary film about the dangers of sailing tall ships in the late nineteenth and early twentieth centuries.

One of the most revealing songs recorded for *Dream Street Rose* didn't wind up on the album. "Forgive Me Lord" was an acknowledgment of past sins. Almost Calvinistic in tone, it was the kind of repentant number churchgoers like his parents could appreciate. Lightfoot cites his "shame" and "foolish pride" and asks God to take his hand and lead him to salvation. And he makes the candid admission that he was "caught in the act," likely a reference to Brita's adultery charge that she had found him in their bed with another woman. Although Lightfoot performed the song for years, the recording remained in the vaults until 1999, when it finally appeared on his *Songbook* box set.

By keeping things mellow musically on the new album, Lightfoot sealed his fate with critics. He'd become pigeonholed as an easy listening artist—a label that dogged him throughout the 1980s. To clear the house after a concert by punk rockers X, staff at the Greek Theatre in Los Angeles once played Lightfoot's music over the sound system, emptying the venue in record time. His new songs were good, but the music was playing it safe, trying to fit comfortably into radio's new adult contemporary format. The result was, as one critic put it, "frightfully ordinary." The most damning review came from the *Los Angeles Times*, once one of Lightfoot's biggest champions, which described *Dream Street Rose* as "middle-of-the-road music for adults who don't want to rock but aren't ready for Vegas."

Lightfoot could always count on his Massey Hall concerts for comfort. "It's nice to be back on these hallowed boards," Lightfoot, wearing his embroidered denims, told the receptive audience. "This is my hometown," he said, "and it's the most important engagement of the year." The Toronto shows were also nerve-racking, because the audiences were filled with family and friends. But they were uniformly successful. If there was any negative note, it came during his performance of his new song "Ghosts of Cape Horn," when Lightfoot had to pucker up and whistle the sea chantey's refrain. He'd recovered most of his facial motor functions after his affliction with Bell's palsy, but he still couldn't smile or whistle properly. "It was, to put it bluntly, lousy whistling," wrote one reviewer, who otherwise found no fault with a performer who "oozes talent, reeks of perfection and doesn't even have the decency to let it go to his head." Lightfoot, who'd just been voted Canada's Male Singer of the Decade, could also be declared the world's most humble pop star.

Cathy Coonley didn't come to the concert. She was staying with her sister in San Diego. "She's about 2,500 miles away now," Lightfoot admitted to the *Toronto Sun*'s Wilder Penfield III, "and there's not too much I can do. She won't come up for the concerts. I was hoping she might." Although he and Coonley shared mutual interests and were seen by friends and family as compatible in many ways, Lightfoot got cold feet about marrying her. He told Penfield: "I always feel [marriage] is going to be an entrapment." During the same interview, Lightfoot spoke openly about his drinking. But he still credited booze with fueling his songwriting and remained in denial about the toll it was taking on his health and relationships. "I've had a problem with alcohol for the last ten years. But I don't know that it did more harm than good: some of my most creative periods have been during this time."

During his month off in July, Lightfoot undertook another canoe trip to dry out. He joined fellow paddlers Ted Anderson, Paul Pepperall and veteran canoeist Fred Gaskin and flew up to the Northwest Territories for a three-and-a-half-week journey down the South Nahanni River. After arriving at the headwaters by helicopter, the group was only four days into the trek when disaster struck. As Gaskin wrote that year, "Gordon and I were lining his new Old Town Voyageur canoe through some very turbulent water down a drop between two boulders when, without warning, the canoe spun broadside to the current and swamped. We pulled the packs from the canoe just as it submerged and watched horrified as the canoe bent backward and wrapped tightly around the boulder. We spent the balance of the day trying to salvage the boat, but it was no use. The combined strength of four men, a strong rope, pry bar (log), and sophisticated applications of all the physics we knew were to no avail. We were now four men with one canoe. Things couldn't have looked worse!" Just as the four were contemplating how to carry on, another canoe team arrived with a block and tackle, and the combined strength of all the men managed to pull free Lightfoot's canoe, which miraculously returned to its original shape and form. Lightfoot later paid tribute to his indestructible watercraft (made of ABS Royalex) and its journeys in his song "Canary Yellow Canoe."

During one of their reunions Coonley, along with Bev, encouraged Lightfoot to try his hand at film acting—something his friends Dylan, Ronnie Hawkins, Johnny Cash and Levon Helm had all pursued. (He'd once been considered for the lead role in the 1976 remake of *A Star Is Born*, co-starring with Cher, but the part eventually went to his friend Kris Kristofferson, while Barbra Streisand took the female lead role.) Lightfoot agreed. With the ICM talent agency in Los Angeles representing him, he was offered parts in three movies: a Burt Reynolds car-chase flick, a Steve McQueen film, which was canceled when McQueen was diagnosed with cancer, and a Bruce Dern western called *Harry Tracy, Desperado*, about the last surviving member of Butch Cassidy's Hole in the Wall Gang. Lightfoot liked Dern and agreed to go for the part of Marshal Morrie Nathan, who is charged with the task of capturing the notorious train robber and legendary escape artist Tracy, played by Dern. While in Los Angeles for his annual gig at the Universal Amphitheatre, he memorized his lines and auditioned in the Hollywood offices of executive producers Sid and Marty Krofft. Lightfoot won the part but needed acting training. He also had to take horseback-riding lessons at Toronto's Humber College, where he developed a bad case of saddle sore.

Shooting for *Harry Tracy* began in December on location in Alberta and British Columbia. Coonley had a small part as a prostitute, so she was along for the entire shoot. Lightfoot remembers that on the night John Lennon was murdered, he and Coonley were snowed in at their motel room in Canmore, Alberta, where they watched the grim news on television. In the script, Lightfoot's unsmiling lawman suffered several indignities. One scene called for him to sit naked in a bathtub with Coonley's hooker scrubbing his back, only to have two shocked townswomen burst in on him. In another, Lightfoot's US marshal gets thrown off a hurtling train in his long underwear and lands in a snowbank, leaving Tracy once again to make his getaway. The most humiliating scene involved him being dumped into an outhouse trench filled with what Lightfoot describes as "drilling mud and Oh Henry! chocolate bars."

The eight-week shoot was sometimes wild and dangerous. On location one day, Lightfoot almost got himself killed by a train. "It was backing up, and I was looking the other way and didn't see it coming," he says. On another occasion, he and the rest of the cast and crew had to withstand bone-chilling temperatures in the Cariboo Mountains in British Columbia, in a place called Barkerville. Lightfoot's fondest experiences were on horseback in the majestic forests. "We had an Indian guy who was in charge of the horses, and he really looked after them well, keeping them warm and fed. I had a soft spot for those horses. Mine was called Harmony. I'll never forget the beautiful rides I got to do on her through these forests full of huge trees."

Harry Tracy provided Lightfoot with no shortage of adventures. He also got to sing "My Love for You," written by Red Shea's brother Les Pouliot, on the soundtrack. But when it was released the following year, the $8.3 million movie bombed at the box office and was pulled from theaters. The film was relegated to video release and the occasional broadcast on late-night television.

Lightfoot later landed another on-screen role in *Hotel*, an Aaron Spelling TV series based on a novel by Arthur Hailey, one of Lightfoot's favorite novelists. The series starred James Brolin and Tippi Hedren and a rotating cast of guest stars that included Elizabeth Taylor, Alec Baldwin and Johnny Depp. Lightfoot was offered a part he could certainly relate to: a country singer named Joe Daniels, struggling with alcoholism, who is booked to play in the St. Gregory Hotel's nightclub. Signing on in 1986, he flew out to Los Angeles, where his episode was shot in a Burbank studio. Lightfoot found the work at times fun, but hugely challenging.

My character gets a second chance in his career. As Joe Daniels, I was on a comeback and trying to behave myself and stop drinking. But I wind up hitting the bottle again. The liquor I drank on set was just colored water. I had a couple of lines to do. My main problem was that I don't have a photographic memory and just couldn't memorize lines. So I had to really study and practice over and over again. The worst moment came when they also gave me a guitar solo and I had to learn it. That almost drove me nuts. It took me all night long. Ronee Blakley was playing my wife and was also playing a singer. I had to accompany her. There were fifteen people hanging around on set, and I'll tell ya, I got so nervous that the pressure got to me and I cried. Being able to memorize lines is the real talent of being an actor. You also need to have an actor's voice. In the end, I didn't like what I saw or heard of myself on film.

As the Stetson-wearing, fringe-jacketed Joe Daniels, Lightfoot was far from memorable. His appearance in the *Hotel* episode, which aired the following January, marked his last acting role.

Touring took Lightfoot to Nevada twice in 1981, playing Harrah's casinos for multiple nights in both Reno and Lake Tahoe. With better paying dates—well more than $100,000 a week for Lake Tahoe—and a desire for a fuller sound, he added Mike Heffernan to the band, a bookish-looking keyboardist who'd most recently accompanied singer-songwriter Shirley Eikhard. As usual, Lightfoot's schedule included a full week at Massey Hall, where he proudly pointed out his children, Fred and Ingrid, now seventeen and sixteen, in the audience. The *Toronto Star* sent its classical music and opera critic to review his performances in an attempt to get a fresh perspective on the Canadian icon. William Littler credited Lightfoot with embracing "the sophisticated pop music mainstream without losing the folk spirit that seems to energize his best work" and called him "a master storyteller in song." He cited narratives like "Ghosts of Cape Horn" and "The Wreck of the Edmund Fitzgerald" for their "directness of statement."

In May, Lightfoot was booked to play concerts in Dublin and Belfast. At the time, Northern Ireland was facing a hunger strike by imprisoned members of the Irish Republican Army and protests on both sides of the Irish border by IRA sympathizers. Heffernan, as the first of his immediate family to visit the homeland, arrived in Dublin proudly touting his Irish heritage. "It was a big deal for me, being Irish on both sides," he says. "Plus, I was touring with Gordon Lightfoot, so I was filled with this sense of mission and Irish pride." But that quickly dissolved as he found himself tossed headlong into the "Troubles." "The day we got there, [hunger striker] Bobby Sands had already died," says Heffernan, "and when Francis Hughes died, all hell broke loose, because the British government obviously wasn't doing anything to avoid it." What started as a demonstration in front of Dublin's General Post Office turned into an all-out riot. As Lightfoot sang his songs of Canadian railroads and shipwrecks to a packed house at the National Stadium, angry crowds roamed the downtown streets just two miles away, smashing windows even in the hotel where Lightfoot and his band were staying.

"After the concert, some of us went out to a restaurant and saw the chaos firsthand," says Heffernan. "Gord didn't come. There was tear gas, guys running past with blood running down their faces. Terry [Clements], who'd had US Navy training, showed us how to deal with it, telling us to keep our backs to the walls as we made our way back to the hotel. It was pretty terrifying."

Tensions escalated the next night in Belfast, as hunger striker Francis Hughes lay in state before burial. Lightfoot and his band and crew arrived to find a barbed-wire fence around their hotel and a guard post for body checks outside the entrance. The concert at Grosvenor Hall was equally fraught, with police in flak jackets patrolling the lobby and the sound of gunshots a few blocks away. That night, an

IRA member killed one police officer and wounded three others. "As events unfold around us we'll try to carry on," Lightfoot told the audience, to great applause. "I don't know what to say. I only wish you all well—and peace." Following the concert, Lightfoot stayed for two hours to sign autographs for hundreds of Catholic and Protestant fans who'd happily shared an evening of Lightfoot's music. "After all they've been through, it's the least I can do," he told Paul King, a *Toronto Star* reporter who'd flown over for the tour and was planning a Lightfoot biography. Like Markle's, it never materialized.*

Lightfoot enjoyed King's company, and with Clements they bonded over Irish whiskey. Lightfoot was developing a habit of having at least two stiff Irish coffees before every concert. Before the British tour ended, his heavy drinking would once again be his downfall. Following dates in Liverpool, Glasgow and London's Royal Albert Hall, promoter Andrew Miller added another London concert at the Dominion Theatre. That final show, according to Rick Haynes, was a disaster. "There was a lot of consumption going on, and it got out of hand," he says. "I always told Gord not to let song requests or hecklers throw him off. But he liked to do things his way and on that night let a couple of hecklers get to him. He took the bait." Barry Keane remembers it being even worse. "Gord would ramble a bit when he was drunk," Keane says. "Somebody in the crowd said, 'Shut up and sing.' So Gord answered him back. At one point, he said, 'You're stupid people; you live in a stupid country.' I would call that verbally abusive. There was an F-bomb or two as well." Lightfoot, by his own admission, lost control of the show and his temper.

---

* King was a colorful character who moved easily among the rich and famous. Before he became a writer, he'd worked in the Rome office of a talent agency, looking after visiting celebrities. King was often mistaken for a Hollywood star himself. When he died in 2008 of cancer, his obituary described him as having "John Wayne's swagger, John Huston's drawl and Humphrey Bogart's toughness."

There was a problem at the Dominion. We'd been on the road for ten days and I was thoroughly drunk. I got into an argument with one of the patrons. I didn't like his attitude. He was right at the back of the theater, and he kept yelling at me, "Play 'The Patriot's Dream'!" It was one of those songs we weren't doing. But he kept yelling for it all through the show. I lost it, walked off the stage and didn't come back.

This was the first time in his career that Lightfoot had ever abandoned his audience. Some accounts say he was already bad-tempered over a negative review of his Royal Albert Hall concert in the *Daily Telegraph*, where critic John Coldstream criticized Lightfoot's sound system and his voice. "The Canadian singer has an indistinct voice at the best of times but, at the outset last night, it appeared as if he had undergone extensive dental surgery." John MacLennan, a Canadian stockbroker who attended the Dominion concert, complained that Lightfoot bad-mouthed English people, the country and its radio stations. "He said he was never coming back, got angry over the fact that his [previous] concerts had not sold out and then walked off saying, 'I don't feel well enough to go on,'" MacLennan told one reporter, adding that Lightfoot's exit was met with a chorus of boos.

Fans at the sold-out concert were furious that the show had been cut short after a little more than an hour, and Miller, the promoter, offered to refund their money. He also convinced Lightfoot to return to the stage and play for the people still in the theater lobby. About twenty fans came back and sat on the stage as Lightfoot gave them an intimate performance of another half dozen songs. Paul King gave an off-the-record account to a Canadian Press reporter, saying that Lightfoot was "very tired, had just gone through riots in Ireland and spent all day arranging for himself and his crew to get home through Paris because it looked as though the British airports were going to be closed by a strike." All of which was true, but it was

Lightfoot's bad behavior onstage that ultimately made news—even in his hometown, where the *Orillia Packet & Times* declared, "Brits Bid Gord Good Riddance." For a man as proud as Lightfoot, that headline hurt deeply. Ashamed of the London debacle, he privately vowed never to perform again in Britain. It was only in 2016— thirty-five years later—after repeated pleas from fans and offers from promoters, that Lightfoot returned to London for a concert at the Royal Albert Hall, after performing ten other dates in the United Kingdom.

Lightfoot continued recklessly drinking, fully aware that he had a serious problem. "I knew I was becoming an alcoholic at that point," he says now. At LA's Greek Theatre in August 1981, it threatened to jeopardize his relationship with his Warner bosses, Mo Ostin and Lenny Waronker. "Playing in front of big audiences at the Greek, Mo and Lenny left early because they could see I was so drunk. I know, because Cathy Coonley told me about it. I was always a bit of a horse's ass when I drank." That fall, Lightfoot's conviction for drunk driving was yet another warning sign. Coonley and his sister, Bev, begged him to give up the booze. And Lightfoot's daughter Ingrid says that even Brita called and implored him to quit.

Rick Haynes remembers how the drinking was ruining Lightfoot's health. "His liver numbers weren't great and he was overweight," says Haynes. "For a while, he was drinking Brandy Alexanders, which is like drinking ice cream. And he and Terry were drinking Bloody Marys, to the point where they were carrying around a Bloody Mary kit, pounding them back all day long. Then Gord took to drinking rum—Myers's Rum with Coke. Man, he could drink. Terry and Gord were enabling each other. A lot." Barry Keane recalls a tour with concerts in Alaska and Hawaii where Lightfoot and Clements were completely drunk for the whole trip. "Gord and Terry were serious drinkers, had their own inner circle," Keane says. "Rick was in and out. Pee Wee was in there sometimes. I'd be ordering Perrier water, and Gord would tease me, saying 'Are you drinking that *paranoid* water again?' I wasn't making a stand, it was just a personal choice."

Before the year was out, Lightfoot faced tests of both his professional and his personal resolve. First, he negotiated a long-term contract renewal for four more albums with Warner. The first album under the deal was due in the new year, and Lightfoot was going to have to prove to Ostin and Waronker that despite his drinking problem he could still deliver marketable recordings with original songs.

On the personal front, Lightfoot had to prove his commitment to Coonley. The two had endured a rocky relationship that rivaled even the fractiousness of Lightfoot's affair with Smith. But during their last reconciliation, Coonley had become pregnant. Lightfoot was going to become a father again. On December 30, Coonley gave birth to a nine-pound son, Eric.

When his next album, *Shadows*, was released, Lightfoot put out a promotional interview disc to explain the origin of some of the songs. The title track was a love song to Coonley that he'd completed on his last canoe trip. "Baby Step Back" was a rock-tinged number whose title came from an expression Bev's husband, Bob Eyers, used before teeing off at golf. Most telling was what Lightfoot revealed about the meaning behind the album's first single, the boldly confessional "In My Fashion." "It recognizes my responsibilities as a human being, the people I've been very closely related to in my life, like my family, my relatives, my two kids by my former marriage and that sort of thing," he said. "It's a song about where you recognize that you've not cut all ties, even though things have not worked out the way people would have liked, that everything is being looked after and things have not just been cast to the wind." One critic cleverly described "In My Fashion" as Lightfoot's "My Way," concluding that despite everything heard to the contrary, he was not such a bad guy.

The early 1980s was the era of music videos, when getting airplay on MTV was crucial for commercial success. Although grandstanding in front of cameras was not his style, Lightfoot desperately wanted to stay in the game and get his new music heard. Reluctantly, he agreed to make promotional videos. He and his band showed up at a suburban TV studio and shot videos for four songs from *Shadows*: the title track, "In My Fashion," "Baby Step Back" and "Blackberry Wine." The videos, directed by Les Pouliot, were embarrassingly bad, with Lightfoot and his band members dressed in comical costumes and lip-synching onstage, in a poker game and alongside actors that included a nymph and a midget. None gained any airplay, and *Shadows* reached a disappointing number 87 on the *Billboard* chart.

Commercial failure did not sit well with him. Like his father, who always looked after his staff at Wagg's laundry, Lightfoot had employees to take care of and was not about to let them or their families down. "I'm just a very conscientious guy," he said, "and we run a big business here, a big company. A lot of people work in this company. There's all the guys in the band, the sound people, everybody, and we try to do what we can to keep things rolling."

Lightfoot had no choice but to throw himself into another year of touring. The sixty-nine dates included some of his most inconsistent performances, several of them sullied by drunkenness and outright bizarre behavior. His August 17 concert at Saratoga Springs, in upstate New York, was so strange and uneven that it prompted one fan, Edward Livingston, to write a lengthy letter, titled "The Death of a Hero," to the *Schenectady Gazette*. "I became increasingly aware of some peculiar aspects of [Lightfoot's] performance," wrote Livingston. "First, he slurred and drawled his words, making even the familiar hard to understand. Second, he salted the moments between songs with comments about them, which were often banal and unnecessary, and brandished statements that threatened to expose his personal life to thousands of fans. Then he turned his back to the audience, apparently to change guitars or say something to his band, but he stayed turned away for a full minute. When he faced us he was in tears, and in broken sobs repeated that he could not continue the concert, that he was sorry, we could have our money back if we so desired. His cool, his professional composure, disintegrated before our eyes and we were facing a man whose personal tragedies had gotten him in the wrong place at the wrong time."

Livingston had no idea just what personal tragedies Lightfoot faced, but they were myriad. And drinking was at the heart of them. As he'd done many times before, he set off on another northern canoe trip to dry out and get back in shape. This time, he chose to travel the George River, which flows from northern Quebec into Ungava Bay. But the canoe trip failed to work its usual magic, and he fell right back into his pattern of heavy drinking. The toll his alcohol intake and increasing irrationality was taking on Coonley finally proved too much. On Labor Day, she took Eric and left Lightfoot forever. As Lightfoot watched his partner and their son leave, the cost of his reckless drinking hit him full force. "Seeing them disappear down the driveway in a taxicab at five o'clock in the afternoon, with Eric just nine months old, it damn near tore the heart right out of me. I knew then that I just had to quit. I lost a relationship and my son—that snapped me out of it." He immediately emptied his liquor cabinet and methodically poured each bottle down the drain in his kitchen sink.

FOURTEEN

A Lot More Livin' to Do

To quit drinking, Lightfoot knew he was going to need help. He turned to Larry Green, one of his closest associates at Warner's Canadian office. Green was an alcoholic who had found sobriety with the help of a Toronto doctor. Based on his friend's recommendation, Lightfoot began seeing Dr. Jack Birnbaum, a psychiatrist and author of *Cry Anger: A Cure for Depression.*

We talked about my problems, my personal life, my remorse about having caused Cathy to leave. [Dr. Birnbaum] made me commit to not having a drink and asked me to come back in a week's time. I went there every week at first, then every two weeks. It wasn't what people call a twelve-step program. It was just me making the commitment not to drink and seeing him on a regular basis. A lot of the time that doesn't work for people, but in my case it did. I got all the booze out of the house and started going to the gym more frequently.

Part of Lightfoot's workout involved running three miles a day, either on the treadmill at the Cambridge Club or the quarter-mile track that circled Toronto's City Hall across the street. It wasn't long before Lightfoot, age forty-four, lost more than twenty-five pounds.

Quitting drinking and adopting daily workouts required astonishing willpower. But that was Lightfoot: disciplined and determined.

Staying sober had its challenges. After flying out to the West Coast in November for the year's final seven concerts, Lightfoot found himself in a bar in Victoria, BC. Sitting on the table in front of him was some rosé and white wine. The temptation proved too much: he promptly drank a half bottle of each. At the show that night, he fell into his old pattern of drinking Irish coffee before going onstage. "That was always my drink at concert time," he says, "never vodka or anything else."

When he returned to Toronto, he had another appointment with Dr. Birnbaum and owned up to his transgression. The doctor started writing on his prescription pad, says Lightfoot. "He said, 'Gordie, I'm going to put you on Antabuse [a medication that triggers a severe hangover immediately after alcohol consumption].'" Lightfoot knew what it was—"Boy, did I ever"—and pleaded, "Please don't put me on that."

"The threat of Antabuse really scared the shit out of him," Rick Haynes confirms. "He was so terrified that he promised his doctor he wouldn't drink again." Lightfoot picks up the story: "The doctor listened to me and said, 'Okay, Gordie,' and he tore up the prescription. I asked him, 'What happens if I really can't stay sober?' and he simply said, 'I'll see you next week.' I realized I didn't need alcohol and didn't want it. After that, I didn't have another drop."

In the summer of 1982, Lightfoot undertook his ninth canoe trip, this time on the Kazan River in what is now Nunavut. At first, he attempted to do it with his Malaysian-born gardener, Choon Goh, who lived with his wife, Amy, in Lightfoot's coach house. Goh wasn't an experienced paddler. When the canoeing proved too difficult, the pair waited until other paddlers joined them and took Goh's place.

*We're doing the Kazan River, from the Snowbird Lake—north of Flin
Flon, Manitoba—to Baker Lake. It's a good trip. I wouldn't advise it
though—it's a trip for experts. We plan to start about July 1 and hope we
don't run into ice, because it's been a cold winter. What you have to do is
just simply carry everything around the ice if you ever encounter ice. It's
usually ice that's drifting out of lakes and into the rivers. In some of these
lakes that are long and narrow, the ice will collect, as in a funnel. But you
take the number of days into consideration. The rule of thumb is you should
go about twenty miles a day regardless of what kind of obstructions you
might run up against, which could be rapids, any number of things. So it's
an interesting thing. It's really good for your health, and now I've done
about 3,500 miles of it, but I'm pushing for the 4,000 mark this summer on
the Kazan, which is about a 500-mile trip.*

He made his five-hundred-mile target and returned home revital-
ized and ready to get back to his music. A new contract with Warner
meant Lightfoot had another album to deliver and needed new songs.
He returned to his writing room at Beaumont Road and sat at the
Quebec table in his wicker chair. Armed with just a guitar and writing
pad, he began composing, pulling melodies out of his head and jotting
down words as they came to him. It was a familiar pattern for someone who had already written more than 250 songs. The difference this
time: there wasn't a drop of alcohol involved. For a man who'd previously relied on booze as a songwriting lubricant, it was a remarkable
feat. Today, Lightfoot says proudly, "I did it with just a lot of coffee
and cigarettes."

The first songs Lightfoot wrote while sober, "Broken Dreams,"
"Someone to Believe In" and "Salute (a Lot More Livin' to Do),"
were among the most upbeat numbers he'd ever composed, full of
chiming guitars and peppy tempos. Others, like "Knotty Pine" and
"Whispers of the North," were relaxed tunes that harked back to his
acoustic heyday. All would be featured on his next album.

When it came time to record the songs, Lightfoot desperately wanted a contemporary sound. He was reaching for what he called "the brass ring" of Top 40 radio. To achieve it, he enlisted Dean Parks, a Los Angeles–based session guitarist who played on prominent albums like Steely Dan's *Katy Lied* and *The Royal Scam* (most significantly, he later contributed guitar to Michael Jackson's monumental *Thriller* album). Working together as co-producers at Toronto's Eastern Sound Studios, Lightfoot and Parks went for a rockier sound, using synthesizers and prominent electric guitars.

Salute was released in July. The title came from a Spanish travel poster that Lightfoot had seen in Dr. Birnbaum's office. Sales were insignificant and the album did poorly on the *Billboard* chart, coming in at number 178. Lightfoot believes the weak showing was at least partly due to the title and now wishes he'd called it *Whispers of the North*, after the song he'd written while prepping for his last canoe trip. "To that wild and barren land / Where nature takes its course," he sings on the track, which opens and closes with the haunting sound of a loon. Along with "Christian Island (Georgian Bay)" and "Seven Island Suite," it ranks among Lightfoot's strongest expressions of love for the Canadian outdoors. But aside from several good songs, *Salute* was disappointing. The album lacked cohesiveness, and its slick production didn't suit Lightfoot's material, which was more compatible with a warmer acoustic sound.

Lightfoot had sold his beloved *Golden Goose* sailboat to a buyer in Hamburg, Germany, in 1981. Now forty-five, he focused his recreational time on canoeing and a new adventurous activity: auto racing. He wasn't about to get behind the wheel of a high-speed racing car himself (although he did once own and race a go-kart), but he allowed himself to get roped into sponsoring driver John Graham, thanks to his friend Brian Good. They'd met over a golf game.

Graham's Cobra, equipped with a Ford Cosworth V8 engine and emblazoned on the side with the insignia "Lightfoot Racing," started competing in the Canadian-American, or Can-Am, Challenge Cup. The big Can-Am winners at the time were American driver Al Unser Jr. and Canada's Jacques Villeneuve Sr. Actor Paul Newman was Can-Am's most illustrious driver. The Lightfoot-sponsored car qualified for half a dozen races. Its best result was a fifth-place finish at Mosport, in Bowmanville, Ontario. But Lightfoot enjoyed the competitive nature of the sport and never regretted his investment.

We had a good car, a tight little model that ran well. Nobody was expecting to set the world on fire. We were just doing it for fun, but we did it in a professional manner. We raced at Mosport, Riverside and Laguna Seca, in California, and in Las Vegas, where we got to meet Paul Newman. My job was to stand right beside the straightaway and hold up the time card so John Graham knew what his time was on the previous lap. In one of the races, our guy had a spin-out where he injured his shoulder badly enough that we had to take him to hospital for X-rays. I remember riding in the ambulance with him. He was okay, but I remember thinking, How are we going to pay for this? I was the guy with the resources, so I was having to worry about these kinds of things.

Graham took part in the Canadian Grand Prix in Montreal, where Lightfoot reserved a boat for the week of the race so that twenty-five of his guests could watch the competition in comfort while moored on the St. Lawrence River. This was typical of his generosity. He was equally magnanimous that month when his old friend John Denver was performing at Toronto's Kingswood Music Theatre, joining Denver onstage to help him sing "Early Morning Rain." Lightfoot's touring schedule in the fall took him back to his usual haunts, including the Universal Amphitheatre and the Sahara Tahoe, as well as a new three-night booking at Harrah's Marina

Hotel Casino in Atlantic City. Although his record sales were down, there were still legions of fans willing to shell out for tickets to see Lightfoot perform.

The year ended with Lightfoot's sister leaving Early Morning Productions. Bev's departure was not unexpected: she had seen her brother through some of the highest and lowest points in his career, including the rock-bottom low of his heavy drinking. It hadn't been easy for her. Observers couldn't help noticing the strain that working together had placed on their relationship. Bernie Finkelstein, the True North Records founder and Bernie Fiedler's concert-producing partner recalls visits to the Beaumont house when he had to deliver something or discuss a matter with Lightfoot, and it wasn't always pretty. "Gordon was very generous, but I knew he had a lot of troubles with his sister," says Finkelstein. "I remember being at his house when they had huge fights. She had some responsibility. I'm not sure Gordon was ever happy about it. But it was very strange for me to witness that, because I'd put him on so high a pedestal."

In December, Lightfoot gave his sister a farewell party at his home. About eighty friends and associates raised glasses to Bev, and Lightfoot gave a short speech in which he thanked her, saying she'd done a "superlative job but now wants to do something else with her life." Bev told one reporter she had no definite plans except to visit friends in Amsterdam and maybe open her own gift or woolen shop in Barrie, a short drive from the Lightfoot homestead in Orillia. "I've enjoyed Toronto," said Bev, "but my heart's still back home." Bev ultimately retired to a quieter life, happy to have left the music business behind. Her replacement was Barry Harvey, a gruff fellow Orillian, who'd previously been Lightfoot's tour manager. Things were going to be very different around the Early Morning Productions office.

In 1984, with no booze or Cathy in his life, Lightfoot threw himself into an increasingly fanatical fitness regime, traveling daily when in town to the Cambridge Club for his rigorous workouts. Sometimes he drove; other times he took the subway, happy that despite his level of fame he could still move freely about in public without being instantly recognized and accosted. Getting fit felt good. It also meant that the demands of touring and canoeing wouldn't be as arduous on a man now well into his forties.

"March Means Lightfoot" proclaimed a billboard high above Toronto's Yonge and Bloor intersection. The sign was advertising Lightfoot's sixteenth annual Massey Hall stand in March that year. Its purpose, Lightfoot told his writer pal Paul King, was "not to sell tickets, 'cause I think we'll sell out anyway, but to tell the folks here I'm alive, well, and raring to go." He certainly was. Lightfoot appeared onstage during opening night looking fit and handsome. For the show's second half, he wore a white suit, which drew wolf whistles from some in the audience. *The Globe and Mail* reviewed the concert: "If there's a major change, it's that he looks better," wrote Liam Lacey, "slimmer by a good twenty pounds, so that the cheeks have regained their hollows and the waistline has returned." His review noted that Lightfoot remained hugely popular despite being out of step with mid-'80s Canadian chart-toppers like the big-hair, spandex-wearing bands Loverboy, Glass Tiger and Honeymoon Suite. "He is certainly not fashionable," concluded Lacey, "but, in some senses, he never was. In his awkward and romantic way, Lightfoot speaks for Canadians' secret, awkward and romantic selves in a way few artists are able to speak to any audience." Lightfoot's connection with his audience was unshakable, a bond that transcended changing musical tastes, forever held in place by the universality of his songs.

His rejuvenated state did not go unnoticed south of the border either. When Lightfoot's tour stopped at the 1,600-seat Duluth Auditorium at the western tip of Lake Superior, *Duluth News-Tribune* critic Bob Ashenmacher drew connections between Lightfoot's fitness and his performance: "The Canadian singer has had mean times in recent years. The records haven't been selling. The drinking was becoming a problem in concert—there was a listlessness, a puffiness around the eyes and in the music. Today, the man has dried out. The surplus weight is gone and he's even developed a muscular upper body (he's taken to lifting weights). He's also upgraded his stage appearance. Gone are the baggy, faded jeans with the rose patch. On Saturday he walked out in cream cowboy boots, black slacks and shirt, a red velvet waistcoat and—Gordon, you hound—a red bowtie." Added Ashenmacher, "Of course, appearances don't necessarily matter. But they were indicative of his new attitude. He was positively frisky—the joker of old, but with new energy to the playfulness. And with a focus to his gaze that had been missing in recent years." For the first time in ages, Lightfoot's mood was positive. Could it be that he was actually happy for a change?

Lightfoot was due to deliver another album to Warner Bros. The company desperately wanted to see him back on the charts after his lengthy absence, so label head Mo Ostin suggested he cut something with Canadian-born David Foster, a keyboardist who'd become one of the leading hitmakers of the day. Foster was a shameless self-promoter and commercial in all the ways Lightfoot wasn't. He also had a reputation for taking an aggressive role in the studio, insisting not only on arranging material but also often writing or rewriting it. *Rolling Stone* that year dubbed Foster "the master of . . . bombastic pop kitsch." Even Lightfoot's mother, Jessie, had sounded a warning, telling her son, "Gordie, don't let David Foster steal your thunder." Still, to keep Warner happy, he agreed to work with Foster on one track during the album sessions.

While discussing the collaboration with Lightfoot, Foster got a call from Quincy Jones, his producer and mentor. Jones had just finished recording a song called "We Are the World" with a cast of US pop stars to benefit African famine relief. Written by Michael Jackson and Lionel Richie, it was a direct response to Bob Geldof's charity single "Do They Know It's Christmas?," which had featured English pop stars under the name Band Aid and raised millions for the same cause. Jones threw the challenge to Foster: if he quickly pulled together a Canadian equivalent, it could be packaged and sold with the US song. Foster already had a melody, and with Bryan Adams, Jim Vallance and others came up with lyrics for a song titled "Tears Are Not Enough." Foster enlisted Adams's manager, Bruce Allen, to assemble performers and booked a Toronto recording studio. Allen lined up Joni Mitchell and Neil Young first. Lightfoot was the next call. On a flight to Toronto, Foster, Adams and Loverboy's Mike Reno looked over the lyrics and the list of artists to determine who would sing what. Foster suggested that the all-important opening line, "As every day goes by, how can we close our eyes," should be sung by an instantly recognizable voice. Everyone agreed that that voice should be Gordon Lightfoot's.

On a bitterly cold Sunday in February, Lightfoot drove to Manta Studios at 311 Adelaide Street East in downtown Toronto. It's an urban legend that he pulled up in a pickup truck; in fact it was his cream-colored Oldsmobile Toronado. Neil Young and Joni Mitchell arrived in a taxi with Young's manager, Elliot Roberts, while the band Platinum Blonde showed up in a white stretch limo. Foster, following Quincy Jones's example, taped a sign to the studio wall inside that read "Leave Your Egos at the Door." Forty-five of Canada's top entertainers, including Burton Cummings, Anne Murray and Oscar Peterson, entered Manta that frigid day to take part in the session. Foster was thrilled with Lightfoot's performance and remembers him "killing it" on the song's opening line. He was less than thrilled with Young's contribution, commenting that he'd sung the word "innocence" flat, to which Young replied, "That's my sound, man," a crack that sparked howls of laughter and loosened everyone up. With Lightfoot's buddies Liona Boyd, Murray McLauchlan and Sylvia Tyson also present, it was like Old Home Week.

Everybody was there, everybody you could possibly think of. Ronnie [Hawkins] was there—even people from Country Hoedown *like Tommy Hunter. There was Geddy Lee [of Rush]. I remember him saying a couple of times, "This is so strange." And it was. But it was one of those things you should do and get involved in. They wrote such a great song, a good little tune that was easy for everybody to learn. I was happy to do it. [Foster] could have had anyone start off the song. I wondered at the time, Why am I number one? But we were working together, so I guess that's why I started.*

In fact, Foster wouldn't produce Lightfoot's album track until late in the year. Lightfoot was consumed by work on the rest of the new album, to be called *East of Midnight*, and spent much of the year in the studio. He'd written fifty new songs and recorded demos and full tracks of many of them, then agonized over which ones he should include. It would prove to be the longest recording project Lightfoot had ever undertaken. At times, he wondered if he should even bother putting out a new album, given how poorly his last three had sold. "When I started to make [it], there was a question mark about whether it was practical to make another album or not," he told Wayne Francis, who runs a popular Lightfoot fan website. "So I went down to Los Angeles and told the record company people, 'If I'm going to do this, then give me the ball and let me run with it.' I wanted to make this album myself and I wanted to do it here in Canada. So I didn't have anyone to answer to or anyone to mess around with; I just got into it and made sure it was done right." For Lightfoot the perfectionist, having full control was the best possible scenario.

Warner's Mo Ostin and Lenny Waronker agreed. But at one point during the studio sessions, Waronker called Lightfoot to ask if he wanted to record something with Dylan for the album. Lightfoot demurred. "I told Lenny, 'I'm not sure. Let me think about it,'" he says. "I wondered if I'd be able to rise to the occasion. I've always been a relatively shy individual. And there are quite a few people I've met in this business who I find overwhelming." Dylan was one of them. Waronker saw the marketing value of a duet with Dylan where Lightfoot saw only an awkward and stressful situation, and Dylan was already on the hook to pay tribute to him in an upcoming award presentation. Lightfoot didn't pursue it.

Taking a respite from recording, Lightfoot broke his own tradition and moved his annual Massey Hall stand to November. The schedule change didn't hurt—all nine concerts sold out. Lightfoot mixed plenty of new songs from his latest sessions with old favorites. Reviews were positive. Of the new material, *The Globe and Mail* and the *Toronto Sun* singled out the ladies-praising reverie "Let It Ride" and the dreamy, sax-drenched "A Lesson in Love." The latter was a standout, inspired by a biography Lightfoot had read about the showman P.T. Barnum, who brought Swedish singer Jenny Lind to America in 1850 for her stagecoach tour. As the *Globe*'s Liam Lacey wrote, "The tale, with its implications about the music business, the circus and the misunderstood artist, has some personal resonance with Lightfoot." Filled with inspired writing of the enigmatic, Dylanesque variety, the song remains a poetic high-water mark in Lightfoot's extensive catalog.

> *You look like the moonglow that follows me home*
> *Always makes me turn around, won't leave me alone*
> *First to come are the midgets, a monkey and a kid*
> *Followed by those two one-armed jugglers, the ego and the id*

In December, Lightfoot flew to Los Angeles and finally started working with Foster. "[David] called me and said, 'Let's write the greatest love song that two Canadians have ever produced up to now,'" says Lightfoot. "He sent me a melody. I wrote the lyrics, which I kept refining. We produced 'Anything for Love' in short order and had a lot of fun doing it."

Back in Toronto, Lightfoot spent the next several months in post-production at Eastern Sound, remixing potential singles and choosing which tracks to include on the album. His preoccupation with the project had left him no time to book concert dates for 1986. That meant that for the first time since he began performing Lightfoot would not play a single concert in a calendar year. Sacrificing the stage for the studio wasn't an easy choice, but that was how much importance Lightfoot placed on the new album.

East of Midnight was released in July 1986. Along with "A Lesson in Love," the ten-song collection also featured two fine songs that touch on sailing. The cascading "Morning Glory" references Biscayne Bay, off the Atlantic coast of Florida, where Lightfoot once sailed with Fred Neil. The majestic "A Passing Ship," with a typically fluid guitar solo from Clements, describes a sunlit ocean and blowing gales but is actually a metaphor for feeling lost at sea. As Lightfoot later revealed, "It's about a guy on the outside looking in, who wants to have a family but can't get into that secure situation, even though he wants to. I've been there, so I know how it feels."

Lightfoot was thrilled with *East of Midnight*. "The best piece of work I ever did," he now says, "my all-time favorite album." But he feels it was spoiled by the perception created by Foster's involvement on "Anything for Love." The song was released as the single and reached number 13 on the Adult Contemporary chart. It still sticks in Lightfoot's craw. "That was the only track that David produced," he says, "but everyone thought the album sounded so damn good that he must've produced the whole thing. People don't bother reading the album credits." The words of Lightfoot's mother—"Don't let David Foster steal your thunder"—had proven prophetic. Lightfoot kept any bitterness aside when *Billboard* asked for a comment on working with the producer for the magazine's special issue on Foster. "There was really so much to learn and I paid close attention," said Lightfoot. "It was uplifting, one of the greatest experiences of my life. His attitude is one of positivity at all times."

East of Midnight was a stylistic shift for Lightfoot. Its cover depicted him wearing his flashy white suit and looking more like Spanish crooner Julio Iglesias than Canada's famous folk singer. The album's glossy production sound was too slick by half, giving it the whiff of a commercial sellout. It simply didn't suit his image or material. Striving to stay relevant, Lightfoot was guilty of aiming too hard for the polished adult contemporary sound favored by radio at the time. But there was no doubting the herculean effort behind the album. He had poured his heart and soul into the project, recording in three different studios over a fifteen-month period. He'd even sacrificed a year of touring. There were some strong songs on the album, including several that have since become concert favorites: "Morning Glory," "I'll Tag Along," "A Lesson in Love" and "Let It Ride." But *East of Midnight* was ultimately another misstep for Lightfoot, who remained musically lost and rudderless in the '80s.

They were hardly friends, but when Foster asked him to take part in the David Foster Celebrity Softball Game, Lightfoot obliged. Playing before a crowd of 5,500 at Royal Athletic Park in Victoria, BC, Lightfoot, Rob Lowe, comedian Tommy Chong of Cheech & Chong and various other screen stars and professional athletes raised $100,000 for children in need of organ transplants. The game featured some strange shenanigans, including Wayne Gretzky attempting to steal a base: when the Great One was called out, he simply uprooted the bag and walked off with it. Female stars, with the umpire on their side, were allowed to breeze around the bases. The good-natured game ended in a 12–12 tie, although Lightfoot remembers it a little differently.

The final score was 12–11. My team lost. I ran on an infield fly and there was [hockey player] Tiger Williams at first base, in a crouching position with the baseball in his hand, just waiting to tag me out. It was a wonderful day. Wayne Gretzky, Rob Lowe and the guy that wrote and performed the theme for Ghostbusters *[Ray Parker Jr.] were all there. Alan Thicke had brought along a whole bunch of hockey players, and there were movie people, musicians and celebrities playing in this team. I was playing right field, and center field was Olivia Newton-John. There were people crowding the fence in the outfield, and Olivia and I went back there, trying to hold the fence up, because the people were pressing it and it was getting ready to fall.*

For years, the Canadian Academy of Recording Arts and Sciences (CARAS) had been lobbying Lightfoot to accept an induction into the Canadian Music Hall of Fame. Each time he was asked, Lightfoot declined. He simply wasn't ready. "I always felt that it had a 'gold watch' kind of feeling to it and that it sort of implied a condition of semi-retirement," he told a reporter in the fall of 1986. The hall of fame had previously inducted the likes of Oscar Peterson, Hank Snow, Glenn Gould, Wilf Carter and Joni Mitchell. It was Neil Young's acceptance a few years earlier that changed Lightfoot's mind. Young was still going strong, very much "in commission," he said, "and he helped to jog me a bit."

What ultimately sealed the deal was Dylan's agreement to take part in the ceremonies at the November Juno Awards in Toronto. In fact, Lightfoot had told CARAS that accepting the induction was conditional on Dylan presenting him with the award. Dylan had recently sung Lightfoot's praises in the liner notes to his *Biograph* box set: "Every time I hear a song of his, it's like I wish it would last forever." Dylan was at the lowest point in his career at the time. His *Knocked Out Loaded* album that year was awful—a "career-killer," *Rolling Stone* called it. When he took to the stage at the Harbour Castle Hilton, in Toronto, wearing an earring and glittery gray jacket, Dylan seemed to have a chip on his shoulder. He told the audience that his presence was instrumental in Lightfoot's decision. "I know he's been offered this award before," Dylan said, "but he's never accepted it because he wanted me to come and give it to him." Whether he was being coy, playful or just plain weird, Dylan's remark came off like a backhanded compliment. Bart Beaty, the head of the University of Calgary's English Department who runs the Dylan-obsessed blog *Long and Wasted Year*, felt Dylan's attitude was very patronizing. "It's hard to imagine how he could have been more obnoxious on an important night for one of his friends," Beaty wrote. "It must suck to be friends with Bob Dylan if he acts like this." Maybe Dylan was just being as egotistical as Lightfoot had been in holding out for Dylan's participation. At any rate, a tuxedoed Lightfoot came out to accept the award and was overheard saying to Dylan, "Thanks for doing it." Afterward, the pair retreated to Lightfoot's home for another one of their private jam sessions. They still hadn't performed together publicly, and the awkward dance between the two cele-brated songwriters continued. Perhaps they'd never be close, having grown too guarded and too insular. But their respect for each other never diminished.*

The late Alan Thicke, however, was a famous friend who did get close to Lightfoot. He first encountered the singer-songwriter at col-lege. "When I was at the University of Western Ontario, I noticed

---

* Paul Simon and Lightfoot also shared a mutual admiration. They'd met on the set of *Saturday Night Live* and following Simon's 1980 concert at Maple Leaf Gardens, he dropped by Lightfoot's house where the two played songs for each other.

that the guys who were doing the best with girls all knew a few Gordon Lightfoot songs on guitar," said Thicke. "I thought if I learned to play a few of them, my social life would improve—and it did. I became a Lightfoot fan. He was the most popular artist universities could book in the late 1960s. I had the bright idea that if I volunteered for the university's entertainment committee and got involved in booking, then I could score front row seats and maybe even meet the guy. That's how I first met Gordon."

Thicke, who later starred in the TV sitcom *Growing Pains,* often called on Lightfoot to appear on his talk show or take part in charity events. Their friendship deepened over the years. Thicke remembered Lightfoot and the Good Brothers coming over to his LA home when his wife, Gloria Loring, was pregnant with their first son. "Gloria was a couple of weeks late, and the doctor was concerned that she was sleeping too much and might never deliver," said Thicke. "I spoke to Gordon and suggested he come over after his show in LA. 'I've gotta keep Gloria awake all night,' I told him. So we played guitars and sang into the wee hours, and wouldn't you know it, Gloria goes into labor!"

Thicke and Lightfoot had attended the 1976 Canada Cup hockey final in Montreal, which was Bobby Orr's last game. When Canada won and pandemonium ensued, a police escort was arranged for the two biggest celebrities—Orr and Lightfoot—and Thicke got to tag along in the police van, which whisked them off to a series of official Team Canada parties. Said Thicke, a hockey enthusiast and amateur player himself, "Who could ask for anything more?" When Thicke was hired to book the talent for the NHL All-Star Game and awards gala in Los Angeles five years later, he invited Lightfoot to perform, along with comedians Rich Little and George Burns. He also roped his friend into performing at a benefit for his personal charity, the Alan Thicke Centre for Juvenile Diabetes Research. The benefit was such a success that Thicke was able to convince the NHL awards show to become a major sponsor for his charity.

Over the years, Thicke got to see sides of Lightfoot few did. "He's a sensitive guy!" said Thicke, who organized celebrity pickup hockey games in LA. "At one of my annual Christmas family gatherings, where we play a little shinny hockey, Gordon was in town and played on the same team as my brother Todd. Gord's a very competitive guy. He hadn't been on the ice in quite a while, but he's out there very energetically going into the corners and grinding it out. We didn't have formal uniforms or anything. In one instant, he lifts my brother's stick and steals the puck, not recognizing they were both on the same team. Gord started apologizing about it and was apologizing at the after-party we had. And to this day he still talks with misgivings about taking the puck away from someone on his own team!"

Hockey was also involved the next time Thicke called on his friend. In February 1987, Thicke was the master of ceremonies for Rendez-vous '87, an international gala held in Quebec City as a cultural exchange between Canada, the United States and the Soviet Union. Along with two hockey games between the NHL All-Stars and the Soviet national team, there were two days of concerts, featuring performances by Paul Anka, David Foster, Glass Tiger, the Russian rock group Autograph and the Red Army Choir. It wasn't a brilliant lineup, but Lightfoot was happy to have a big audience, a nice paycheck and the chance to help his friend Thicke, who'd booked him and his band to appear on both shows. Dressed in a navy sports jacket with shirt and tie, Lightfoot performed sets that included songs like "Morning Glory," from *East of Midnight*. It kicked off a busy year of touring that would see him give seventy-two concerts across Canada and the United States. Lightfoot was far from retirement and still very much "in commission."

————

In his 1987 concerts, Lightfoot dispensed with the electric guitar he'd flirted with on his previous tour and stuck to his trusty six-string Martin and twelve-string Gibson. He'd taken to singing "Anything for Love" guitar-less, ambling across the stage Sinatra-style and crooning to prerecorded accompaniment. Fortunately, this was an affectation he quickly abandoned. Lightfoot had been wryly introducing the song in concert as "Dave's ditty," an indication of his attitude toward the David Foster collaboration. He was still unsure of his place in the '80s music scene and admitted to *Maclean's* that he'd toyed with the idea of retiring from songwriting and recording altogether. "When your albums aren't selling, it's not practical for a man to spend his life chained to a desk and to a recording studio," he told the magazine. "You have to grow up and realize that there is a new generation of recording artists out there."

A new generation, it turned out, had grown up on Lightfoot's music. In July 1986, Lightfoot got a call from MCA Records. Would he be willing to meet one of the label's fastest rising stars, a singer-songwriter from Nashville who was a huge Lightfoot fan? Steve Earle, in Toronto to perform at the Diamond Club, had shaken up the music world with his debut album, *Guitar Town*, and hard-hitting songs like "Good Ol' Boy (Gettin' Tough)." Although he'd previously written songs for country legends Waylon Jennings and Carl Perkins, the Texas-born Earle was a dyed-in-the-wool folkie who'd absorbed the songs of Dylan, Jerry Jeff Walker and Ramblin' Jack Elliott. He'd also known Lightfoot's work for as long as he could remember, even learning to play "Canadian Railroad Trilogy" in its entirety. "You couldn't find anything less relevant in San Antonio," says Earle, "but I just thought it was so cool."

Lightfoot agreed to meet the country-folk-rocker and invited him to his Beaumont Road home. "Dave Watt from MCA Canada dropped me off," says Earle, still amazed at his luck, "and I went up, rang the bell and fucking Gordon Lightfoot comes to the door. He invited me in, asked if I wanted anything to drink and handed me his Martin D-18. I was in awe, and I'm not like that very often. He picked up another guitar, and we sat and traded songs back and forth in his solarium for several hours. Finally, he decided it was time for me to go, but he didn't know who to call and I didn't either. So I just wandered down his street. There I was, stranded in Rosedale! But it remains one of my favorite memories ever. When you meet one of your heroes and you're not disappointed in them, then it's something else."

Earle invited Lightfoot down to his show that night at the Diamond but had no idea whether he'd make it. It turned out he did: Lightfoot was there in the balcony, stage left. When Earle and his band, the Dukes, came back out for a second encore they decided on the spot to play "Sundown." Says Earle, "We'd never played it before and never since, but it felt like the right thing to do."

Lightfoot's recent records might not have been selling, but he could still warm a frozen crowd with one of his classics. At the opening ceremonies for the 1988 Winter Olympic Games, he and Ian Tyson belted out Lightfoot's "Alberta Bound" and Tyson's "Four Strong Winds" in near zero temperature to the outdoor capacity crowd at Calgary's McMahon Stadium. Lightfoot wore a thick sweater and jeans, while Tyson sported a cowboy hat and duster coat, matching the outfits of hundreds of men who square-danced around the stadium with their female partners. A huge cheer rang out at the mention of Alberta in Lightfoot's song. As he and Tyson sang about chinook winds and Rocky Mountain sunsets, Olympic athletes and audience members sang and clapped along. The performance by the two musical icons was a highlight of the ceremonies and a quintessentially Canadian moment that even an American TV announcer found moving because it was "so real." For Canadians, the performance struck a far deeper emotional chord. "Four Strong Winds" was Canada's unofficial national anthem, while "Alberta

Bound" served as a rallying cry for people in the West and anyone who'd ever ventured there.

Lightfoot had performed with Ian Tyson two years earlier, after getting a call from his old friend Sylvia Tyson. She and Ian were organizing a reunion concert at Kingswood Music Theatre at Canada's Wonderland, a theme park north of Toronto. It was going to be taped for CBC Television, with special guests Judy Collins, Linda Ronstadt, Emmylou Harris and Murray McLauchlan. Would Gordon join them? "Gordon wasn't sure," recalls Sylvia. "He wasn't performing that year. I called him again and said, 'I don't want to put any pressure on you, but the minute you know either way, let me know, because we need to promote it. Just barely the week before [the concert], he phoned up and said, 'Well, you can go ahead and advertise it.' It was that tight." She adds, "Gordon's very mercurial. The minute he said yes, it almost became the Gordon Lightfoot show. He'd become a vessel that Canadians placed so much on because he came to represent Canada and the land."

For his appearance on the *Lovin' Sound* TV special, Lightfoot donned his white suit and strode out onto the stage at Kingswood to sing "Early Morning Rain" with Ian and Sylvia. He then played "Knotty Pine" by himself and joined everyone for "Four Strong Winds." Although he'd initially dithered about taking part, Lightfoot was pleased to credit the two friends who had helped kick-start his career by introducing him to Albert Grossman.

Ian and Sylvia weren't Lightfoot's only folk-singer friends on television. Murray McLauchlan was hosting a special called *Floating Over Canada*. The show's conceit saw McLauchlan, a licensed airplane pilot, fly a Cessna 185 floatplane across the country, dropping in on musical friends like Buffy Sainte-Marie, Levon Helm, Edith Butler and Ian Tyson along the way. McLauchlan invited Lightfoot to take part, thinking he'd be thrilled to participate in a TV show in which he got to demonstrate his canoeing skills. It should have been

Dylan inducting Lightfoot into the Canadian Music Hall of Fame at the 1986 Juno Awards. © Bruce Cole, Plum Communications.

Cowboy shirts and tuxedos: with the Good Brothers (from left) Bruce, Brian and Larry Good. Courtesy of Bruce Good.

Early morning parenting: with son Eric. © Cathy Coonley.

With longtime friend Alan Thicke. © Tom Bert.

Galen: Lightfoot's California-born
son with Joanne Magee.

At the Toronto Maple Leafs' home opener in 1992, with Steve Yzerman, Darryl Sittler and Wendel Clark.

Discussing the *Edmund Fitzgerald*'s sinking with Great Lakes captains Fred Leete and Tom Allor.

Preparing for the next leg of the journey: Great Slave Lake, Northwest Territories in July 1984.

Saving the Amazon rainforest: with David Suzuki near Manaus, Brazil, in 1989. Courtesy of David Suzuki.

Family time: with Elizabeth Moon and son Miles in the ravine below Beaumont home, 1992. © Rick McGinnis.

Looking on, admiringly, at daughter Meredith, Occupy Toronto, 2011. Material republished with the express permission of the *Toronto Sun*, a division of Postmedia Network Inc.

Gords of a feather: with Gord Downie at Canadian Songwriters Hall of Fame evening, 2010. © David Chan.

The Tower of Song: with Leonard Cohen at Cohen's 2006 induction into the Canadian Songwriters Hall of Fame. © Anjani.

With longtime friend Ronnie Hawkins at the launch of "Christmas Must Be Tonight" in Toronto, December 2015. © J.P. Moszulski.

Tying the knot with Kim Hasse at the Rosedale United Church, December 2014. © Kate Hood.

The band: Carter Lancaster, Mike Heffernan, Rick Haynes and Barry Keane with Lightfoot outside Graceland, Memphis, in March 2016. Courtesy of Rick Haynes.

a classic Lightfoot appearance. "At the time, he was renaissance Gord," says McLauchlan. "He'd forsworn alcohol and was sober. He looked like an expedition guy, very fit from all his wild river paddles in northern Canada. I told him, 'I'll come out of the sky in a float-plane, you'll be in Muskoka in a canoe, and we'll meet.' He agreed but then worried about which canoe he should bring. In the end, he brought this beautiful antique canoe and showed up at our location on this rock island all by himself."

But Lightfoot's mood turned ugly shortly after he arrived, possibly over a disagreement about which of his songs he was to sing. "Something had gotten under Gord's bonnet," McLauchlan says. "The producers and I had a long list of his well-known songs, but he adamantly refused to play any of them; he wanted to sing his 'Knotty Pine' and really got himself revved up over it. He became kind of abusive to some of the people on the shoot, the cameraman and the production assistant, being snarky and occasionally profane. I had to take him aside and say, 'Listen, if you don't behave yourself, I'm gonna have to throw you in the fucking lake.' He behaved himself after that." What McLauchlan and his producers hadn't taken into account was that the perfectionist in Lightfoot meant he never liked being outside his comfort zone. Throw him a last-minute curveball, like suggesting he perform a song on camera that he hadn't rehearsed, and he'd likely go all squirrely on you.

When at home, Lightfoot continued his daily visits to the Cambridge Club on the eleventh floor of the Sheraton Hotel. He'd become quite a fixture around the place, one of the few members whose photograph hung on its walls among other national icons and Canadian-themed posters, maps and paintings. One day, while working out in the gym, Lightfoot heard a song on the sound system that sounded strangely familiar. It was Whitney Houston singing "The Greatest

Love of All," a song composed by Michael Masser. Lightfoot felt its melody had an uncanny resemblance to "If You Could Read My Mind." "It really rubbed me the wrong way," Lightfoot told *Maclean's* writer Brian D. Johnson. "I don't want the present-day generation to think that I stole my song from him." He promptly launched a lawsuit claiming Masser's song stole twenty-four bars from "If You Could Read My Mind," but he later dropped it. "I let it go," Lightfoot explained, "because I understood that it was affecting Whitney Houston, who had an appearance coming up at the Grammy Awards and [it] wasn't anything to do with her. I said, 'Forget it—we're withdrawing this.'"

One of the people Lightfoot had met at the Cambridge Club was Rob Caldwell, a financial adviser from Kitchener, Ontario, who'd become one of his canoeing buddies. In 1985 the two, together with others, undertook a trip along the Back River, in Canada's Northwest Territories. It was Lightfoot's second time on the Back and would be the last of the eleven trips he made over fourteen years. "Gord is a very good paddler, very good in the bush," says Caldwell. "He's as tough as they come. If you're hitting an oncoming wind, he would just put his head down and grind it out. He's very comfortable in a tent. Didn't mind rough conditions—sometimes the stormier the better. Often, we'd paddle for four or five days, then take a day off. He was more inclined to forge ahead." Did it surprise Caldwell that Lightfoot was so comfortable in the wild? "Not at all. I could tell he was adept at it, very well organized, every detail mapped out: supplies, emergency equipment, the whole bit. He could even use needle and thread to put a button back on a shirt."

Caldwell remembers that Lightfoot's celebrity—even in remote places in the North—caused a stir. At the end of the Kazan River trip, the canoeing crew arrived in a small village of a few hundred people who were anxious for the famous musician to entertain them at the school gymnasium. "I have a picture of Gord playing guitars with a bunch of children at three or four in the morning, because everyone would be up all day at that time of year," Caldwell says. "And he was surprised that people up there knew his music." On another occasion, in a Yellowknife restaurant, the crew met the owner of a metal scrapyard who was keen to show them his operation. "Gord really enjoyed going with him in his big Caterpillar dump truck and crushing some of the old cars in the yard."

Lightfoot has always valued the friendships he formed on his canoe trips. The extreme experiences of those expeditions seemed to cement friendships for him. He and Caldwell have stayed friends ever since, and Lightfoot visits him at his rural property in Powassan, near North Bay, Ontario.

For a man so closely connected to the Canadian wilderness, it was natural that Lightfoot would embrace environmental causes. He had performed benefit concerts for Earth Day and Greenpeace early on, but he'd been largely absent from the environmental scene in the '80s. It took a phone call from scientist and environmentalist David Suzuki, host of CBC's popular *Nature of Things* TV series, to renew Lightfoot's commitment to the cause. Suzuki challenged him to take part in the fight to save British Columbia's Stein Valley, threatened by government logging plans. With its glacier-fed lakes and old-growth forest, the Stein was a sacred place for First Nations people and one of the last major undeveloped wilderness tracts in western Canada. Suzuki was working with an environmental group called Voices for the Wilderness and knew the cause needed more celebrity power to raise its profile. Not only did Lightfoot agree to take part in a festival at the mouth of the Stein River, he flew his band out to perform for free. According to Suzuki, Lightfoot later also donated a large sum of money that pulled the festival out of debt. The following year, 1989, Lightfoot again headlined the festival, with Bruce Cockburn, Blue Rodeo, Valdy and Colin James, attracting more than twenty thousand people—double the number expected. Cockburn's environmental anthem "If a Tree Falls," a song Lightfoot greatly admired, served as the festival's unofficial theme.

The number of benefits Lightfoot performed over the next few years was impressive. He took part, along with Murray McLauchlan, Mary Margaret O'Hara and Margo and Michael Timmins of Cowboy Junkies, in a Toronto fundraiser to help the fight against logging of the Temagami pine forest in northeastern Ontario. Then he teamed up with Ian Tyson and McLauchlan in southern Alberta to oppose the damming of the Oldman River. Lightfoot's ecology activism peaked in the late 1980s when Suzuki enlisted his support for saving the Amazon rainforest in Brazil. He joined Suzuki, writer Margaret Atwood and Paulinho Paiakan, a leader of the indigenous Kayapo people, to protest the damming of Brazil's Xingu River at Altamira and the clear-cutting of the surrounding rainforest. Lightfoot sang at fundraisers in Toronto and Ottawa, where he promised Paiakan he would go to the Amazon and sing for him.

Lightfoot was as good as his word. In the winter of 1989, he and a Canadian contingent that included Suzuki and future Green Party leader Elizabeth May flew into the Amazonian town of Manaus. They arrived in the middle of the night and took taxis to an inexpensive downtown hotel, where everyone was registered two to a room. "We were all exhausted, but I was so impressed with Gordon Lightfoot," Suzuki wrote in his memoir. "Here was a superstar who had his own jet to fly from gig to gig. I am sure he was accustomed to going to the airport in a limo and used to being taken care of, but here he was, one of the gang. A young man said to him, 'Gord, you're bunking with so-and-so and there's your bag and here's your key,' and Gordon hauled his luggage without complaint." The protest at Altamira drew worldwide attention to the Kayapo cause. Paiakan invited the Canadians, along with Sting, whose celebrity put the struggle onto the pages of *People* magazine, to visit his village. There, they ate traditional food cooked on fires and were

· treated to a Kayapo concert of singing, drumming and dancing. For Lightfoot, the trip led to a song that eventually appeared on his 2004 album *Harmony*. The place where he stayed in Manaus was called the Nobo Hotel, but the *b* and the *o* in the sign were burned out, so he called the song "The No Hotel."

Lightfoot rounded out the decade with three benefit concerts in his hometown, the first time he'd sung publicly in Orillia in eighteen years. It was a cause close to his heart. Proceeds went to the Orillia Opera House and Soldiers' Memorial Hospital, where his father had been cared for before his death. As he told the *Orillia Packet & Times*, "There wouldn't be a 'Pussywillows, Cat-Tails' without Orillia. I think about Marchmont [the countryside to the west of town] when I'm singing that—where the North River goes through. We used to fish out there when we were boys." Lightfoot also told the local paper that getting involved in environmental activism felt like the right thing to do. "An inner voice told me to work with David Suzuki," he said.

Inspired by Suzuki's commitment to going green, Lightfoot started riding the bus and subway to his fitness club downtown. "I felt so guilty. I was working for Dr. David Suzuki trying to save the Stein Valley in BC and he asked why I was driving halfway across the city so I could run my butt off at the club," he later told the *Toronto Sun's* Jean Sonmor. "Nobody bothered me [on the bus or subway] but sometimes I got so lonely I wished they would." Loneliness didn't suit Lightfoot.

Cathy Smith was having a hard time. She'd been in and out of the news over the past four years as the Belushi case lurched its way through the US courts. But Lightfoot hadn't abandoned her: in fact, he'd helped cover her legal costs. Smith had pleaded no contest to a charge of involuntary manslaughter and three counts of furnishing and administering dangerous drugs to the comedian (the *National Enquirer* had paid her $15,000 for her story, which ran with the headline "I Killed John Belushi," although Smith's lawyers claimed the *Enquirer*'s interviewers had supplied her with alcohol when she was already stoned on drugs). A judge sentenced Smith to three years in prison, saying she had supplied the "poison" that led to the death of Belushi from an overdose. She served eighteen months at the California Institution for Women. The association with Smith dogged Lightfoot, putting him in awkward situations at parties and even his health club, where members asked about her in hope of hearing salacious details.

Lightfoot still refused to bad-mouth the woman he once loved. "I've been called arrogant many times because I would not open up," he told the *Toronto Sun*'s Liz Braun. "I was reluctant to do it the whole time Cathy Smith was on trial—it was not my place to speak out on it at all. I was helping to finance her costs, but I wasn't gonna start yakking about it. The simple fact of the matter is that she and I lived together for three years in a relationship that ended thirteen years ago. She's a great lady. She and I had a wonderful time. It just didn't work out, and at the time she wasn't into any of the hard drugs or anything like that."

It would have been understandable if Lightfoot, having given up booze, had put up a firewall between himself and Smith. Seeing her again could only bring back memories of all their nights together, when alcohol had been a constant presence in their lives. But rather than cut her off when she got out of jail in March 1988, as so many others did, Lightfoot helped Smith get back on her feet. He gave her money, encouraged her to write about her experiences and even made introductions that led to the publication of her memoir, *Chasing the Dragon.*

In the midst of all the chaos of his personal life, Lightfoot relied on the stability of his band. He liked having the same people around.

Haynes and Clements had both been with him for nearly twenty years, Keane and Ringwald (aka Pee Wee Charles) for almost as long. Lightfoot had formalized their commitment years before, paying his sidemen an annual salary whether they played or not. During the 1980s, those salaries exceeded $50,000 for each musician. It was an arrangement that suited Lightfoot. So, when his pedal steel player Ed Ringwald told him in July 1987 that he wanted to leave the band, Lightfoot was not happy. This was the musician who'd brought such a distinctive sound to "The Wreck of the Edmund Fitzgerald" and other songs for sixteen years. During a short break in touring, Ringwald drove to Lightfoot's Beaumont Road house from his home in Kitchener, Ontario, to explain himself. "I told him how thankful I was for all he'd done for me and the awareness that he'd brought to me as a player," says Ringwald. "I told him that deep down it was time for me to get off the road and be with my family. He was a bit shocked, but said he understood, shook my hand, gave me a hug and said, 'Pee Wee, I'll never replace you.' And to this day he hasn't, which is a pretty big honor, given the legendary minstrel that he is. It was very emotional for both of us."

Lightfoot had been mostly alone since Cathy Coonley had left with their son, Eric. He'd gone on a few dates and had spent time with Judy Heard, an Eaton's sales clerk whom he'd met at one of his concerts. But it wasn't serious. Lightfoot was able to build an amicable relationship with Coonley and had shared custody of their eight-year-old son. Eric would spend weekends with his father every couple of weeks and today remembers his dad taking him to Toronto Blue Jays baseball games or monster truck shows at the SkyDome. "Mostly we'd just go places," Eric says. "There was always this conveyance aspect to our time together, driving up Yonge Street in his Cadillac, riding the subway or the ferry boat across to the islands and back—even going up in the elevator at the CN Tower. Getting around with no real goal. Just hanging out."

He made time for his other children as well, visiting fourteen-year-old Galen and his mother, Joanne, whenever he was in Los Angeles. As for his eldest kids, he arranged to regularly see Fred, by then a graduate of the University of Toronto, and Ingrid, who already had two children of her own. They'd have occasional meals together. Lightfoot tried his best to maintain good relations with their mother, Brita, although it wasn't always easy. Brita had never remarried and divided her time between a year-round cottage on Lake Simcoe and a condo in Montego Bay, Jamaica.

One day, around the time he was working with David Suzuki, Lightfoot walked into Bernie Fiedler's office and recognized the pretty blond woman who was working as Fiedler's receptionist. It was Elizabeth Moon, whom he'd first met backstage at Ian and Sylvia Tyson's reunion concert. They'd dated once, but Lightfoot had found her cold and unexciting. This time was different. "I could see she was beautiful," he later admitted to a female interviewer, "but when I found out she was nice, too, then I really got interested." Lightfoot and Elizabeth, eighteen years his junior, began dating, and the romance snowballed. "The next thing I knew, she was living with me," Lightfoot says today. "She got pregnant pretty quick, and five months later I married her." The wedding, on January 14, 1989, took place in the living room at 5 Beaumont Road, in a small cere-mony attended by a few close friends and family. Right afterward, Lightfoot flew to the Amazon on his Brazilian rainforest–saving mission. It didn't sit too well with his new wife. "Liz likes to say I spent my honeymoon with David Suzuki," Lightfoot admits, "but I had to go, because I'd promised to make the trip, had all the shots and everything."

The arrival of his fourth son, Miles, on July 23, 1989, was a turn-ing point for Lightfoot. He was a father again and now in a stable relationship. No longer rattling around, alone, in his big old mansion, he was happy. Domestic bliss clearly suited him. At fifty-one, life was good—so good that he was even laughing more freely. Most of all, Lightfoot was thrilled by his romance with Liz. His new young bride became his next muse, inspiring him back into songwriting throughout the following decade.

FIFTEEN

A Painter Passing Through

At the dawn of the 1990s, Lightfoot's status shifted from admired veteran performer to revered living legend. While he'd already won more Juno Awards than any of his compatriots, in the new decade tributes and accolades for Lightfoot's entire body of work began pouring in. Not all of this made him especially comfortable. Like the Hall of Fame induction, Lightfoot, ever humble, usually felt such recognition was undeserved or best left for when he retired. And he wasn't yet prepared to hang up the microphone.

But Lightfoot was particularly pleased to receive the William Harold Moon Award from the Society of Composers, Authors and Music Publishers of Canada (SOCAN). He'd had a connection to the late Harold Moon (no relation to Elizabeth Moon), and this award brought it full circle. Lightfoot had been just seventeen when he pitched "The Hula Hoop Song"—his very first composition—to Moon, then the general manager of BMI Canada. The prestigious prize was bestowed on Lightfoot at a formal gala on September 25, 1990, at Toronto's Inn on the Park. Dressed in black tie, Lightfoot attended with his new wife, Elizabeth, and rubbed shoulders with Ontario premier-elect Bob Rae, a songwriter himself, and with members of Blue Rodeo. Host Ian Thomas joked that "with a musician as premier, we'll expect him to sleep in till three. Public appearances will include a concert rider—cold cuts and Heinekens!—[and] two forty-minute sets with a half-hour break and a lightshow." Lightfoot himself got laughs, telling the audience that he genuinely thought when he wrote it that his Hula Hoop composition was a "hot song."

At fifty-two, Lightfoot was happier than he'd been in years. He was enjoying life with his attractive young wife and their newborn son, Miles. He looked fitter than ever and felt invigorated enough to perform forty-six concerts in 1990, most of them in the United States. His commitment to environmental causes remained strong. The issue of Native land rights was prominent in the news that year with the crisis in Oka, Quebec, where Mohawks were trying to preserve their sacred lands. Lightfoot, whose name had led some to believe he had indigenous roots, felt a strong kinship with First Nations people and supported their land-rights fight. He often sent checks when a First Nations group called Early Morning Productions asking for his support.

That summer, Lightfoot performed at another benefit festival to help save the old-growth forest in the Stein Valley. (A threatened blockade by local loggers forced a last-minute venue change, and with the move to the Tsawwassen First Nation, south of Vancouver, the festival drew only 23,000 of the expected 30,000 people.) The efforts of indigenous leaders, David Suzuki, Lightfoot and other artists finally paid off five years later, when the Stein Valley was protected as parkland. BC premier Mike Harcourt held a ceremony with Lytton First Nation chief Ruby Dunstan and Lil'wat chief Leonard Andrew to mark the entire watershed's preservation as Stein Valley Nlaka'pamux Heritage Park, administered by the Lytton First Nation and BC Parks.

Lightfoot found another cause to support. He already had a bond with the people of Superior, Michigan. The town had made him an honorary citizen because his song "The Wreck of the Edmund

Fitzgerald" had drawn attention to those who died on the ore-carrying ship, many of whom had been Superior residents. When he heard the town was struggling to raise money for a new hockey arena, Lightfoot sent them a check for $2,500 to help with construction.

Sometime in 1991, the producers of TV's *The Simpsons* contacted Lightfoot's Early Morning Productions office. Matt Groening's staff was interested in licensing "The Wreck of the Edmund Fitzgerald" for use in an episode, called "Radio Bart," in which a character would sing the song through Bart Simpson's Superstar Celebrity Microphone. According to *Simpsons* writer Jon Vitti, Lightfoot's licensing arrangement would have required the producers to get permission from the families of all twenty-nine crew members who died in the Great Lakes tragedy. Faced with that daunting prospect, the producers opted instead to license C.W. McCall's "Convoy." When asked about this, Lightfoot guesses that his office manager Barry Harvey likely made up the story about the complicated licensing to discourage the producers. While it would have been cool to have "The Wreck" featured in the popular animated series, Lightfoot was always protective of the families of the *Edmund Fitzgerald*'s victims.

With a better outlook on life, Lightfoot began writing again. And despite his charitable efforts, his focus was not on topical songs. "I'm getting into a more ethereal thing now," he told one reporter before an Atlanta concert in July. "The other day, I told my producer about a new lyric and he asked me what it was about. I said, 'It's about nothing.' What else could I tell him? The last thing the world wants is another song about a current issue. I'm still telling stories, but they're between the lines, you know?" In concerts that year, Lightfoot also began performing Dylan's "Ring Them Bells," a gospel-like cautionary tale about the need for moral renewal. Lightfoot gave Dylan's lyrics and references to saints and sacred cows all the necessary solemnity—and got the thumbs-up from the song's composer. "I played it for Bob when he was in

Toronto recently," he acknowledged at the time, "and he liked it just fine."

The following year, Lightfoot opened his tour in New Orleans and moved north through Memphis and Detroit. He appeared at Chicago's outdoor Ravinia Festival, where folk pioneer Bob Gibson was in the audience, and gave a shout-out to his old songwriting mentor, whose "Civil War Trilogy" had influenced "Canadian Railroad Trilogy." His new songs that night included several that would feature on his next album: an urgent sea chantey called "Fading Away," a pretty ballad for Elizabeth, "Only Love Would Know," and an oddball number known as "Wild Strawberries," written for his son Miles. The latter, Lightfoot told a *Chicago Tribune* reporter, is "whimsical and philosophical and has one laugh in it," referring to a line in which he reveals an alleged penchant for polka-dot underwear. "Miles has a good sense of humor," Lightfoot said. "My sense of humor lay buried until 1982," he added, referring to the year he quit booze. "It's funny— as you get older, you complain less because you get mellower, and with that mellowness comes a bit of humor."

In September 1991, Lightfoot returned to Carnegie Hall. *The New York Times*'s Stephen Holden noted that the Canadian singer-songwriter had "changed remarkably little." Lightfoot, he wrote, "remains the master of a low-key pop style that is two parts folk to one part country while incorporating light brushstrokes of rock. Mr. Lightfoot's music extends the traditional folk format of Pete Seeger by discreetly seasoning it with a touch of Bob Dylan's grit." Holden added that at fifty-two Lightfoot was "no longer the suave folk crooner he used to be," but that his voice was now better suited to singing "battle-scarred" love songs like "If You Could Read My Mind" and historical yarns like "Canadian Railroad Trilogy" and "The Wreck of the Edmund Fitzgerald." "A cragginess and a tense astringency of timbre have crept into his singing that is carefully understated. But these middle-aged seams add emotional depth to a voice that at one point sounded almost too smooth to be recounting such rugged adventures."

When he returned to Toronto in early November for his Massey Hall stand, Lightfoot was debuting more new songs. One of them, "Drink Yer Glasses Empty," was inspired by the Persian Gulf conflict. Neither pro- nor anti-war, it simply reflected the call to duty for enlisted men and women. Lightfoot performed it on CBC Radio's *Morningside* and gave a revealing interview to the show's host, Peter Gzowski. Gzowski told Lightfoot, "Your songs are our songs," and pressed him about his notorious shyness and reluctance to do interviews.

GZOWSKI: You've never been comfortable in this situation, have you?

LIGHTFOOT: It was always, what have I got to say, really, that will make your coffee taste any better.

GZOWSKI: Yet the world is clamoring to rap with you, and you insist you don't have anything to say.

LIGHTFOOT: That is precisely correct.

GZOWSKI (CHUCKLES):   Well, thanks for coming by, Gordon.

LIGHTFOOT: It has to have some educational value to it for it to make any sense.

GZOWSKI: Why can't it be like a song, just something that goes out . . .

LIGHTFOOT: That's what it is! It is the song. That's why I don't talk. I just like to sing about it, just sing.

GZOWSKI: The reticence about interviews is surely a key to you. All the stuff about the private Lightfoot— you really are private.

LIGHTFOOT: I could be called reclusive, I suppose, but no more
                 than anybody else.

Even after thirty years as a performer and easily one of the
biggest stars ever to come out of Canada, the man from Orillia
had not shaken off his small-town reserve or grown comfortable in
the media spotlight. Onstage was different. As long as he was able
to sing, play guitar and not talk, he was fine. But offstage, in front
of a TV camera or radio microphone, he was his own worst enemy:
shy, humble and, by his own admission, likely to put his foot in his
mouth. In his heavy drinking days, he was particularly liable to
"shoot himself in the foot" when doing interviews. What booze
did succeed in doing, apart from provide fuel for songwriting, was
loosen him up in social situations. Longtime friend Bernie Fiedler
remembers that well: "Gordon was the most fun guy to hang out
with when he was drinking. When he stopped drinking, he totally
got into himself." Fiedler adds, "I've always said, if I was ever
asked the question 'Do you think Gordon Lightfoot was a happy
person?' I would actually have to say I don't think he was ever
entirely happy."

Lightfoot was at least professing to be happy—happy in his
marriage to Liz, happy to be a father again and happy with his life
in Toronto, riding the subway to his health club whenever he was
in town. Workouts at the Cambridge Club involved a strict routine of lifting weights, running on the rooftop track in fair weather
or running on a treadmill and doing other aerobic training. "I got
in this exercise class and it does wonders for the diaphragm," he
told one reporter. "You do a few exercises and you feel like Luciano
Pavarotti." He also said he was happy with his career, adding,
"There was a time when I hated it," meaning when booze was
compromising his songwriting. That was all a thing of the past,
and with two albums left on his contract with Warner Bros. he was
starting to chalk up more new compositions. But as he told the

Toronto Star, "The world doesn't necessarily need to see another album from me until I'm ready to give them one."

There were certain songs in his catalog that Lightfoot now refused to play. These included "Nous Vivons Ensemble (We've Got to Stay Together)," his 1971 plea for national unity amid the threat of Quebec separatism, and "Black Day in July," his 1967 response to the Detroit race riots. Of the former, he told the *Star,* "I can't be a politician; I'm not qualified to be a politician. The first thing that happens when you get involved is they stick a camera in your face, and as soon as they do that, I'm finished." Of the latter, he said he felt it was too "preachy" for a Canadian to be commenting on American affairs.

A third song banished from his repertoire was "For Lovin' Me," his breakthrough song that was a hit for Peter, Paul and Mary in 1965. Lightfoot's daughter Ingrid, had once scolded him for its macho attitude. "I didn't want him to sing it, because it made me angry," Ingrid says. "I knew it was about my mom. It's pretty self-explanatory. 'I'm not the kind to hang around' and 'the new love that I've found.' My dad was going through a lot of women. My mom didn't need to be reminded of that." Lightfoot agreed and stopped performing the song altogether. "It's as chauvinistic as hell," he said, "and I've tried not to be chauvinist."

Unlike Dylan, who often renders his songs unrecognizable in concert, Lightfoot could always be counted on to deliver live exactly what he offered on record. When he and his band performed in Washington, DC, at the Kennedy Center in 1993—one of only twelve tour dates that year, all of them in the United States—the *Washington Post* commented that his show "wasn't just a reasonable facsimile of his recordings, it was nearly note-perfect." The perfectionist in Lightfoot meant that he continued to spend an obsessive amount of time on tuning instruments with his band. Their preshow ritual involved

Lightfoot getting his six- and twelve-string guitars in tune with the help of Heffernan's keyboard. There was always a lengthy sound check with a run-through of many of the songs to be performed that night. Haynes jokes that every concert day they would perform a matinee as well as an evening show. Then Lightfoot would return to his dressing room for more tuning.

That year, Lightfoot booked time at Toronto's Eastern Sound to record new tracks for his next album. The few public appearances he made included attending the Juno Awards at Toronto's O'Keefe Centre and the Warner Bros. after-party at the top of the Four Seasons Hotel. There, he mingled with label mates k.d. lang, Alannah Myles and the members of Blue Rodeo. For Blue Rodeo's Jim Cuddy, just being in Lightfoot's presence was a thrill. One of the first songs he learned to play at age nine was "For Lovin' Me." "Lightfoot's songs were always part of the landscape," says Cuddy. "And it really meant something that Gord never moved to the States and you would see him around Toronto. He's not a myth—he's a reality. And a very interesting reality." His bandmate Greg Keelor recalls listening to Lightfoot's *Gord's Gold* on his Walkman in 1984, when he and Cuddy were living in New York, and how the music inspired him: "Its harmonic resonance, the artistry of the songwriting, made me want to live deeper, to feel more, so that I might write a better song. And because the music was Canadian, it was like a message from home."

Lightfoot was seen around Toronto on at least two other occasions that year. During the summer, with Liz at his side, he attended the official opening of Renascent House, a downtown rehabilitation clinic for alcoholics. Funded by the Ministry of Health, the center provides a twenty-eight-day program for patients. "I have a history of similar problems of my own," Lightfoot told a CBC reporter, adding that Renascent offered a much more effective source of help than was available when he was dealing with his addiction. "I had to go to other means. I had to seek medical help. I had to promise the doctor that I wouldn't drink and then go back and visit him each week."

Lightfoot got a big thrill on October 6, when the Toronto Maple Leafs, the hockey team he'd supported since he was a boy, made him an honorary captain. At the season opener at Maple Leaf Gardens, he dropped the ceremonial puck at center ice for Leafs captain Wendel Clark and Detroit Red Wings' Steve Yzerman, as tuxe-doed former Leafs great Darryl Sittler looked on. "I was so awe-struck by the whole scene that I just dropped that puck and got the heck out of there," he later said. "I've been a Leafs fan all my life and keep the faith. When we're on the road, we follow the games. Sometimes at intermission, when we're playing a concert and the Leafs are playing a game at the same time, we ask, 'How are the Leafs doing?'" That night, Lightfoot was tickled to receive an official Maple Leafs hockey jersey with his name emblazoned on the back.

In 1993, Lightfoot released *Waiting for You*, his first new album in seven years. The blue-tinged images on the front and back cover showed a smiling, lean-looking Lightfoot sitting outdoors with gui-tar in hand. The previous fall, Barry Harvey had hired Rick McGinnis, a young punk photographer, to shoot images for the album and instructed him to show up at Lightfoot's Rosedale address precisely at ten one morning. McGinnis arrived, a little in awe of being in the legendary musician's house, and spotted Lightfoot's guitars lined up in the sunroom. Lightfoot offered him a coffee, and McGinnis remembers him brewing it on his stovetop. "Here's this rich guy making me a coffee in an old aluminum percolator, the kind you take camping. That really impressed me." McGinnis then asked if there was somewhere outside they could use for the photo shoot. Lightfoot suggested a spot down in the ravine behind the house. As the two made their way down the hill, McGinnis says he had an epiphany: "There I was, walking a path through the woods behind a guitar-carrying Gordon Lightfoot, thinking, 'This is the most Canadian fucking moment of my life.'"

Lightfoot liked the images and agreed to a more formal photo session a couple of weeks later at McGinnis's studio in Toronto's pre-gentrified Parkdale neighborhood. He arrived in his Cadillac, carrying his guitar and suit bag. After commenting on the colorful street life outside, Lightfoot took a seat with his guitar and McGinnis got to work shooting. Later, McGinnis played Lightfoot a raucous cover of "Sundown" by a California punk outfit called Claw Hammer. "They were a really loose band," says McGinnis, "and I was sure Gord was going to hate it. But to my surprise, he said, 'Not bad, not bad, some tough changes on that song.' He was amused by it." McGinnis cherishes the memory of his encounter with Lightfoot and his photos being featured on *Waiting for You*. "Within my circle of musician friends, Gord was held in very high esteem. I got to shoot a musical icon and had a great time doing it."

Waiting for You was greeted by Lightfoot's most positive reviews in years. "His most consistently good piece of work since *Sundown*," wrote the *Toronto Star*. *Now* magazine, a Toronto alternative weekly, stated that "there is a classic Lightfoot sound to the new material, unfettered by lofty production or gushing strings," while the Canadian Press commended Lightfoot's "most personal songs he has ever written." The US press was equally effusive. "Lightfoot has rediscovered the virtues of understatement in his vocals and arrangements—his best album in twenty years," said the *Washington Post*. The *Los Angeles Times* called it "among the most honest personal efforts in his catalogue, a heartfelt, minimalist return to the singer-songwriter's folk and country roots that recalls his early, more traditional work." Best of all was the cheeky review from *Rolling Stone*, which felt that "it's comforting to know that the passage of time has done little to diminish either the artistic spirit or the patriotic fervor of the bard of the Great White North."

All of which was hugely gratifying to Lightfoot, who had truly wondered if his writing days were over. "I had a dry spell there," he admitted. "I didn't feel compelled to do an album. But after a while, I put my nose to the grindstone. It took about two and a half years to come up with ten real good songs." Lightfoot dedicated *Waiting for You* to Liz and Miles and included at least two songs written specifically for his wife. But he confessed that finding the space necessary for writing wasn't easy. "When you're in a position of having the responsibility of a new marriage and a new child, what I found was that the only time I could work was to get up at three in the morning and work for five hours because it was the only time there was any real peace and quiet around the house." Sitting in the early hours at the Quebec desk between two old tape recorders, his office wall adorned only with a large map of Canada, he collected all of his best song ideas on cassette and then wrote them out methodically in his tidy handwriting with pencil on yellow lined pads of paper. Lightfoot's muse was back.

Some serious midlife soul-searching had produced *Waiting for You*'s most autobiographical songs. The confessional "Welcome to Try" details the rough-and-tumble days of alcohol binges and sexual conquests and mentions his children and his admonishing mother. "I'll Prove My Love" was Lightfoot's earnest commitment to Liz, while "Restless" expressed the itchy feeling he'd always felt, married or not. Lightfoot sings about his "on-again off-again style" in the stirring title track, which has the rolling, tossed-at-sea feel of "The Wreck of the Edmund Fitzgerald." And he gives his solemn cover of Dylan's hymnlike "Ring Them Bells" a stately elegance.

Despite his creative rebirth, Lightfoot was still in no mood for tributes or books about him. "I'm not worthy," he told a surprised Nick Krewen of the *Hamilton Spectator*. "I don't need tributes. I don't need books. All I need is my guitar, my songwriting and some people to play for." Then he emphasized the reason for his reticence: "You know what? I'm too humble. I'm humble to the point of feeling inferior most of the time." The odd confession served to explain why Lightfoot had quashed a planned tribute album by CBC Radio. Although his compatriots Neil Young and Joni Mitchell, as well as his buddy Dylan, had all received the tribute treatment by various artists, Lightfoot vetoed the nearly completed project, saying, "It didn't seem like it was a very good idea—I mean, why?"

In fact, a whole new generation of artists had been discovering his songs. Art-rockers the Rheostatics recorded a hauntingly atmospheric rendition of "The Wreck of the Edmund Fitzgerald" on their 1991 album *Melville*. Acclaimed singer-songwriter Ron Sexsmith, one of Lightfoot's biggest fans, was often performing his version of "Sundown" in his sets. Sarah McLachlan, a future three-time Grammy winner, recorded a hushed, reverent version of "Song for a Winter's Night" for John Hughes's 1994 remake of *Miracle on 34th Street*. Then bluegrass star Tony Rice delivered an entire album of Lightfoot covers. The coolest tribute came a few years later when an indie supergroup that consisted of Blue Rodeo's Greg Keelor, Rick White of Eric's Trip, and the Sadies' Dallas and Travis Good (sons of Lightfoot's friend Bruce Good, of the Good Brothers) recorded four stoned-out, backwoods takes on Lightfoot songs. They called themselves the Unintended, a play on the fictional band the Intended that Lightfoot referenced in "Go Go Round."

Lightfoot did seem happy to accept more honors from the songwriters' association. In November, the organization presented him with SOCAN Classic Awards for twelve of his songs, including "Early Morning Rain," "If You Could Read My Mind," "Sundown" and "Carefree Highway," all of which had received more than one hundred thousand airplays on radio. Lightfoot received a standing ovation from his peers after Murray McLauchlan introduced him by saying, "Gordon is crazy in a way that all songwriters should be crazy." Then Lightfoot rounded out his busy touring year with two benefits. The first saw him and his band perform on a bill with Simon & Garfunkel and Blue Rodeo before 54,000 people at Toronto's SkyDome in support of the United Way charity. After that, he returned to Orillia to perform three shows to benefit Soldiers' Memorial Hospital and the Orillia Opera House programming fund. Getting hit up by his hometown was becoming a habit.

Of the thirty-nine concerts Lightfoot performed in 1994, only one was in Canada. On June 14, he was invited to take part in Massey Hall's centennial celebrations, performing in a diverse lineup that included the Toronto Symphony, opera singers Maureen Forrester and Lois Marshall, Blue Rodeo and comedian Dave Broadfoot. He could hardly say no: the Grand Old Lady of Shuter Street, as the concert hall was affectionately known, was to Lightfoot as the Grand Ole Opry was to Hank Williams. His entire family—which grew that year with the birth of a daughter, Meredith, on May 11— attended the special concert. Lightfoot was strong on tradition, and there was none stronger than Massey.

Lightfoot's regular Massey Hall springtime concerts resumed in 1995. "I feel like a tulip coming up every March," he once quipped, which led him to stagger his appearances there and to bloom instead on a May and November rotation. When he appeared there on March 16 for the first of six nights, Lightfoot could look down from the stage and see his daughter Ingrid's two children, seven-year-old Amber and five-year-old Johnny, in the front row. He told the *Toronto Star*'s Sid Adilman that he was doing his best to make amends for having been an absentee father in the past. "In my first family, I'm afraid, at that particular time I guess I wasn't around long enough to be a service to them, and I do regret that a great deal to this day," he said. "[I] keep the lines of communication open at all times and see them regularly and the two grandchildren as well. And the child from the common-law marriage, Eric—who's thirteen now—we go to movies. We stay around the house and play Nintendo. He's only with me every three weeks." Lightfoot continued, "My new family is growing and needs more attention. Since I won't be following the same route as I did in my first marriage, I will be dealing with it practically. I hope I can handle it." Making amends for past mistakes had become a priority. Responsibilities to his children were now paramount. If he'd sinned in the past, Lightfoot's future was going to be all about redemption.

Family wasn't the only thing on his mind. So was the *Edmund Fitzgerald*. Lightfoot had become an honorary member of the extended family of the ship's survivors and heard regularly from them. When the ship's bell was raised in July, after lying undisturbed 538 feet below the surface of Whitefish Bay, off Michigan's Upper Peninsula, there was a distinctly Canadian angle to it. Two Canadian Navy mini-submarines had helped raise the bell from the lake floor. As a dozen relatives of the twenty-nine victims looked on, the relic was brought on board the Canadian Navy ship *Cormorant*. It became the centerpiece of a memorial at the Great Lakes Shipwreck Museum at Whitefish Point, Michigan. Lightfoot had done more than anyone to keep alive the memory of those lost at sea. In November, he was the special guest at the ceremony there to mark the twentieth anniversary of the *Fitz*'s sinking. With many family members of the crew in attendance, Lightfoot was proud to have been chosen as the person to ring the ship's resurrected bell.

As Lightfoot embarked on a new year, it was clear that he was at a harmonious point in his life: happy in his marriage with Liz and their children, Miles and Meredith—and a new addition, a Hungarian sheep dog named Ivory.

In interviews and during his concerts over the next couple of years, Lightfoot did start to offer more glimpses than usual into his personal life, perhaps a sign of his new contentment. When he performed "A Lesson in Love," his 1986 song about P.T. Barnum and Jenny Lind, he introduced it as a "little trip down shrink alley." Going to his therapy sessions in his post-drinking days, he had been amused to find that numerous psychiatrists all had their offices on the same street in Toronto.

After performing two nights in his hometown for the Orillia Opera House's hundredth anniversary and just before a four-night stand at Massey Hall, Lightfoot welcomed two reporters on separate occasions into his Rosedale mansion, made them coffee in his old campfire percolator and offered each what sounded like a frank confession. The *Toronto Sun*'s Jean Sonmor asked about his notorious shyness. "Conversation," she wrote, "lurches around unexpected corners and rarely connects in a straight line." Sonmor then quoted Lightfoot: "I've asked myself many times if the shyness is really arrogance. One of my worst fears is that, in my unconscious, I'm one of the most arrogant people who ever lived and I don't even know it. If I am, I'm sorry for every faux pas." With the *Toronto Star*'s Peter Howell, he was equally self-critical: "I've made a few mistakes in my career, I'll admit them. For the last many years, I've been in a process of atonement. Honestly, I really try hard to please, particularly when it comes to my family. I feel a really strong responsibility to them." It's hard to imagine a more humble or self-effacing superstar. Ever since he'd quit drinking, making amends preoccupied Lightfoot. Sometimes he called it a process of atonement. Later, he took to saying he was in a state of repentance. Either way, the duty weighed heavily on him.

His extended family, including his mother, Jessie, and sister, Bev, were all there with him when his hometown renamed the Orillia Opera House auditorium after him. One of the local papers reported that Lightfoot sat "nervously, tapping his chair while local dignitaries reviewed his career and paid tribute to him." Another significant honor came Lightfoot's way in November, when he received the Governor General's Performing Arts Award in Ottawa. At the reception following the ceremony, Ian Tyson performed a medley of Lightfoot's songs. For chronicling Canadian history in song, Lightfoot had been called the "aural Pierre Berton." In a feature article in *The Globe and Mail*, Berton, who'd seen the singer-songwriter regularly at the Cambridge Club, where they were both members, was asked to comment on Lightfoot. "Gordie is a taciturn kind of guy," the celebrated author replied. "I think he cares about his music, but I don't think he cares about his image."

More accolades followed. Lightfoot received a star on Canada's Walk of Fame in Toronto, and "If You Could Read My Mind" became a disco hit for the second time, recorded on this occasion by Stars on 54 for a movie about New York's famed Studio 54 nightclub, starring Canadians Mike Myers and Neve Campbell. Viola Wills's sultry disco version had topped the US dance charts back in 1980. Why Lightfoot's lovelorn folk classic lent itself so well to booty-shaking club mixes remains a mystery and one of the quirkier footnotes in his story.

In the spring of 1998, Lightfoot released *A Painter Passing Through*, his nineteenth studio album. It featured eight original songs, along with covers of Ian Tyson's "Red Velvet" and Steve McEown's "I Used to Be a Country Singer." The latter was Lightfoot's way of lending a helping hand to his nephew Steve Eyers, Bev's son, who was singing in a bar band with McEown called Even Steven. Lightfoot's own compositions included two numbers about dreamers, seekers and schemers, "Drifters" and "Much to My Surprise," and another about a street busker, "My Little Love." Also featured were two Canadian-specific numbers, "On Yonge Street," a tribute to Toronto, and "Ringneck Loon," which conjured up the eerie sound of the birds he'd heard countless times on canoe trips up north. Lightfoot had previously included actual recorded loon calls on two songs from 1983's *Salute* album, "Whispers of the North" and "Gotta Get Away," and a loon is also heard on his "Canary Yellow Canoe."*

But the album's best song was the autobiographical title track, a backward-glancing number in which Lightfoot contrasts being in his prime—"in demand, always in control"—with facing his sunset years. By turns wistful and melancholic, it suggested that Lightfoot, in his sixtieth year, was coming to terms with his life and perhaps his place in pop's pantheon. Recorded at Grant Avenue, the studio Daniel Lanois had opened in Hamilton in 1976, and where the likes of U2, Brian Eno and many others had made recordings, *A Painter Passing Through* featured Lanois's piercing guitar on two tracks, "Boathouse" and "On Yonge Street." Meanwhile, acclaimed folk musician Willie P. Bennett added chugging harmonica to the album's quirkiest track, "Uncle Toad Said," Lightfoot's stab at comic surrealism.

Spring was a tough time for Lightfoot. He was upset during the early months of 1998 by news that his mother was dying. A smoker all her life, Jessie had developed emphysema and wasn't given long to live. When Lightfoot played Massey Hall for four nights in early May, he spoke about his mum at every show—about her influence on him, her insistence that he make use of his voice and how she'd attended every concert he ever played at Massey. Then, after telling the audiences that his eighty-eight-year-old mother was gravely ill, he played what he said was her favorite of all his songs: "The House You Live In." On May 26, Jessie Lightfoot died at the Royal Victoria

---

* Lightfoot licensed the loon calls from Canadian sound recordist Dan Gibson.

Hospital in Barrie, Ontario. Three days later, the Lightfoot family held services at Mundell Funeral Home in Orillia and Jessie was laid to rest at St. Andrew's Cemetery.

My mum had been sick for a long time. Bev did most of the work over the years, getting her into various homes. Finally, we got her back into her own house and found a nurse for her. But it became too much. I walked in there one afternoon and I could tell she was having trouble breathing, trouble getting her breath. The doctor said, "She's working hard, real hard." She always did work hard, come to think of it. She was a good mother. Never missed one of my Massey Hall shows. Always just pure love taken for granted. There was never even a question. She always told me, "Be honest, don't lie and don't use bad language," which I always did. I was with her at the end. When she died, she was out cold. The nurse came in and said, "Yeah, that's it, she's gone." I felt relief. I know she went to a better place.

At year's end, Lightfoot put his beloved Rosedale mansion up for sale. He really didn't want to leave 5 Beaumont Road, his home for a quarter of a century and the place where he'd rehearsed with his band and written so many of his hits. But Liz wasn't happy there. Repulsed by centipedes found in the building's nineteenth-century basement, she insisted they move uptown to a more modern home. So the stately brick house, which had witnessed the birth of songs like "Carefree Highway," "Rainy Day People" and "The Wreck of the Edmund Fitzgerald" and been the scene of memorable parties, including the notorious Rolling Thunder Revue gathering, went on the market. It was the end of an era.[*]

---

[*] One post-Mariposa bash went on for ten days because, Lightfoot told *The Globe and Mail*'s Liam Lacey, "we just couldn't seem to stop it."

Lightfoot, Liz, ten-year-old Miles, five-year-old Meredith and their dog, Ivory, moved into a sprawling Italianate modern mansion in the upscale Bridle Path neighborhood in Toronto's North York suburb. With neighbors that included former newspaper baron Conrad Black and, later, rap superstar Drake, the area is known as Millionaires' Row and ranks as Canada's most affluent neighborhood based on household income and property value. Lightfoot wasn't certain he was going to be able to settle. "The move went well," he told one reporter, "but I'm not sure about my new surroundings. We used to live downtown and now I've moved about five miles out to the northeast." It did have one distinct advantage over his Rosedale home: plenty of parking for his band members when they came to practice.

Aside from performing across Canada and the United States that year, Lightfoot stayed busy preparing the release of a career-spanning retrospective. The four-CD box set *Songbook* came out in November and contained eighty-eight songs, ranging from 1962's "Remember Me (I'm the One)" to 1998's "A Painter Passing Through." Lightfoot, always hands-on and meticulous in his choices, suggested or agreed to the inclusion of sixteen previously unreleased tracks. These were no second-rate castoffs. Two are excellent train songs. "Station Master" was recorded in Nashville for *Summer Side of Life*. With its chugging rhythm and cryptic lyrics about a "disowned and ragged princess," it's one of Lightfoot's most Dylanesque numbers. "Borderstone," from the *Sundown* sessions, is a Woody Guthrie–inspired tune. Full of twang and aching pedal steel, it tells of hopping a freight "a hundred boxcars long" on a night "as black as the coal dust on the tracks." Another pair of standouts, "Too Much to Lose" and "Never Say Trust Me," were written for Paul Newman's *Cool Hand Luke* and Kenny Rogers, respectively but never used. As an overview of Lightfoot's huge body of work, *Songbook* was long overdue and well received. Respected UK music magazines *Mojo* and *Uncut* both heaped praise, with the former writing, "As a voyage of rediscovery it can hardly be bettered," and the latter declaring it simply "magnificent."

SIXTEEN

Inspiration Lady

Lightfoot entered the new millennium well aware that things had changed. Top 40 radio, which once embraced his music, was no longer receptive to his sound. The generation of singer-songwriters who came up in the 1960s and '70s were now relegated to golden-oldie stations, pushed aside by auto-tuned divas, hook-savvy rappers and big-beat producers. Lightfoot's "Sundown," however, received a cool update thanks to one rapper's hip-hop version. Elwood, a New York producer-artist (real name: Prince Elwood Strickland III), covered the song with Lightfoot's blessing and added his slacker rap over some slick beats. Sounding like a cross between the Beastie Boys and Beck, Elwood's "Sundown" scored airplay on contemporary hit radio in Canada and college and alternative stations in the United States. Meanwhile, an American ad agency had wanted to license the original "Sundown" but Lightfoot turned them down, saying, "I don't want a beer commercial to be my epitaph."

When it came to songwriting, Lightfoot was far from finished; he'd already completed several new compositions and recorded demo versions of them. He told one reporter early in the year that a new album wasn't entirely out of the question. "I don't have as much time as I'd like to do it," he said about songwriting, "but I'm still doing it.

I can think about lyrics when I'm in the shower, tuning up in the dressing room or while I'm driving. I keep track of things. I write things all the time on slips of paper. Then I go back to the room where I work and get it together." Those close to him knew that, with all his various family commitments, it was a wonder Lightfoot had any time for songwriting at all.

But if radio spurned his music, his fans were still legion. With forty-eight concerts booked for 2000, retirement was the furthest thing from Lightfoot's mind. The prospect of a new album was his incentive to keep going, but it was the rewards of touring that kept him motivated. "Each concert is another challenge to see if I can keep the quality and the energy up," he explained to one interviewer that year, and to another he enthused, "Everybody [in the band] loves to play and when you've got people like that around you, you want to get out there and keep on doing it." He added, "There's a presence of mind all around. The degree of concentration is unbelievable. We're like a team. We're out there to win, and winning means doing a great show."

The sports analogy was in keeping with Lightfoot's competitive spirit. At sixty-one, he hadn't lost any of his drive to stay in the game. And comparing his band to a team was certainly appropriate. Like seasoned ballplayers or hockey old-timers, Rick Haynes and Terry Clements had been with Lightfoot for thirty years or more, while Barry Keane and Mike Heffernan had been part of the band for at least twenty. Together, they had one goal in mind: delivering the best sound, as seamlessly as possible, in support of their captain and in service to his songs.

That game plan was executed perfectly when Lightfoot taped an hour-long American TV special—his first since he'd launched his career—in April of that year. Before a capacity crowd of 1,500 at the Pioneer Theater in Reno, Nevada, he and the band performed his biggest hits and personal favorites like "Waiting for You," which he introduced with a grin as being about "making babies in the north country." Lightfoot, with mustache and looking trim in shirt and jeans, stood at the microphone like he meant business and sang one instantly recognizable song after another. There were no theatrics, no flashy pyrotechnics, just studied professionalism as Haynes, Keane, Clements and Heffernan provided immaculate, unobtrusive backing. "Sometimes we were criticized for looking like wooden Indians," says Haynes, "but we were always just about the music." The resulting *Live in Reno* remains the best Lightfoot concert, after the BBC's *In Concert*, ever captured on television. It aired later that year on PBS before going to video.

Although middle-aged, Lightfoot could still turn heads. When he appeared in August at New York's Town Hall for the first time in thirty-two years, *The New York Times*'s music critic Ann Powers compared him to a movie star, with "the same laconic appeal that allows wrinkling leading men like Peter Fonda and Nick Nolte to maintain careers." Lightfoot, she added, is "a rugged guy who knows how to melt. The slow thaw defines his music and his enduring charm. Few of Mr. Lightfoot's folk-rock peers could fall back so easily on the masculine stereotype he embodied. This Canadian outdoorsman, who has spent much of his nonmusical life working for environmental causes, easily taps into the lineage of the singing cowboy." Citing "Minstrel of the Dawn" and "Don Quixote," Powers noted that Lightfoot's "most flowery songs are saved from utter corniness by his reserve as a musician and a personality. Such understatement is his gift." She singled out his most famous song, "The Wreck of the Edmund Fitzgerald," observing that it "captures high drama in sepia tones" and was "perhaps the only sea chantey to become a major hit in the arena rock era."

The high drama of that song continued to pull Lightfoot into its swell. He couldn't escape it. Since 1977, he had supported a scholarship at the Great Lakes Maritime Academy in Traverse City, Michigan, and every year since the song became a hit, he'd been invited to services at the Mariners' Church of Detroit. "It's a song I just can't walk away from," he told one newspaper. "Whether I attend services or not, I know when we're on tour, doing engagements, we're constantly meeting blood relatives [of the victims]." That November, Lightfoot took part in the many remembrances surrounding the twenty-fifth anniversary of the sinking. "It's my way of showing my worth," he said. "That was one of the songs that kept my career going."

The *Edmund Fitzgerald* wasn't the only cause Lightfoot continued to support. The early 2000s saw him giving and receiving in almost equal measure. He continued to give benefits for myriad causes, from a concert to assist farm families in crisis to a surprise performance for Renascent, the alcohol rehab facility he'd helped officially open in 1991. At the same time, the honors, tributes and awards kept coming his way. He was inducted into the Canadian Broadcast Hall of Fame and received a Lifetime Achievement Award from the Toronto Arts Council. Then, to acknowledge his lifelong connection to their instruments, C.F. Martin & Co., the guitar manufacturers, produced a Gordon Lightfoot Limited Edition Signature guitar.

In September 2001, Lightfoot was inducted into the Canadian Country Music Hall of Fame. He hadn't always been comfortable with the country tag. In the 1970s, when *Playboy* magazine's annual music poll named him top country and western male vocalist-composer for several years running, Lightfoot didn't attend the awards. Believing sales would be better if his music were more firmly in pop or adult contemporary territory, Warner executives had pressured him during the '80s to tone down the pedal steel sound and other country-ish elements.

But Lightfoot was happy to accept the honor now. Performing tributes to him at the Hall of Fame celebration were Anne Murray ("Cotton Jenny"), Ian Tyson ("Early Morning Rain") and Ron Sexsmith

("If You Could Read My Mind"). When asked about his admiration for Lightfoot, Sexsmith admitted to having "probably an unhealthy affection for [his] music." He added, "My band mates are always making fun of me, because when you're on tour, everybody always brings their little CD carrier with all these different CDs in it. They'll go through mine and find ten Gordon Lightfoot CDs. I just find his voice very comforting when I'm away from home."

Lightfoot had played fifty-three concerts the previous year and was well on his way to exceeding that number in 2002 when fate intervened. It was the afternoon of September 7, a Saturday, and Lightfoot was driving north to Orillia to play the second of two concerts at the Opera House, with his guitars safely stored in the trunk of his Oldsmobile. He'd driven Highway 400 countless times in his career, beginning in his days as a boy soprano and continuing when he was trying to get established as a folk singer. He'd also made the trip frequently during his parents' illnesses. Lightfoot had finished the previous night's show with severe stomach pain. Ingrid told him he didn't look well. In the morning, after he had spent the night in agony, Liz urged him to forget the show and go straight to Sunnybrook Hospital, a few minutes' drive from their suburban Toronto home. But he was determined to keep his concert date, so he took a couple more painkillers and headed north.

Ever since his mother stood him on the kitchen table as a toddler to sing and he'd soaked up the applause of his aunts, uncles and cousins, Lightfoot has been hooked on performing. It defined his childhood and dominated his life through its numerous peaks and valleys. Even when marriages were on the rocks or the bottle got the better of him, Lightfoot never let anything get in the way of his concert commitments. He lived and breathed the old theater expression "The show must go on." The searing pain in Lightfoot's stomach

worsened as he pulled into Orillia and made his way to the Opera
House. He knew the town was counting on him. Money raised from
the two shows was earmarked for local charities, the Sunshine
Festival Theatre Company and Soldiers' Memorial Hospital, where
he had a special connection: he was born there and his father had
died there.

When Lightfoot entered the Gordon Lightfoot Auditorium,
inside the 102-year-old Opera House, it was still four hours to curtain. Before sound check, he made his way down two flights of stairs
to the dressing room, wincing with each step. His band members
were already onstage, cracking jokes while waiting for the boss. All of
them had been concerned about his condition the previous night.
Haynes had told him he should cancel the next show, but Lightfoot
waved it off. There was no talking to him.

Time ticked on. Lightfoot still hadn't appeared onstage.
Lightfoot's sister, Bev, arrived in the auditorium. Seeing everyone
twiddling their thumbs, she asked in her no-nonsense way, "What
the fuck is going on around here? Where's Gord?" Racing downstairs, she opened the dressing room door and saw her brother pros-
trate on the floor. "Gord, ya stupid fuck, what the hell are you doing?"
"Well, I don't feel good," he managed to say. Bev launched straight
into big-sister mode: "You're going to the hospital right now." She
and Haynes helped him to his car and they drove the six blocks to
Soldiers' Memorial, a hospital with just two emergency beds.

Lightfoot's blood pressure was right off the charts. Bev stayed
with him. Haynes and Keane waited nervously outside. When a hospital alarm went off, Lightfoot's bandmates knew something dire
had happened. Twenty minutes later, Bev emerged looking worried.
"Gord went into some kind of convulsion. They're not sure what it
is." "There is not gonna be a show," Haynes declared. "We'll be lucky
if he lives." Everyone knew Lightfoot needed to be moved to a bigger, more advanced facility, but no beds were available. Just then,

another alarm and flashing lights signaled a new crisis. The doors to Lightfoot's room flew open and in went the nurses with heart paddles. They'd lost him, but were able to bring him back. Lightfoot was suffering from massive internal bleeding and required immediate surgery to save his life. Suddenly, news came that a bed had opened up and, at one-thirty Sunday morning, he was airlifted to Hamilton's McMaster University Medical Centre.

Lightfoot was conscious but in critical condition when he arrived in the intensive care unit. The medical team, led by Dr. Michael Marcaccio, chief of surgery and a gastrointestinal specialist, stepped in. Lightfoot had suffered an abdominal aortic aneurysm, a rupture of the garden hose–sized vessel that supplies blood to the body. Few survive the trauma. Albert Einstein, Lucille Ball and Conway Twitty all died from abdominal aortic aneurysms. To halt the flow of blood and allow Marcaccio to operate, Lightfoot was put into a coma using the barbiturate propofol. The surgeon performed a tracheotomy to assist his breathing.

Despite all efforts, it was touch and go. Liz, Bev and Rick Haynes kept a vigil at McMaster. On Sunday, the hospital held a news conference stating the barest of facts about Lightfoot's condition. But the media demanded a comment from the family. "Elizabeth wanted to keep it all quiet," said Haynes. "She said, 'Don't tell anybody anything—it's private, this is family.' But I said, 'If you don't tell them something, it's going to be "Gord was in a hotel with a bag of blow and a hooker—just like the Who's John Entwistle."' So she said, 'Okay, you tell them.'"

Haynes was not a man accustomed to being front and center. But later that day, shaken and red-eyed, he faced the media cameras for his friend. "I've known Gord for thirty-five years," he told reporters, "and I can't remember the last time he was in hospital. This is a very difficult experience and everybody has been up all night. He's definitely getting better. He's not in as much pain as he was, and he's being very well attended to." Added Haynes, "Gord's a strong guy, he's a fighter." It was the kind of positive message fans needed to hear. But no one actually knew if Lightfoot was going to make it.

On the Friday night before his collapse, Lightfoot had debuted one of his new songs, "Couchiching." It was, on the surface, a simple portrait of his hometown and the pleasures of its lakeside setting. Although he hadn't lived there in over forty years, Orillia always defined him, shaping and carrying him through life the way the soil sustains a tree. The song was meant as a straightforward tribute to his roots, but with its droning vocal and hypnotic rhythm, the tune evoked a stark and, strangely, haunting feeling. And the song's last verse took on an eerie foreshadowing. "When I get my final slumber, when I pawn my diamond ring / I will do my final number, by Lake Couchiching." That prophecy was almost fulfilled that night.

The near-death experience shocked fans around the world, many of whom flooded the hospital and Early Morning Productions with cards, flowers and good wishes. Lightfoot's coma lasted six and a half weeks. When he regained consciousness, on Halloween, there was a tube down his throat. The first thing he heard was music.

On the morning I woke up, the sun was shining and I heard, right out of thin air, a beautiful rendition of my song "Minstrel of the Dawn." It was a sort of hallucination. Happened just as I came to and one of the nurses was filling up my feeding apparatus. The whole song with me singing, but sounding much more pristine than on the record. It was the most amazing thing.

More amazing was Lightfoot's recovery. He was in hospital for three months and returned several times for additional procedures. Some of these involved taking muscle tissue from his legs to repair his stomach wall. The speed with which he bounced back impressed his doctors, who attributed his survival and fast healing to his fitness from regular gym workouts.

There was another factor: work. With eighteen new songs written and demoed, Lightfoot's attention—as soon as he regained consciousness—turned to how he was going to record his next album. It proved highly therapeutic: rather than dwell on his condition, including the fact that he had no abdominal strength to sing and had temporarily lost the ability to hear himself, he focused on the challenge of completing a recording while still being largely out of commission.

He was in and out of McMaster throughout the following year. During his final hospitalization, in 2003, when doctors reconstructed his abdominal muscles using tissue from his thigh, band members Haynes, Clements, Keane and Heffernan, along with a returning Red Shea and engineer Bob Doidge, began working on completing the demos at Grant Avenue, adding their respective parts. Haynes would then bring their recorded efforts on CD to the hospital and Lightfoot would make suggestions and changes that Haynes took back to the studio to work on.

Lightfoot gave two significant interviews in the year following his abdominal hemorrhage. To the *Toronto Star* he vowed he would return to touring in eighteen months. "I plan to fight my way back," he told the paper. "My goal is to get out there and do it again, whatever that takes." Sounding like a motivational speaker, he added, "The most important things to me now are: Don't spin your wheels! Keep trying! Don't give up! There's always hope!" More shocking was the news he revealed to *The Globe and Mail*. Whether it was because of his renewed obsession with recording and touring or because of the toll his illness had taken on him (Lightfoot was then living with an ileostomy, similar to a colostomy but involving the small intestine, and walked with what the *Globe* described as "the ginger shuffle of someone taking care with his bones"), Liz and he had separated. She left as soon as he was out of the hospital, taking Miles and Meredith with her. His second marriage had lasted fourteen years but in the end had fallen victim—as all his significant relationships with women had—to his career and his health. "We're living under separate domicile" was the terse way Lightfoot explained it to the *Globe*, trying to put a brave face on it but with a divorce lawyer's choice of words.

Liz's departure couldn't have come at a worse time, and Lightfoot was deeply hurt. Privately, he was despondent over the breakup. Although they'd had their difficulties, Lightfoot loved Liz and had remained completely faithful to her throughout their marriage. Carrying on without her, alone in a massive house he never wanted to move into in the first place, wasn't going to be easy. But he had no choice except to press on: work was aiding his recovery, and he planned to keep up the momentum. At the same time, Lightfoot's "Comeback from Death's Door," as one headline bluntly stated, was intensifying all the accolades and appreciations. First, Dylan called to wish him well, followed by the federal government, elevating his Order of Canada status to Companion, the highest ranking. Then came *Beautiful: A Tribute to Gordon Lightfoot*, a star-studded compilation featuring artists from Murray McLauchlan, Maria Muldaur and Ron Sexsmith to such bands as Cowboy Junkies, Blue Rodeo and Blackie and the Rodeo Kings, all covering Lightfoot songs. Among the standout tracks were Bruce Cockburn's eerie "Ribbon of Darkness" and the Tragically Hip's urgent "Black Day in July." By year's end, Lightfoot was the first inductee into the Canadian Songwriters Hall of Fame.

A sense of melancholy, a mixture of heartbreak and regret, had always been present in Lightfoot's work. Love and loneliness permeated the songs on *Harmony*, his first post-Warner album, which came out in the spring. Although he didn't perform at the launch party for the album in Massey Hall's downstairs lounge, he proudly attended and appeared upbeat. Now signed to Linus Entertainment, a Canadian independent label, he had emerged from what he called his "dark slumber" with a surprising amount of energy, buoyed that fate had granted him a second chance. As he wrote in *Harmony*'s liner notes, "A feeling of confidence was in the air."

Themes familiar to Lightfoot fans, including travel, nature and lost love, figured in the new material, especially "Sometimes I Wish," "No Mistake About It" and "End of All Time." Lightfoot made a video for the album's single, "Inspiration Lady," a melodic gem of a tune clearly inspired by Elizabeth. The album also included "Couchiching" and live performances of two songs recorded in 1998, "Shellfish" and "The No Hotel," about his trip up the Amazon. But *Harmony*'s standout was "River of Light," a relaxed, free-flowing number in which outdoor imagery conveyed interior emotions—in other words, classic Lightfoot. The album was hailed as a return to form by many music reviewers, including Tim Sheridan of England's *Mojo* magazine. "Over the last four decades, Gordon Lightfoot has been the bard of simple pleasures and overlooked beauty," wrote Sheridan. "Judging by his latest disc, it would seem that a brush with death made this appreciation and insight even keener. It may not be his masterpiece, but it's an honest, often gorgeous statement by a still formidable singer-songwriter." If nothing else, the album, with its new and previous recordings cobbled together from his hospital bed, was a testament to the man's indomitable strength and remarkable work ethic.

But Lightfoot's greatest fear remained. Had he entirely lost his singing voice? If his voice was gone, it would put an end to performing. "That would've been worse than death for Gord, not being able to sing," says Barry Keane. Although Lightfoot had worked briefly with a speech therapist, he had quit, finding it embarrassing to do the rudimentary exercises. His fear was laid to rest that summer at the

Mariposa Folk Festival in Orillia. The festival was presenting a tribute to him, so he decided to attend. Murray McLauchlan remembers Lightfoot backstage sheepishly asking whether he thought it would be all right if he played a song. "It was funny," says McLauchlan, "but also quite charming, because he clearly didn't want to impose. So I joked, 'Jeez, I don't know, Gord, we might need to ask permission.' This was a guy who'd just come back from the dead. He knew it wasn't going to be all that great, he just wanted to do it. Watching him connect with people that really loved him was unbelievably powerful—almost spiritual." Lightfoot sang just one of his songs, "I'll Tag Along." It was a signal to everyone, including himself, that he was back.

Emboldened by his Mariposa comeback, Lightfoot went on to give three more performances in 2004. In August, he sang five songs, including "Couchiching" and "Inspiration Lady," at a benefit concert in Peterborough, Ontario, for flood relief, organized by his buddy Ronnie Hawkins. Lightfoot also acted as music mentor when he appeared on TV's *Canadian Idol* and coached the final six contestants on their renditions of "If You Could Read My Mind." Then in late November, to thank the medical staff at McMaster University Medical Centre who helped save his life, he performed two full-length concerts, his first after being struck down two years earlier. The sold-out shows at Hamilton Place were to benefit the hospital. Midway through each concert, he personally thanked Dr. Michael Marcaccio and the nurses at McMaster, some of whom, he said, gave him positive feedback on his new songs when he was playing them back in his hospital room. During the opening night show, Lightfoot's voice was noticeably thinner, his guitar playing a bit rusty, and he even forgot an occasional lyric. But the crowd didn't care; they were witnessing a remarkable recovery.

Barry Keane remembers well just how big a deal it was for Lightfoot to perform when he was in such a weakened state. "This was a proud man, and he knew it was going to be, for him, a lesser performance," says Keane. "But he wanted to perform for the doctors and nurses to show his gratitude. It took so much courage and a tremendous amount of strength and character to do it." Keane also believes that Lightfoot's return from the brink changed him for the better: "It showed in his everyday demeanor. He was a lot less angry, less impatient and just seemed thankful for the extra time on the planet and that he could continue doing what he wanted to do."

Lightfoot worked hard to get himself back in shape. His exercise routine at the Cambridge Club was a little different: he no longer ran on the treadmill, focusing instead on sit-ups to strengthen his abdominals. Following a program worked out for him and approved by his doctors, Lightfoot returned to his almost fanatical—he calls it "religious"—approach to fitness. After stopping in at Early Morning Productions to attend to day-to-day office demands with office manager Anne Leibold, he drove daily to the health club for a two-hour session—a practice that continues still.

Lightfoot was feeling strong when his tour opened that April in California. After four nights at the Orleans Casino in Las Vegas, he was back in Toronto preparing for the resumption of his Massey Hall stand. The week before the first of four sold-out shows, he was back at his favorite restaurant, Bigliardi's, on Church Street, to celebrate Meredith's eleventh birthday. When opening night came, Lightfoot stepped out on the Massey Hall stage at 8:10 P.M. with the words "Sorry I'm late." The audience jumped to its feet and gave a prolonged standing ovation with whoops and whistles before he played a single note. Critics noted that he seemed "a little short of wind" and found his baritone "thin on the top end," but it didn't matter: Lightfoot was bathed in love from his first song to his last.

While his friends and fans were celebrating Lightfoot's comeback, the man himself was mourning the death of his first wife. Brita died in June of complications from a stroke. Ingrid surprised fans with a posting online about her mother, who was "Granny" to her two teen-age children. "Mom was definitely not the senior type," she wrote. "She was still beautiful at sixty-nine, looked sixty. She took care of herself and had no bad habits. She was a very happy person and lots of fun. Very stable. She loved her grandchildren dearly and devoted a lot of time to them. Her passion was always gardening. She had a serious green thumb! She also studied antiques. In the winter she was a snowbird and myself and my two kids would join her every year for a week or two. She was a fabulous cook too—Scandinavian style! She had her cottage on Lake Simcoe raised and converted into a home and lived there for several years. There, she gardened to her heart's content." Until Ingrid's posting, little had been known about the private woman for whom Lightfoot had written such evocative songs as "Beautiful" and "Spanish Moss." With her passing, the curtain was pulled back just a little.

On July 2, just a year after his Mariposa comeback, Lightfoot faced the biggest audience of his career—solo. He was invited to perform for Live 8, a series of one-day benefit concerts held in multiple cities with the call to "Make Poverty History." The Canadian concert took place in Barrie, Ontario, and featured such stars as Bryan Adams, Neil Young and the Tragically Hip along with international acts that included Mötley Crüe. Dan Aykroyd and Tom Green introduced Lightfoot with suitable awe as a "Hall of Famer and a part of our national spirit." With the afternoon sun low in the sky, Lightfoot walked out onto the stage with just his Martin guitar and stood before a sea of people. "Nice to be here," he told the crowd, "to provide a small musical interlude." Then he launched into "Restless," "If You Could Read My Mind" and "Let It Ride." With people cheering as far as the eye could see, Lightfoot gave the crowd a wave and a thumbs-up. Afterward, he returned for a rousing finale with Neil Young on "Rockin' in the Free World."

Lightfoot's appearance at Live 8 had been a triumph—and a surprise.

I was asked by [promoter] Michael Cohl to do it, and while I was trying to make up my mind, it came on the radio that I was part of it. So I said, "I guess I'm doing this." I went up there with just Barry Harvey and Red [Shea], who came along as my roadie, and knocked out three tunes just solid. I proved I could still do it. I had two rock bands on either side of me and I went on about five o'clock in the afternoon. It proved to be the perfect spot for me.

A few weeks after Live 8, Lightfoot, Clements and Haynes took the stage at Mariposa in a throwback to the trio days of the early 1970s. They delivered an eleven-song set that included "Couchiching" and "Clouds of Loneliness" from *Harmony* and chestnuts "Sundown," "The Wreck of the Edmund Fitzgerald" and "Early Morning Rain." His "Canadian Railroad Trilogy" was one of the highlights of the festival.

In December, the trio returned to Orillia for an afternoon performance at St. Paul's United Church in celebration of its 175th anniversary. It was the first time Lightfoot had performed there since he'd sung in the church as a boy. After an eight-song set, he sat for an interview with Rev. Karen Hilfman Millson, who asked him about his earliest memories of Orillia, and entertained questions from the audience. Bev, sitting in the front pew, recalled how her brother sang for nickels as a three-year-old in front of relatives at their grandmother's house. She also remembered him singing at her wedding in the same church at age thirteen, just before his voice changed. Bev then told the audience that she often accompanied young Gordie on organ when he was a boy soprano. "He was way better than anybody in the whole wide world," she said, still bursting with pride all those years later.

———

Lightfoot suffered another health crisis the following year while in the middle of a fifty-four-date tour. This time it was a TIA, a transient, or minor, stroke. It occurred during his sound check at the Island Resort and Casino in Harris, Michigan, and it affected the use of his fingers on his right, guitar-picking hand. But Lightfoot soldiered on. "It was a bit of an inconvenience," he told one reporter, with typical Lightfoot understatement. "The band carried the back up and I just fingered chords with the left hand. After about the fifth day, I started to get the strum back. We got some rosin, the kind you put on a bow for a fiddle, put that on and it helped me hold onto the flat pick. I just used the thumb on my right hand for the next two months." It was yet another example of the lesson he'd learned from Albert Grossman: never give fans anything less than they expect. Few would have noticed any difference in the music.

By February the next year, his playing was right back to normal. But others around Lightfoot weren't so lucky with their health. In December, Barry Harvey died of a sudden heart attack at fifty-six. It would now fall to Anne Leibold to run the Early Morning Productions office. Then Red Shea, the guitarist who helped shape Lightfoot's early sound, died the following June at the age of seventy, of pancreatic cancer diagnosed just two weeks before. Only two years younger than his former sidekick, Lightfoot showed no signs of slowing down.

Lightfoot greeted his own seventieth birthday on November 17, 2008, more determined than ever to keep going. He'd already performed sixty-two concerts that year, most of them in the United States. And the next year, he booked even more. The seventy-four shows in 2009 were as many as he'd played in his heyday in the 1970s. Lightfoot, grateful to be alive, couldn't get enough of it. "He lives to work," says Ingrid. "What makes him happiest is being on stage." Outside of touring, he was leading a pretty quiet life, dividing his time between going to the gym and seeing his children and grandchildren more frequently. "He definitely changed after the aneurysm," adds Ingrid, "paying more attention to all of us and calling more."

And his iconic stature kept growing. Artists from Johnny Cash to the Tragically Hip's Gord Downie were continuing to cover his songs. There were now regular tribute nights in Toronto celebrating his music. The government of Canada had chosen him as one of four Canadian artists whose face was featured on a postage stamp. His legend was secure. But Lightfoot—modest to a fault—seemed either unaware or unfazed by all the attention. For him, the real test of his worth would be whether he could keep on performing.

SEVENTEEN

Going the Distance

Lightfoot was hooked on touring. His addiction to performance—and applause—was the hardest habit of all to break. And why would he want to? Lightfoot never felt more alive than when he was onstage. Between 2010 and 2016, he performed an average of seventy dates a year. In 2014, perhaps inspired by his pace horse, Bob Dylan, who played ninety-two shows on his Never Ending Tour that year, the seventy-one-year-old Lightfoot undertook an astonishing eighty-seven shows, surpassing his career high of eighty-six concerts in 1974.

A creature of habit and routine, Lightfoot started his day on February 18, 2010, the same way he did whenever he wasn't on tour: driving down to Early Morning Productions and tending to any pressing business matters before heading on to the Cambridge Club for his workout, which he'd been doing daily since the '70s. But first he had to pay a visit to his dentist for a routine checkup. After his appointment, while driving to his Yonge Street office, Lightfoot was listening to an all-news radio station and was surprised to hear "If You Could Read My Mind" being played. Surprise turned to shock when the song was followed with a startling report: Gordon Lightfoot had died. As soon as he arrived at his office, Lightfoot called the station to disprove it. But he was too late—the news of his death had already circulated to radio stations and major newspapers across Canada. He was the latest victim of a celebrity-death hoax, joining the likes of George Clooney, Miley Cyrus and Matt Damon. With the phone ringing off the hook with concerned calls, he didn't make it to the gym that day.

Lightfoot quickly telephoned his children to assure them he was fine. Ingrid had heard the reports and was deeply upset. Eric was on his way by train from Halifax to Montreal when he got the news. All were relieved to hear it was just a sick joke. Then the *Toronto Sun*'s Joe Warmington called and asked if Lightfoot would take a selfie to let the world know he was alive. The photo ran the next day with the headline "Dead Wrong."

The origin of the story, bizarrely, could be traced to Ronnie Hawkins, whose management office had received a phone call from someone claiming to be Lightfoot's grandson saying that Lightfoot had passed away the night before. Hawkins called to tell his wife, Wanda, who in turn told her friends. Then a post appeared on Twitter, which Canwest News picked up, and it went viral from there. Hawkins was horrified that he'd been duped and was inadvertently the source. Knowing what a real brush with death was like, Lightfoot was able to be philosophical. "I think it's rather amusing, actually," he said. "I'm just happy that it's not so." And the Sault Ste. Marie news website *Soo Today* had the wit to update the story with "Gordon Lightfoot Is No Longer Dead." Ultimately, the hoax gave Lightfoot a standing joke he has used in concerts ever since, quoting Mark Twain's famous line "Reports of my death have been greatly exaggerated."

Since his brushes with death—real and invented—Lightfoot had made family a bigger priority. Juggling all his commitments to see each of his children at arranged times on different days almost required a weekly flow chart. Visiting his eldest son involved spending time not only with Fred and his wife, Leynie, but their two children, Kristina and Ben. Says Fred: "In my younger years I didn't really see much of Dad, but he's been very supportive of my kids, especially Ben, who's extremely autistic, and comes to visit a lot." Lightfoot's eldest daughter, Ingrid, had broken up with her husband and was raising her kids, Amber and Johnny, with financial help from their "grandpa." Lightfoot also continued visiting Galen whenever he passed through Los Angeles.

Eric, Lightfoot's son with Cathy, was very much influenced by his father. For years, Lightfoot had kept drums in his basement, a reminder of his early stint as a drummer. Eric played the kit whenever he visited and developed a passion for drumming that led him into music, joining the electronic Toronto band Madrid (he also drummed with the group Minority and hip-hop artist Cadence Weapon). Airplanes were another connection between father and son. Eric had fallen in love with flying from the times he'd accompanied his dad on tour flights in the Lear jet. When he decided to become a commercial pilot, Eric moved in with his father for six years, beginning in 2004, so he could be closer to Buttonville Airport, where his Seneca College instruction took place. "Dad really cherishes his space," says Eric, "but there was enough room for both of us. I had my own apartment downstairs. When he wasn't on tour, we'd have dinner together, always with CNN on in the background. It was all very relaxed, and we'd talk only when we felt like it." After graduating, Eric moved out to Squamish, BC. He now flies with Sea to Sky Air, a local flight operator.

Most of Lightfoot's fatherly duties involved his two children with Liz. Miles would come over for dinner before Lightfoot took him to tae kwon do classes. Meredith had taken up music and was learning to play the guitar and banjo. She was also developing political views. In 2011, she joined Occupy Toronto, the local chapter of the international movement against social inequality, and was camping with about a hundred other protesters in downtown Toronto's St. James Park. After living in a tent for a month the cold nights made her sick, forcing her to return home briefly; and when she was back in the park, now a muddy bog from the rain, Lightfoot dropped in on her with an extra blanket. Confronted by news cameras, he was put on the spot and asked what the protest was about. "Too many young people and not enough jobs," came Lightfoot's terse reply, though he was rarely inclined to offer political opinions. When the cameras turned to Meredith, her hair in dreadlocks, the seventeen-year-old spoke confidently of "fighting for people and wanting a better world." Lightfoot put his arm around Meredith, clearly proud of his daughter's spirit. She is still pursuing a music career, playing Appalachian folk music on the banjo and performing as Meredith Moon, using her mother's name. Although she has tried not to trade on her father's fame, she has become a regular performer at Mariposa in Orillia and taken part in Lightfoot tributes at Toronto's Hugh's Room, organized by singer-songwriter Jory Nash. Some of her favorite times, she says, are spent just jamming at home with her dad. "One of the things that I admire about him is that he realizes he has room to grow," says Meredith. "He's still learning things about himself."

Lightfoot has always been a stickler for accuracy. Whenever he wrote a historical song like "Canadian Railroad Trilogy" or "Ballad of Yarmouth Castle," he'd taken pains to get the facts of the story right. Lightfoot had written "The Wreck of the Edmund Fitzgerald" in late 1975 after carefully researching every detail about the ship's sinking. Based on what he knew at the time, he wrote the now-famous words "At seven P.M. a main hatchway caved in, he said / Fellas, it's been good to know ya," suggesting that the ship's crew members had failed to secure the rear hatch cover. In 2009, two Toronto film producers, Mike and Warren Fletcher, had approached Lightfoot for permission to use his song in their TV documentary called *Dive Detectives*. The filmmakers planned to conduct a thorough investigation into the sinking of the iron-ore tanker, so Lightfoot agreed to a licensing arrangement for the song, something he'd rarely ever done.

After watching the finished film the following year, Lightfoot learned that the wreck was most likely caused not by human error but a rogue wave. The revelation prompted him to rewrite his lyrics. "There's been a lot of controversy about that," Lightfoot told one reporter. "There's no hatch cover involved, so a couple of guys are off the hook there. The mother of one of those guys, she'd worried about that for years—a lady called Ruth Hudson, her son Bruce died. He was one of the guys that was supposed to be checking the hatch covers." In a statement Lightfoot issued, he said, "This finally vindicates, and honors, not only all of the crew who lost their lives, but also the family members who survived them." Although he wouldn't rerecord the song, from then on, whenever Lightfoot performed it, he sang, "At 7 P.M. it grew dark, it was then he said / Fellas it's been good to know ya." No more mention of the hatchway. Few songwriters would have cared enough to make the correction.

In early March 2010, Lightfoot took part in an evening of music and conversation with another famous Canadian Gord—the Tragically Hip's Gord Downie. The Gord-a-thon, called If You Could Read My Mind, was presented by Canada's Songwriters Hall of Fame and intended to showcase the craft of songwriting. Clearly, Downie, himself a published poet, was in awe of his veteran counterpart. Downie praised his "austerity and economy of words" and thanked him for being a "great teacher." Moderator Laurie Brown asked both how they viewed themselves: songwriter or entertainer? "I think of myself as Gordon Lightfoot," joked Downie. Lightfoot didn't hesitate in answering: "First and foremost, I like to perform." Lightfoot played four songs, with guitarist Clements and bassist

Haynes accompanying him, while Downie played solo. Downie asked Lightfoot how he dealt with writer's block, and the former heavy drinker answered quickly: "Alcohol." Equally honest, if more cryptic, was his answer to a question about whether certain songs were too personal to sing. Lightfoot said no, before adding, "My life has been quite complicated."

There was nothing complicated about receiving major songwriting honors. In October 2011, Lightfoot learned he was to be inducted into the American Songwriters Hall of Fame. He was especially pleased by the news, because he'd be joining his peers Leonard Cohen, Kris Kristofferson and Dylan, all of whom had been inducted. The following year, Dylan paid Lightfoot the ultimate tribute: performing Lightfoot's song "Shadows" in concert (he'd done the same thing in 1998 with "I'm Not Supposed to Care"). Dylan told MTV's Bill Flanagan that Lightfoot was among his favorite songwriters. "You and Lightfoot go back a long way," Flanagan noted. "Oh yeah," replied Dylan, "Gordo's been around as long as me." When asked which were his favorite Lightfoot songs, Dylan listed "Shadows," "Sundown" and "If You Could Read My Mind," before adding, "I can't think of any I don't like."

Although a proposed tour with Dylan years earlier never materialized, Lightfoot did get invited to join him onstage at Dylan's Toronto concert on July 13, 2013. This would be the first time the two had ever performed together. The prospects were tantalizing: Lightfoot could take the lead on Dylan's "Ring Them Bells" or maybe "Just Like Tom Thumb's Blues," while Dylan could cover Lightfoot's "Early Morning Rain" among several others. In the weeks leading up to the concert at Molson Amphitheatre, a fierce debate raged within Lightfoot's family. Who would attend the Dylan concert? Lightfoot had a new girlfriend, Kim Hasse, a Mason City, Iowa, native twenty-three years his junior whom he'd met on the road. Hasse had been introduced to Lightfoot's music many years earlier by her brother and met him periodically at his concerts. A background actor in Hollywood, she'd introduced herself to him again in Tampa, Florida, and this time something clicked. The two began dating, with Hasse flying up to stay with Lightfoot in his Bridle Path home. But tensions began immediately between Lightfoot and Liz over the new woman in his life, which came to a head that summer.

That's why I missed my chance to sing at the Dylan concert. I was supposed to go down there and be a guest. I had to choose which woman I was going to take to the show. It was Elizabeth who first asked me if she could go. Then Kim found out about it and said "Why can't I go? Why can't we all go?" "Because Liz doesn't want you to," I told her. Kim then said, "We could sit in one area and Liz could sit in another." It got out of hand. So finally, three weeks before the show, I said, "That's it, I'm not going." I got so pissed off at myself for worrying about how to handle it, I canceled. Kim called it a tragedy. But I made the decision and just removed myself from the whole situation.

It *was* a tragedy. Lightfoot and Dylan had long admired each other as songwriters and had covered each other's work. They'd also played together many times, but only privately. Fans had long hoped that the two might perform together. What song would they sing? What would it sound like? Would the song be one of their own or something by one of their peers? Those questions remain unanswered. A duet between the two titans of popular song has so far never happened and now falls into the speculative category of "what if?"

Lightfoot lost two musical friends in 2011. David Rea, who'd played lead guitar on 1966's *Lightfoot!* and had toured with him for two years before its release, died at sixty-five after a summer-long illness. Lightfoot had always admired Rea's intricate guitar picking, best remembered on the opening of "For Lovin' Me," and he later became a fan of his songwriting talent, especially "Shorty's Ghost," a humorous number Rea wrote about a ghost that hangs around a brothel.

A greater loss on a personal level was the death of Terry Clements, who died of a heart attack at sixty-three. Songs like "Sundown," "Carefree Highway" and "The Wreck of the Edmund Fitzgerald" all bear his inventive solos. Clements had been much more than just his loyal sideman for almost forty years. "Terry was a terrific guy, a wonderful friend and a great guitar player," Lightfoot told the Canadian Press, adding that the two shared many adventures together, including sailing, and had rehearsed two days before the guitarist entered the hospital, where he died two weeks later. "He had many friends throughout North America who really admired his playing and had a great deal of respect for him," Lightfoot said.

Although Lightfoot stated that there was no replacing Clements, the truth was his longtime guitarist's heavy drinking had made him an unreliable band member. "He was messing up real bad," says Rick Haynes, "and it's a wonder he didn't get fired." Clements had been living alone north of Toronto, in Aurora, and Lightfoot did his best to help him, offering to get him an apartment downtown and pay for his rehab. But according to Haynes, Clements's alcoholism had gone too far. Lightfoot quietly recruited Carter Lancaster, a Hamilton, Ontario, guitarist, to take Clements's place and began secretly rehearsing with him. When Clements died, Lancaster was ready to step in.

Clements's last contributions to the Lightfoot sound appeared on the 2012 album *All Live*, a CD of nineteen songs recorded at Massey Hall between 1998 and 2001. It was Lightfoot's first live recording in forty-three years and only the second of his career. He'd originally intended to save the live album until after he'd died but then had a change of heart. After all, there were no studio recordings on the horizon (although "Plans of My Own," an unused track from *A Painter Passing Through*, was discovered and released in 2016) and no new songs. Well, hardly any new songs. Filmmaker Spike Lee had called Lightfoot to ask if he could contribute a song along the lines of "The Wreck of the Edmund Fitzgerald" for his documentary *When the Levees Broke*, about the destruction of New Orleans from Hurricane Katrina. Lightfoot responded with "Prayer to the Oil Field," a bluesy topical number, but the song never made it into the film. He also composed a number called "24 Hour Blues" and another, "It Doesn't Really Matter," for his latest muse, Kim. Both remain unrecorded.

Mostly, Lightfoot kept his focus on concert work and geared up for his 2013 tour, which he dubbed "50 Years on the Carefree Highway." In March, he appeared at the Grammy Museum in Los Angeles and took part in an onstage interview before performing a forty-five-minute set with his band. "Despite [Lightfoot's] frail appearance," noted one reporter, "his voice was still hearty and distinct, folksy and filled with haunting and self-aware reflection." It's true that Lightfoot looked worn out and weak, but showing the energy of a performer many years younger, he went on to deliver seventy-one concerts that year. Late in the summer, Lightfoot replaced Neil Young at the Greenbelt Harvest Picnic, near Hamilton, Ontario, and at the Ottawa Folk Festival. Young and his band had been scheduled to appear at both events but canceled due to an injury to Crazy Horse guitarist Frank "Poncho" Sampedro. The following spring, Young recorded stark, almost ghostly renditions of Lightfoot's "Early Morning Rain" and "If You Could Read My Mind" for his *A Letter Home* album, a lo-fi but strangely powerful recording of songs by some of Young's favorite songwriters, including Dylan, Ochs, Willie Nelson and Bruce Springsteen.

"If You Could Read My Mind" was easily Lightfoot's most covered song, with more than three hundred recorded versions. Lightfoot himself never failed to perform it. But, as he'd done with "The Wreck of the Edmund Fitzgerald," Lightfoot rewrote the song slightly and sang it differently from the recorded version. Years earlier, Ingrid had challenged him on the sentiment expressed in the lyrics. "She said, 'Daddy, it's not "the feelings that *you* lack," it's "the feelings that *we* lack."'" She was clear that I was pointing at her mum. She said, 'Wasn't it a two-way street, Daddy?' And I said, 'You know, you're right.'" He couldn't do anything about the record, but he promised Ingrid that for the rest of his life he would sing "the feelings that we lack." Recalls Ingrid, "He listened to me, and I'm still a bit shocked that he did."

By the time Lightfoot and his band pulled into Beverly Hills for a sold-out September show in 2014 at the Saban Theatre, a historic 1,897-seat art deco facility, he and his band were running like clockwork. Big cheers greeted "Beautiful" and "Carefree Highway," while "Sundown" had the crowd clapping along. The audience, mostly white-haired and likely retired, knew a lot of the songs. Some had been coming to see Lightfoot since the 1970s. Others remembered his romantic ballads as the soundtrack of their first dates. A few even had pictures of themselves with the Canadian legend on their cell phones. All seemed pleased that their favorite troubadour was still able to conjure up his music magic.

Lightfoot was relaxed enough during the two-hour concert to joke that "we're all from Toronto, and we don't smoke crack cocaine," a reference to the city's notorious mayor, Rob Ford. Before launching into "Baby Step Back," the up-tempo number he always quaintly referred to as a "toe-tapper," he quipped, "Meet me at the Rock Pile, honey, and I'll get a little bolder." Polite chuckles and a few groans followed. The audience was there for the songs, not the jokes, and responded as they might to a beloved but corny old uncle. After encores of "Canadian Railroad Trilogy" and "Rainy Day People," Lightfoot left the stage and its ornate proscenium arch and headed backstage. It was time for the usual after-show meet-and-greet.

Galen and his mother, Joanne, were there, and he dutifully chatted with fans and posed for a selfie with Carla Olson, of 1980s Americana new-wavers the Textones. Even Joe Wissert, producer of *If You Could Read My Mind* and *Summer Side of Life*, dropped by. Lightfoot hadn't seen him in years and was thrilled to catch up.

Four days later, after sound check and before his show at San Francisco's Louise M. Davies Symphony Hall, Lightfoot was busy warming up in his dressing room, doing some arm stretches and focusing on the songs he'd chosen to perform that night. The last time he and his band had played in the building, he noted, was thirty-three years earlier, when the venue first opened. "It's good to be back," he said. A few doors down, drummer Barry Keane was leading his bandmates through a series of limbering-up exercises. Standing in a circle, following Keane's instruction, they looked a lot like veteran ballplayers getting loose before a game. Promptly at 8 P.M., Lightfoot and his team strode onto the stage and launched into two sets of crowd-pleasing hits mixed with a few surprises. He prefaced "Clouds of Loneliness," a rarely performed song from his post-aneurysm *Harmony* album, with the explanation that it was about his marriage falling apart. With just keyboardist Mike Heffernan at his side, Lightfoot opened the second set with his solemn salute to those called on to fight in wars, "Drink Yer Glasses Empty." Before finger-picking his way through "All the Lovely Ladies," he looked down admiringly at his 1948 six-string Martin guitar. "It's been around," he told the audience with a grin.

The year's touring finished, as it often did, with a four-night run in late November at Massey Hall. Lightfoot, as usual, was nervous on opening night. He snapped at Bernie Fiedler, his oldest friend, who'd been producing the Massey shows since 1967, over some sort of ticket mix-up. "I don't need to be dealing with this," Lightfoot screamed before the show. Then he and the band were delayed making their entrance onstage when a radio personality, fancying himself a stand-up comedian, took too long with his introductions. "Who the hell is this guy?" Lightfoot bellowed from behind the curtain. "Get him off!" He hated surprises, and the presence of a lot of family and friends always added extra stress to the Toronto shows.

But the reason for Lightfoot's edginess became apparent immediately after intermission. Lightfoot was presented with the inaugural Massey Hall Honours Award in recognition of his 152 performances in the historic venue—the most by any solo performer. Wearing a royal-blue cropped velvet jacket, he stood onstage and listened as Massey Hall president Charlie Cutts and Ontario's lieutenant governor, the Honourable Elizabeth Dowdeswell, spoke of his legacy. Before his second set could begin, Lightfoot also had to pose with Cutts and Dowdeswell and the standing audience in the background for a ceremonial photograph. It was an occasion worth marking. From his first boy soprano appearances to his many sold-out concerts, the Grand Old Lady of Shuter Street was where he always shone. Lightheads from all over the world flocked to the Church of Gord just to see their hero perform in that sacred space. Ron Sexsmith was usually in the audience, with his friend and fellow singer-songwriter Andy Kim, of "Sugar, Sugar" fame. Sexsmith hadn't missed a Lightfoot Massey Hall show since 1987. "Every year you see him, it becomes more dear in a way," he said, "because he's in his seventies now and you hope he'll be around forever, but no one is." Fact is, Lightfoot plans to continue appearing there until he can no longer summon the strength to walk out onto the hall's broad wooden stage.

The latter half of 2014 saw not one but two weddings in Lightfoot's life. First, he and Kim flew out to British Columbia to witness the marriage of Eric to his girlfriend, Ashley Keenan; the young couple would later have a daughter, Lennox. Lightfoot had always felt close to the son he had with Cathy Coonley and was impressed by the focus and motivation Eric had shown as a young man, first with music and now as a licensed pilot flying sightseers around the picturesque BC coastline. At the reception, attended by eighty people, Eric provided his father with a guitar and asked him to sing a song. Lightfoot chose Ramblin' Jack Elliott's "Diamond Joe." "I could've played something schmaltzy or romantic," he explained, "but I chose a toe-tapper instead."

A much quieter but far more significant wedding later that year was Lightfoot's own. He and Kim tied the knot on December 19 at Toronto's Rosedale United, the same church where Lightfoot had been singing at Christmas services most years since 1976. It was a small, intimate service performed by Reverend Doug Norris and a lone pianist. Now married for the third time, Lightfoot sought to balance his romantic and professional lives and avoid the fallout from touring that had ruined his previous relationships. The best way to do this, he found, was to take Kim with him on the road, but this involved relaxing one of his longstanding rules of travel with his band: no wives. Still, Kim proved to be an asset. She was a positive, reassuring presence and was able to act as his personal assistant.

Lightfoot continued to have health issues that needed attention. In March 2015, he had to cancel eight US dates when he was hospitalized with food poisoning. A regular smoker, he'd also developed emphysema, the same lung disease that had killed his mother. To get through a full concert now, he required a few hits from an oxygen tank at intermission.

Even during the months when he wasn't touring, it was hard to keep Lightfoot away from the stage. In July, he was back in Orillia to make his now annual cameo appearance at Mariposa and sang his ode to his hometown, "Couchiching." In September, he and Kim attended the David Foster Foundation Miracle Gala and Concert at Toronto's Mattamy Athletic Centre, formerly Maple Leaf Gardens, on a double date with Ronnie and Wanda Hawkins.* Foster staged these annual events for his charity to raise money for children in need of life-saving organ transplants. The headliners were Stevie Wonder and Michael Bolton, but Foster gave Hawkins and Lightfoot each a turn to sing. Hawkins sang his old battle cry "Forty Days," while a tuxedoed Lightfoot strolled among the tables singing "If You Could Read My Mind" before arriving at a grand piano onstage next to an admiring Foster. "Gordon has always been kind of shy," says Wanda, "but not in front of a mike. You should have seen him work that room!"

Orillia had begun to realize the heritage value of its most famous son, who'd once been scoffed at in the town for daring to go to Hollywood. Two years earlier, it had launched Lightfoot Days, a celebration with tribute bands, memorabilia displays and walking tours of Lightfoot-related places of interest, including his childhood home. Already Orillia had the Lightfoot Trail, a nine-mile (15 km) trail that stretched along the northeast end of the community. Then, on a crisp autumn day in October 2015, the town unveiled a thirteen-foot bronze statue to the man on the trail near Tudhope Park, the Mariposa site. Titled *Golden Leaves*, the sculpture depicts a young bearded Lightfoot with guitar surrounded by leaves that portray scenes from his songs. Kim and Meredith joined him for the ceremony. Mayor Steve Clarke spoke to the crowd about the importance of Lightfoot to Orillia, recounting personal anecdotes about his school days at Orillia Collegiate Institute and the impact his music had long had on residents. Lightfoot gave an interview afterward and was typically humble. "When I found out they were working on [the sculpture]," he said, "I thought, Why me? What have I done that is so great that I should deserve a statue?" Even after a half

---

* In 2015, eighty-year-old Hawkins teamed up with Lightfoot to record the Band's holiday single "Christmas Must Be Tonight."

century of stardom, the many awards and the worldwide acclaim, Lightfoot still couldn't understand what all the fuss was about.

The last time Lightfoot performed in the United Kingdom, he was downing several Irish coffees before setting foot onstage and working his way through a forty-ouncer of Canadian Club in the course of each day. At London's Dominion Theatre, Lightfoot, over-refreshed, had been drawn into his infamous exchange with a heckler and stormed off the stage in a huff, the resulting jeers from the English press reverberating all the way back to Canada and, much to his shame, even Orillia.

But by the spring of 2016, Lightfoot was ready to put his troubled past behind him. Thirty-five years after he'd last set foot on British soil, he was booked to play a series of concerts there, including a return to London. In an advance interview with London's *Daily Telegraph*, he spoke of how his mother, Jessie, had always been a huge fan of the Royal Family and of his own meeting with Queen Elizabeth at the 1992 Canada Day celebrations in Ottawa. "[The Queen] told me how much she loved the 'Canadian Railroad Trilogy,'" he told the *Telegraph*. "She looked at me and said, 'Oh, that song,' and then said again, 'that song,' and that was all she said."

After successful shows in Glasgow, Liverpool, Newcastle and Manchester, the tour pulled into London for a concert at the Royal Albert Hall. The famous building, with its majestic dome, red velvet upholstery and blond woodwork interior, had played host to everyone from Wagner and Verdi to Sinatra, the Beatles and Lightfoot himself. On the evening of May 24, the Canadian troubadour sat backstage and went through his usual pre-concert ritual of guitar tuning and looking over his set list. He was more nervous than usual. There was a sense of occasion about the show, which had brought his wife, Kim, his daughter Meredith, his friend Bernie Fiedler, and longtime office manager Anne Leibold across the Atlantic to witness it. The band and crew understood the significance of the London appearance too. Three of his bandmates—Haynes, Keane and Heffernan—had been with him on that fateful night thirty-five years ago. At show time, Kim assisted her husband with some oxygen in his dressing room and gave him some gentle words of encouragement before leading him to the stage.

Haynes, Keane, Heffernan and Carter Lancaster walked out onto the darkened stage and took their places. Seconds later, Lightfoot made his entrance, striding out in his red cropped jacket and low-cut boots, his Martin guitar tucked under his arm. As soon as the spotlight picked him out, he was greeted with a standing ovation. It would be the first of several he'd receive that night. From "Sundown" and "The Wreck of the Edmund Fitzgerald" to "Minstrel of the Dawn" and "I'd Rather Press On," Lightfoot and his trusted band delivered two note-perfect sets of recognizable hits and deep album cuts. By the time they finished with "Early Morning Rain" and an encore of "Waiting for You," the audience, older couples, gray-haired hippies and a smattering of younger music aficionados, was back up on its feet. The appreciation expressed was clearly aimed at the quality of the compositions. As one reviewer noted, his "once velvet voice is now reduced to a muted croak." But those in the hall's red velvet seats didn't mind. Many had waited thirty-five years to see the Canadian legend. They were clearly delighted just to be in his presence.

Lightfoot flew home feeling fine, if a little exhausted. He had succeeded in delivering a series of UK concerts in the most professional way he knew how—effectively curing the longstanding hangover he'd inflicted on himself decades earlier. At this stage in Lightfoot's life, it was important to get his house in order, to right past wrongs and bury old ghosts. He'd always professed not to be especially religious, but guilt, remorse and redemption remained powerful forces for the man who once sang "Forgive me Lord for I have sinned." Lightfoot's "sins" were a heavy burden—his bad concert behavior, his neglect of the women in his life, his absence in the lives of his children—and he desperately wanted to atone. He was doing a pretty good job.

As he had long proven, Lightfoot was a survivor. He'd withstood the shifting sands of musical tastes. While his contemporaries were twisting and bending their styles to catch the latest wave, Lightfoot had held firm and stuck with his sound. Aside from some brief flirtations with synthesizers and electric guitars, it was, unapologetically, acoustic folk music. He remained, above all, the quintessential troubadour. Lightfoot had also come through matrimonial storms and found love again. And, most remarkably, he'd survived actual brushes with death, rising again, Lazarus-like, to the relief and joy of family, friends and fans.

Acclaim had long followed him, from his start on the folk scene to his arrival at a legendary status few musicians ever achieve. Except for the elusive Grammy Award, Lightfoot has had every prize imaginable bestowed on him and been hailed as one of the world's foremost songwriters, with more than ten million albums sold. His place in the pop pantheon was secure, although Lightfoot would modestly insist that, like his old friend Leonard Cohen, he too was only paying his rent every day in the tower of song. The true mark of his genius is the vast number and range of artists who have covered his songs. They include legends and veterans like Elvis Presley, Johnny Cash, Judy Collins, Hank Williams Jr., Neil Young, Barbra Streisand, Jerry Lee Lewis, Bob Dylan, Nana Mouskouri, Scott Walker, Eric Clapton, Liza Minnelli and Glen Campbell. There are also younger artists, like Paul Weller, Eva Cassidy, Billy Bragg, Cowboy Junkies, the Dandy Warhols, Mary Margaret O'Hara and Richard Hawley, who have all made Lightfoot songs their own. And the list keeps growing.

In Canada, Lightfoot's status has grown to mythic proportions. No other work by a cultural figure has become so intrinsically linked with Canadian history, landscape and nationhood than has Lightfoot and his songs. Whether capturing the majesty of Canada's outdoors, the thrill of the Rockies, the breathtaking power of the Great Lakes or the teardrops and toil of building the "iron road runnin' from the sea to the sea," his music is pure Canadiana. With a painter's eye for landscape, a poet's taste for romance and a historian's allegiance to accuracy, Lightfoot has inspired comparisons to Canadian icons Emily Carr, Pierre Berton and the Group of Seven. But his indelible melodies and vivid storytelling have made him, perhaps, the most Canadian icon of all.

For all the accolades, Lightfoot remains wholly focused on the stage. He vows to keep performing—"just like Hank Snow, Wilf Carter and Stompin' Tom Connors," as he likes to say—for his faithful fans, who never seem to tire of hearing him. For Lightfoot, a man of mighty talent but modest needs, the greatest reward is still the simple act of being able to go onstage, sing his songs and soak up the adulation of his fans. It is something he will continue to do to the very end.

Notes

Quotes set in italics in the main text are taken from the author's interviews with Gordon Lightfoot. Unless otherwise indicated, all other quotes, including from Lightfoot, are also from interviews conducted by the author and are indicated in the notes below by the subject's name and the date of the interview.

INTRODUCTION: ROLLING THUNDER

3 **"They gave me a buzz"**: quoted in "Rolling Thunder Review," Wayne Francis, www.lightfoot.ca.

4 **"We're gonna do this one for Gordon"**: quoted in Les Kokay, *Songs of the Underground: A Collector's Guide to the Rolling Thunder Revue, 1975–1976*, 2009, www.bjorner.com/RtrBook-Letter.pdf.

1: BY LAKE COUCHICHING

Author interviews with Barry Keane, Marylou Spencer, Tayler "Hap" Parnaby, Marg Barnsdale (née McEachern), Gary Thiess.

10 **"Peter and I set up our huts"**: Lightfoot, July 2014.

11 **"Whenever Gord would be presented"**: Keane, February 2017.

12 **"Orillia in the 1930s"**: Randy Richmond, *The Orillia Spirit: An Illustrated History of Orillia* (Dundurn, 1996).

12 **"Heaven knows Pupkin"**: Stephen Leacock, *Sunshine Sketches of a Little Town* (Bell & Cockburn, 1912).

13 **"The stomp of army boots"**: Marcel Rousseau, in *Mariposa Exposed, Volume 1: Stories for the Sesquicentennial*, Dennis Rizzo and Ross Greenwood, eds. (Le Temps H&S Times, 2016).

13 **paper drives collected seventeen tons**: *Mariposa Exposed, Volume 1*.

14 **"Sometimes Dad's family"**: Lightfoot, August 2016.

14   **"My mum, aunts and other relatives"**: Lightfoot, August 2014.

14   **"I had quite the collection of Dinky toys"**: ibid.

15   **"It was all done with glue"**: Lightfoot, March 2014.

15   **"The place was packed"**: Lightfoot, August 2014.

15–16 **"I remember at one point"**: Lightfoot, February 2014.

16   **"I was called down to the office"**: Lightfoot, August 2014.

17   **"He was the plant manager"**: Lightfoot, March 2014.

18   **"I came face to face"**: quoted in Nick Krewen, "Lightfoot at 54: 'I'm Not Worthy,'" *Hamilton Spectator*, November 6, 1993.

18   **"I even learned how to sing with emotion"**: Lightfoot, February 2014.

18   **"Gordie was a real troublemaker"**: Spencer, February 2016.

19   **"She wasn't a pushover"**: Lightfoot, October 2016.

2: JAZZ 'N' JIVE

Author interviews with Tayler "Hap" Parnaby, Marg Barnsdale (née McEachern), Gary Thiess, Pat LaCroix.

21   **"I was shanghaied right into it"**: Lightfoot, February 2014.

23   **"We did the same thing"**: quoted in John Swartz, "Gordon Lightfoot: Hard Core Quartet Competitor," *The Harmonizer*, September/ October 2006.

24   **"I had to confront my dad"**: Lightfoot, August 2014.

25   **"He did a masterful version"**: Parnaby, August 2016.

25   **"There'd be a carload of us"**: Lightfoot, March 2014.

26   **"I got a call from Charlie"**: Lightfoot, February 2104.

26   **"He sang 'Cry Me a River'"**: Barnsdale (née McEachern), December 2016.

26   **"I can't remember if we actually dated"**: ibid.

27   **"Gord was such a hardworking guy"**: Thiess, August 2016.

28   **"I read about it in *Life* magazine"**: Lightfoot, August 2014.

29   **"They were laughing about it"**: quoted in Roberta Bell, "No Slowing Him Down," *Orillia Packet & Times*, October 12, 2012.

30   **"I remember seeing Blossom Dearie"**: LaCroix, September 2016.

30   **"Gord and I were both vying to be singers"**: ibid.

30   **"It wasn't like barbershop"**: Lightfoot, October 2016.

31   **"I just knew I had to go"**: Lightfoot, February 2014.

3: MOVIN'

Author interview with Tommy Hunter.

34 **"It all had to be written with great care"**: Lightfoot, July 2014.

34 **"I looked at somebody's girl"**: ibid.

36 **"If you listen to some of Gord's"**: Hunter, February 2016.

38 **"Knowing Chet was there"**: Lightfoot, March 2014.

39 **"I just wasn't happy"**: Lightfoot, February 2014.

4: EARLY MORNING RAIN

Author interviews with John Court, Peter Yarrow, Noel "Paul" Stookey, Ramblin' Jack Elliott, Bonnie Dobson, Bernie Fiedler, Wanda Hawkins, Ronnie Hawkins, Jim Mosby, Chuck Mitchell.

43 **"I did Buck Owens's"**: Lightfoot, February 2014.

44 **"When the Beatles burst on the scene"**: ibid.

46 **"Gordie had a good ear"**: quoted in Nicholas Jennings, *Before the Gold Rush: Flashbacks to the Dawn of the Canadian Sound* (Viking, 1997; Penguin, 1998).

47 **"Some nights, we didn't have much"**: Lightfoot, October 2013.

48 **"He looked like Sydney Greenstreet"**: Bob Dylan, *Chronicles: Volume One* (Simon & Schuster, 2004).

48 **"one heck of a songsmith"**: quoted in Jennings, *Before the Gold Rush*.

48 **"I was really impressed with his voice"**: ibid.

49 **"It's a wrenching song"**: Yarrow, February 2016

49 **"I needed to get to a gig"**: Elliott, January 2016.

50–51 **"You knew just listening to him"**: Dobson, January 2016.

51 **"He'd been up all night"**: Lightfoot, February 2014.

53 **"Any way you look at it"**: quoted in Barrie Hale, "Dig That Country 'n' Lightfoot Beat," *Toronto Telegram*, March 4, 1965.

53 **"As soon as he came off stage"**: Fiedler, April 2016.

53 **"guileless manner that is extremely appealing"**: Marvin Schiff, "Lightfoot Appealing with Guileless Air," *The Globe and Mail*, March 10, 1965.

54 **"They're 'mistreating' songs"**: ibid.

54 **"the next Toronto performer"**: Nathan Cohen, "Man to Watch," *Toronto Star*, April 27, 1965.

55 **"When I first heard Peter, Paul and Mary"**: Lightfoot, March 2014.

56 **"It was hot and humid"**: ibid.

57 **"My mother had a big house"**: Wanda Hawkins, January 2016.

57 **"It was a real stretch"**: Fiedler, April 2016.

59 **"There I was in Canada, stoned out of my mind"**: Phil Ochs, "The Ballad of Gordon Lightfoot," *Broadside*, July 15, 1965.

59 **"aiming at a new thing"**: quoted in Elijah Wald, *Dylan Goes Electric: Newport, Seeger, Dylan and the Night That Split the Sixties* (HarperCollins, 2015).

60 **"Pete Seeger and a lot of people"**: Lightfoot, February 2014.

61 **"changed every week"**: Greil Marcus, *Like a Rolling Stone: Bob Dylan at the Crossroads* (PublicAffairs, 2005).

61 **"he looked as if he had jumped"**: Gordon Lightfoot, "Gordon Lightfoot Writes on Bob Dylan," *Toronto Telegram*, September 23, 1965.

63 **"Gordon really had his act together"**: Mosby, March 2016.

63 **"She thought he was a good guy"**: Chuck Mitchell, May 2016.

64 **"A Triple-Decker Musical Treat"**: Claude Hall, *Billboard*, December 11, 1965.

64 **"Gordon Lightfoot in his local debut"**: Robert Shelton, "Folk and Blues Echo Over Holiday," *The New York Times*, November 29, 1965.

5: CROSSROADS
Author interviews with Sylvia Tyson, Charlie McCoy, Burton Cummings, Judy Collins, Marlene Markle.

67 **"Dylan and Phil Ochs are the people"**: quoted in Jack Batten, "I Just Write Songs I Think People Will Dig," *The Canadian*, February 5, 1966.

68 **"He painted, I wrote songs"**: quoted in J.A. Wainwright, *Blazing Figures: A Life of Robert Markle* (Wilfrid Laurier University Press, 2010).

68 **"I'm disappointed there aren't any Mohawk Indians"**: quoted in Frank Kennedy, "Troubadour Gord Lightfoot," *Toronto Star*, January 19, 1966.

69 **"They weren't used to a busload of rowdies"**: Sylvia Tyson, November 2015.

70 **"Gordon Lightfoot, whose UA debut LP"**: *Billboard*, May 21, 1966.

70   **"You never know, someone might get a bit touchy"**: quoted in Douglas Hughes, "Lightfoot: Witty, Wistful and Wise," *Toronto Star*, June 29, 1966.

70   **"It's a good one, Gordon"**: quoted in John Macfarlane, "Lightfoot: The Lyrical Loner," *The Globe and Mail*, June 18, 1966.

72   **"I remember when she sang us a song"**: Lightfoot, February 2014.

73   **"I started with a ballad"**: ibid.

73   **"He listened to the whole thing"**: ibid.

74   **"You did more good with your damn song"**: ibid.

75   **"Folk-rock artists would never come to Nashville"**: McCoy, April 2016.

76   **"country-and-Lightfoot parade of Canadiana"**: Peter Goddard, "Lightfoot Marks Time with Surface Hipness," *The Globe and Mail*, April 1, 1967.

76   **"Gordon came out with his sidemen"**: Cummings, October 2007.

77   **"masterful"**: *Billboard*, July 1, 1967.

77   **"timeless appeal"**: *Hit Parader*, October 1967.

77   **"I heard the sound that Gordon Lightfoot was getting"**: quoted in Jann Wenner, "Bob Dylan Talks," *Rolling Stone*, November 29, 1969.

78   **"Harry came into the Riverboat"**: Lightfoot, February 2014.

78   **"You don't do that kind of thing"**: quoted in John Macfarlane, "Lightfoot: He's *Really* Canada's Own," *Toronto Star*, February 3, 1968.

79   **"I met Gordie in Greenwich Village"**: Collins, May 2016.

6: WHEREFORE AND WHY

Author interviews with Jerry Jeff Walker, John Simon, Chuck Mitchell, Rick Haynes, Elliot Mazer, Sandy Bozzo, Lenny Waronker, Adam Mitchell, Alexander Mair.

81   **"Shrine . . . full of artists"**: Kris Kristofferson, foreword to Paul Colby with Martin Fitzpatrick, *The Bitter End: Hanging Out at America's Nightclub* (Cooper Square Press, 2002).

81   **"When Gordon played the club"**: Paul Colby with Martin Fitzpatrick, ibid.

82   **"Gord said he thought the change"**: Walker, February 2016.

82   **"stockbrokers, mining executives"**: Marq de Villiers, "Gordon Lightfoot: Hurtin' All the Way to the Bank," *Toronto Life*, June 1968.

83   **"cool"**: Simon, March 2016.

84 **"Like all of us, Gordon had genuine self-doubt"**: Chuck Mitchell, May 2016.

85 **"Gord was a very straight Scottish Presbyterian guy"**: quoted in Dave Bidini, *Writing Gordon Lightfoot* (McClelland & Stewart, 2011).

86 **The columnist, Maggie Daley, wrote that Lightfoot**: Maggie Daley, *Chicago Tribune*, February 9, 1975.

86 **Andy Warhol wrote in his published diaries**: Andy Warhol, *The Andy Warhol Diaries*, Pat Hackett, ed. (Grand Central, 1991).

87 **"one of the most arresting and poetic"**: Pete Welding, *Downbeat*, March 6, 1969.

88 **"Writing songs is about finding the time"**: Lightfoot, March 2014.

89 **"as good a poet as a songwriter"**: Marq de Villiers, "Gordon Lightfoot: Hurtin' All the Way to the Bank," *Toronto Life*, June 1968.

89 **"I use the first person a lot"**: quoted in Tony Wilson, "Focus on Folk," *Melody Maker*, March 15, 1969.

90 **"There was so much truth"**: Lightfoot, October 2016.

91 **"It made me feel better"**: Lightfoot, December 2016.

91 **"rich talent"**: Robert Hilburn, "Gordon Lightfoot on Stage at Troubadour," *Los Angeles Times*, September 26, 1968.

92 **"assured, straightforward delivery"**: "Folk Singers: Cosmopolitan Hick," *Time*, November 8, 1968.

92 **"looks like a walk-on from *Bonanza*"**: Robert Shelton, "Gordon Lightfoot: An Emerging Talent," *The New York Times*, December 2, 1968.

92 **"Hi, this is Gordon Lightfoot"**: Haynes, February 2015.

93 **"one of the most exciting"**: Robert Hilburn, "Gordon Lightfoot in Royce Hall Concert," *Los Angeles Times*, January 7, 1969.

93 **"Lightfoot holds the most promise"**: Hilburn, "Gordon Lightfoot Arrives on Scene," *Los Angeles Times*, February 1, 1969.

94 **"I had a real good time with Johnny"**: Lightfoot, February 2014.

94 **"Gord's not pushy"**: Haynes, February 2015.

95 **"Elliot turned to me"**: Lightfoot, March 2014.

95 **"You know, it's really great to be back"**: quoted in Ritchie Yorke, "Home Is the Hall to Gordon Lightfoot," *The Globe and Mail*, March 31, 1969.

95 **"the dollies and the ladies"**: Robert Markle, liner notes, *Sunday Concert*.

96 **"Mo had me come into his office"**: Waronker, February 2016.

97 **"Initially, we'll just be working on packaging"**: quoted in *Billboard*, May 24, 1969.

98 **"I didn't move to the States"**: Lightfoot, March 2014.

98 **Mair organized a lavish press conference**: "Gordon Lightfoot Signs $1 Million Contract," *Toronto Star*, December 2, 1969.

98 **Mair told the gathering**: Dane Lanken, "Lightfoot Plays Pageant, Says It's Not His Thing," *The Gazette* (Montreal), November 29, 1969.

7: BETWEEN THE LINES
Author interviews with Alexander Mair, Dee Higgins, Bruce Good, Brian Good, Lenny Waronker.

102 **"some of the nicest folk music"**: Jud Rosebush, *Rolling Stone*, July 23, 1970.

102 **"Gord didn't do good interviews"**: Mair, November 2015.

102 **"American mining companies are strip-mining"**: quoted in Dane Lanken, "Gordon Lightfoot Rues the Imminent End of Life," *The Gazette* (Montreal), February 21, 1970.

103 **"rapists, murderers, junkies"**: Fraser Kelly, "The Toughest Audience in Canada Loved Lightfoot," *Toronto Telegram*, April 11, 1970.

103 **"Man, they were people"**: quoted in Kelly, ibid.

104 **"an ill-fated karate demonstration"**: *Billboard*, August 15, 1970.

104 **"During the golden era of folk-flavored"**: Robert Hilburn, *Billboard*, Troubadour 20th Anniversary Supplement, August 27, 1977.

105 **"Folks, I've never done this before"**: quoted in Lydia Hutchinson, "Elton John's American Debut," *Performing Songwriter*, August 25, 2015.

105 **"It was just three guys"**: Lightfoot, February 2014.

105 **"devoted audience"**: Mike Jahn, "Gordon Lightfoot Sings His Friendly Tunes," *The New York Times*, October 5, 1970.

105 **"cast a magical spell"**: Gregg Geller, "Lightfoot a Master," *Record World*, October 17, 1970.

106 **"Gord nodded toward someone singing"**: Higgins, June 2016.

107 **"Right away, Gord started working on a song"**: Good, November 2016.

108 **"In the middle of the concert the smoke alarm"**: ibid.

109 **"At about ten to twelve"**: Lightfoot, March 2014.

109 **"It's a highly sophisticated, beautiful song"**: Waronker, February 2016.

110 **"Why are you changing the title"**: Lightfoot, February 2014.

110 **"Albert didn't tend to say much"**: Lightfoot, March 2014.

III   **"Because it is such a warm, personal album"**: Robert Hilburn, "Lightfoot in Step with Public Taste," *Los Angeles Times*, May 16, 1971.

III   **"There are all sorts of temptations"**: quoted in Hilburn, ibid.

8: TILTING AT WINDMILLS
Author interviews with Jerry Jeff Walker, Lee Hirschberg, Rick Haynes, Alexander Mair, Murray McLauchlan.

113   **"was wearing jeans and a denim vest"**: Cathy Smith, *Chasing the Dragon* (Key Porter, 1984).

114   **"drank so much Châteauneuf-du-Pape"**: Smith, ibid.

114   **"drunk and madly in love"**: Smith, ibid.

116   **"I was working so efficiently back then"**: Lightfoot, February 2014.

116   **"I've been through some of life's pitfalls"**: quoted in Loraine Alterman, "If You Could Read My Mind," *Melody Maker*, December 25, 1971.

118   **"I loved that jacket"**: Walker, February 2016.

119   **"strong, gutsy, masculine, erudite singer"**: *Billboard*, January 29, 1972.

119   **"He said he was doing an album"**: Lightfoot, May 2016.

119   **"Don Costa had written a great arrangement"**: Hirschberg, June 2016.

120   **"It pissed me off"**: Lightfoot, February 2014.

121   **"it always comes down to an accusation"**: quoted in Marci McDonald, "The Shy, Withdrawn Singer Whose Music Spans Canada," *Toronto Star*, March 11, 1972.

122   **"He used to whistle"**: Haynes, February 2015.

123   **"Anne and I never sang together"**: Lightfoot, February 2014.

124   **"lived up to every inch"**: Cathy Smith, *Chasing the Dragon* (Key Porter, 1984).

125   **"Dylan was very respectful of what Gord was doing"**: McLauchlan, September 2015.

9: SUNDOWN
Author interviews with Barry Keane, Alexander Mair, Lenny Waronker, Murray McLauchlan, Rick Haynes.

127   **"We were listening to 'You Are What I Am'"**: Keane, February 2015.

128   **"serve to make perfectly decent"**: Stephen Holden, *Rolling Stone*, March 29, 1973.

128   **"It was way up in King Township"**: Lightfoot, March 2014.

129   **"I was hoping that no one else"**: Gordon Lightfoot, Reddit website AMA (Ask Me Anything) question-and-answer session, August 22, 2014.

130   **"spent eight days there getting drunk"**: quoted in Penny Valentine, "Gordon Lightfoot's Mid-Day Madness," *Sounds*, June 2, 1973.

130   **"When [Lightfoot] came on stage"**: Eunice Mouckley, "Gordon Lightfoot's Behavior Was Inexcusable: Former Fan," Letter to the Editor, *Toronto Star*, April 3, 1973.

131   **"I didn't want to get involved"**: Mair, November 2015.

131   **"When did I know the marriage was over?"**: Lightfoot, August 2014.

132   **"It only took forty-five minutes to record"**: Waronker, February 2016.

132   **"maintains all the strengths"**: Geoffrey Stokes, "Poet on a Rising Curve," *The Village Voice*, February 14, 1974.

132   **"Lightfoot's reflections are those of a mature man"**: Stephen Holden, *Rolling Stone*, March 14, 1974.

133   **"I've always had this desire to keep moving"**: quoted in Robert Hilburn, "Lightfoot: Artist Lets the Good Times Roll," *Los Angeles Times*, July 21, 1974.

134   **"A lot of our problems must have been due to drink"**: Cathy Smith, *Chasing the Dragon* (Key Porter, 1984).

134   **"He heard the album"**: Lightfoot, March 2014.

134   **"My dad was very young when he died"**: ibid.

135   **"It's hard work"**: quoted in Karl Dallas, "Lightfoot: Writing Hits by Accident," *Melody Maker*, June 2, 1973.

136   **"I remember we knocked McCartney out of first place"**: quoted in Matt Fink, "Gordon Lightfoot: Extended Interview," *American Songwriter*, January 1, 2008.

136   **"looks at the world through eyes full of questions and doubts"**: Jack Batten, "The Vulnerability of Gordon Lightfoot," *Saturday Night*, July 1974.

136   **"walk down the street without being recognized"**: Robert Windeler, "A Heavy New Star Named Lightfoot," *People*, September 7, 1974.

137   **"We were playing in a big concert hall"**: Lightfoot, February 2014.

137   **"Gordon saw it as a big betrayal"**: McLauchlan, September 2015.

138   **"I'll never forget that"**: Lightfoot, March 2014.

138   **"rotten mood"**: Tom Rogers, "Lightfoot on Wrong Track," *The Tennessean*, December 8, 1974.

139   **"The whole thing—the walkout"**: John Rockwell, "Gordon Lightfoot
      Sings, Fumes, Then Stalks Off," *The New York Times*, December 8,
      1974.

139   **"Gord was having issues"**: Haynes, February 2017.

10: ALL THE LOVELY LADIES
Author interviews with Barry Keane, Murray McLauchlan.

140   **"All of the songs about relationships"**: quoted in Lynn Van Matre,
      "Lightfoot: Flyin' High in a Low Key," *Chicago Tribune*, January 24,
      1975.

140   **"loneliness and remorse"**: quoted in *Songbook* box set liner notes
      (Rhino Records, 1999).

141   **"I find it real difficult"**: quoted in Nancy Naglin, "Gordon Lightfoot
      Rise After Sundown," *Crawdaddy*, April 1975.

142   **"She was a fan"**: Lightfoot, May 2016.

143   **"We had many a pleasurable ride on *Sundown*"**: Lightfoot, February
      2014.

144   **"We were getting near Flin Flon"**: Lightfoot, February 2014.

144   **"It was a fun trip"**: ibid.

145   **"Someone get me a drink"**: quoted in Allan Jones, "Lightfoot on a
      Rampage," *Uncut*, June 11, 2013.

145   **"Mr. Lightfoot has a husky baritone"**: John Rockwell, "Gordon
      Lightfoot in a Relaxed Vein, Offers Folk Songs," *The New York Times*,
      November 24, 1975.

145   **"He's yours"**: Lightfoot, July 2014.

146   **"I walked in the house"**: ibid.

147   **"I remember it so well"**: Lightfoot, March 2014.

147   **"First day in the studio"**: Keane, February 2015.

148   **"It slid sideways in the water"**: quoted in Michael Schumacher,
      Mighty Fitz: The Sinking of the Edmund Fitzgerald (University of
      Minnesota Press, 2012).

148   **"Shipwrecks are different"**: ibid.

150   **"I've never played a club like this before"**: quoted in Peter Goddard,
      "The Ballad of Frankie and Gordie," *Toronto Star*, March 20, 1976.

150   **"Gord likes to be in his comfort zone"**: Keane, February 2015.

151   **"I'm looking at this guy"**: ibid.

151   **"Gord says to the director"**: ibid.

151–152 **"It's a sophisticated work"**: Peter Goddard, "Lightfoot's Musical Growth Results in an Excellent Disc," *Toronto Star*, June 12, 1976.

152 **"Meticulously constructed tunes"**: Billy Altman, *Rolling Stone*, August 12, 1976.

153 **"John was really intense"**: Lightfoot, March 2014.

153 **"I felt sorry for her"**: Lightfoot, February 2014.

154 **"Some of our track and field people are in rags"**: quoted in James Christie, "Lightfoot Heads Gardens Benefit Show to Help Canadian Athletes Drill for Games," *The Globe and Mail*, May 26, 1976.

154 **"McLauchlan Steals Show at the Olympic Benefit"**: Margaret Daly, *Toronto Star*, June 12, 1976.

154 **"Gord was the draw, but I had a great band"**: McLauchlan, September 2015.

11: FLYING HIGH

Author interviews with Ian Tyson, Alexander Mair, Lenny Waronker, Robbie Robertson.

157 **"I see an awful lot of records"**: quoted in *Sault Star*, November 8, 2008.

157 **"doing some cowboy work"**: Tyson, April 2016.

158 **"I would be on the road with him"**: Mair, November 2015.

158 **"I taught Bev about the publishing"**: ibid.

158 **"So I went to see Jerry"**: Lightfoot, February 2014.

159 **"In those days, managers were control guys"**: Waronker, February 2016.

159 **"We're sitting in Weintraub's office"**: ibid.

161 **"Over the years with the Band"**: Robertson, June 2003.

161 **"We walk in, Cathy and I"**: Lightfoot, February 2014.

162 **"I got very drunk"**: ibid.

12: SAILING ON

Author interviews with Paul Body, Liona Boyd, Bruce Good, Brian Good, Steve Eyers.

163 **"Outrageously beautiful girls"**: Robert Markle, "Knowing Lightfoot: A Friend's Portrait of the Artist at Work and Play," *The Canadian*, April 16, 1977.

164 **"I love this place"**: ibid.

164 **"The next ten years"**: ibid.

165 **"the original rugged article"**: *Variety*, July 14, 1977.

166 **"If the audience doesn't like what they hear"**: quoted in Marilyn Beck, "Gordon Lightfoot Says His Music Gets Better as He Gets Older," *Democrat and Chronicle*, July 19, 1977.

166 **"usual supply of corny jokes"**: Robert Hilburn, "Lightfoot/ Amphitheatre," *Los Angeles Times*, August 6, 1977.

167 **"Lightfoot was a major star"**: Body, June 2016.

168 **"avoided any romantic entanglements"**: Liona Boyd, *In My Own Key: My Life in Love and Music* (Stoddart, 1998).

169 **"The immense popularity"**: Dave Laing et al., *The Electric Muse: The Story of Folk into Rock* (Methuen, 1975).

170 **"most radically different"**: Peter Goddard, "Lightfoot Reaches," *Toronto Star*, February 4, 1978.

171 **"more aggression and bite here"**: Colin Irwin, *Melody Maker*, April 29, 1978.

172 **"No one ever measures up in comparison"**: quoted in Ron Base, "Star Track: The Hot Pursuits of Lynne Ackerman," *The City*, February 5, 1978.

173 **"Gordon Lightfoot isn't so much a musician"**: Ray Conlogue, "More of the Same Lightfoot," *The Globe and Mail*, March 20, 1978.

173 **"outrageous egotism"**: Larry LeBlanc, "Lightfoot: On the Record," *The City*, April 2, 1978.

174 **"one of your bigger male chauvinists"**: quoted in Tom Hopkins, "Inside Gordon Lightfoot," *Maclean's*, May 1, 1978.

174 **"made a world of difference"**: quoted in Hardy Price, "The Lightfoot Touch," *Arizona Republic*, May 15, 1978.

175 **"They need the money"**: quoted in Wilder Penfield III, "Lightfoot: A Canadian Legend," *Toronto Sun*, January 29, 1978.

175 **"They could really crack that market"**: ibid.

175 **"He was so generous"**: Bruce Good, November 2015.

175 **"Gord liked hanging with us"**: Brian Good, November 2015.

176 **"Not bad, but he was better at shooting pool"**: Bruce Good, November 2015.

177 **"We were icebound on the Back River"**: Lightfoot, February 2014.

178 **"Orillia Hustler"**: Gary Dunford, "Bobby and Gordie Play Pool," *Toronto Sun*, October 16, 1978.

178 **"You had him leaving with his tail between his legs"**: quoted in Gary Dunford, "No Laughing Matter," *Toronto Sun*, December 14, 1979.

179 **"Like a good craftsman"**: Peter Goddard, "Lightfoot at 40," *Chatelaine*, March 1979.

180 **"Few people in popular music"**: Paul McGrath, "It's the Same Old Concert, and Lightfoot Fans Love It," *The Globe and Mail*, March 19, 1979.

181 **"occasionally short-winded"**: Bob Riedinger Jr., "Talent in Action," *Billboard*, April 28, 1979.

181 **"There was a knock at the door"**: Lightfoot, March 2104.

13: ON THE HIGH SEAS
Author interviews with Mike Heffernan, Rick Haynes, Barry Keane.

185 **"middle-of-the-road music"**: Paul Grein, *Los Angeles Times*, June 29, 1980.

185 **"It's nice to be back"**: quoted in Carola Vyhnak, "Singing Is Great, Whistling Is Lousy," *Toronto Star*, March 16, 1980.

185 **"It was, to put it bluntly"**: ibid.

185 **"She's about 2,500 miles away"**: quoted in Wilder Penfield III, "Lightfoot Down Deep," *Toronto Sun*, March 14, 1980.

186 **"Gordon and I were lining his new Old Town"**: Fred Gaskin writing in Cliff Jacobson, *Canoeing Wild Rivers: Guide to Expedition Canoeing in North America* (Falcon Guides, 2015).

188 **"drilling mud and Oh Henry! chocolate bars"**: Lightfoot, February 2014.

188 **"It was backing up"**: ibid.

188 **"We had an Indian guy"**: ibid.

189 **"My character gets a second chance"**: Lightfoot, March 2014.

189 **"The sophisticated pop music"**: William Littler, "Lightfoot Best at Story-Telling," *Toronto Star*, March 16, 1981.

190 **"It was a big deal for me, being Irish"**: Heffernan, March 2016.

190 **"After the concert"**: ibid.

191 **"After all they've been through"**: quoted in Paul King, "Belfast 'Demonstration'—It's Thumbs Up for Lightfoot," *Toronto Star*, May 15, 1981.

191 **"John Wayne's swagger"**: Tracy Huffman, "Paul King, 72: Colourful Writer," *Toronto Star*, May 13, 2008.

191 **"There was a lot of consumption going on"**: Haynes, February 2017.

191 **"Gord would ramble a bit"**: Keane, February 2017.

192   **"There was a problem at the Dominion"**: Lightfoot, August 2014.

192   **"The Canadian singer has an indistinct voice"**: John Coldstream, *Daily Telegraph*, quoted in Canadian Press story "Atrocious Concert' Angers Lightfoot's Fans," *Toronto Star*, May 22, 1981.

192   **"He said he was never coming back"**: ibid.

192   **"very tired"**: ibid.

193   **"Brits Bid Gord Good Riddance"**: Canadian Press story, *Orillia Packet & Times*, May 22, 1981.

193   **"I knew I was becoming an alcoholic"**: Lightfoot, August 2014.

193   **"His liver numbers weren't great"**: Haynes, February 2015.

195   **"I'm just a very conscientious guy"**: from "Gordon Lightfoot Talks About Shadows," WB Records, 1982.

195   **"I became increasingly aware"**: Edward Livingston, "Death of a Hero," Letter to the Editor, *Schenectady Gazette*, August 23, 1982.

196   **"Seeing them disappear down the driveway"**: Lightfoot, February 2014.

14: A LOT MORE LIVIN' TO DO

Author interviews with Rick Haynes, Bernie Finkelstein, Alan Thicke, Steve Earle, Sylvia Tyson, Murray McLauchlan, Rob Caldwell, Duane Sauder, Ed Ringwald, Eric Lightfoot.

197   **"We talked about my problems"**: Lightfoot, July 2014.

198   **"That was always my drink at concert time"**: ibid.

198   **"He said, 'Gordie, I'm going to put you on Antabuse'"**: ibid.

198   **"The threat of Antabuse really scared the shit out of him"**: Haynes, February 2015.

199   **"We're doing the Kazan"**: from "Gordon Lightfoot Talks About Shadows," WB Records, 1982.

199   **"I did it with just a lot of coffee"**: Lightfoot, February 2014.

201   **"We had a good car"**: ibid.

202   **"Gordon was very generous"**: Finkelstein, April 2016.

202   **"superlative job"**: quoted in Paul King, "A Healthier Lightfoot Vows to Give Best Show," *Toronto Star*, December 7, 1983.

203   **"not to sell tickets"**: ibid.

203   **"If there's a major change"**: Liam Lacey, "Lightfoot Speaks for Our Secret, Romantic Selves," *The Globe and Mail*, March 4, 1984.

204   **"The Canadian singer has had mean times"**: Bob Ashenmacher,

"Lightfoot Dazzles Once Again," *Duluth News-Tribune*, April 21, 1984.

204   **"the master of . . . bombastic pop kitsch"**: Don Shewey, *Rolling Stone*, June 6, 1985.

205   **Foster already had a melody**: Jim Vallance interview in "Tears Are Not Enough," *Canadian Music Blog*, May 30, 2011, https://musiccan-ada.wordpress.com/2011/05/30/tears-are-not-enough-by-northern-lights.

206   **"Everybody was there"**: Lightfoot, February 2014.

206   **"When I started to make"**: quoted in Wayne Francis, "East of Midnight," www.lightfoot.ca.

207   **"I told Lenny, 'I'm not sure'"**: Lightfoot, July 2014.

207   **"The tale, with its implications"**: Liam Lacey, "Generations on Hand as Lightfoot Mixes the Past and Present," *The Globe and Mail*, November 16, 1985.

208   **"[David] called me and said"**: quoted in David Foster Special Issue, *Billboard*, July 26, 1986.

208   **"It's about a guy on the outside"**: "Gord Speaks Out About His Music," *Songbook* liner notes, Rhino Records, 1999.

208   **"The best piece of work I ever did"**: Lightfoot, September 2014.

209   **"There was really so much to learn"**: quoted in David Foster Special Issue, *Billboard*, July 26, 1986.

209   **Playing before a crowd of** 5,500: "Celebrity Softball," *The Victoria Times*, August 26, 1986.

210   **"The final score was** 12–11**"**: Lightfoot, February 2014.

210   **"I always felt that it had a 'gold watch' kind of feeling"**: quoted in "What's Cookin' with Gord?," Liz Braun, *Toronto Sun*, November 17, 1986.

211   **"It's hard to imagine"**: Bart Beaty, *Long and Wasted Year* (blog), July 22, 2014, https://longandwastedyear.com/2014/07/22/live-dylan-1989.

211   **"When I was at the University of Western Ontario"**: Thicke, April 2016.

212   **"Gloria was a couple of weeks late"**: ibid.

212   **"Who could ask for anything more"**: ibid.

213   **"He's a sensitive guy"**: ibid.

214   **"When your albums aren't selling"**: quoted in Brian D. Johnson, "A Troubadour Tracks into the Heartland," *Maclean's*, March 16, 1987.

214   **"You couldn't find anything less relevant in San Antonio"**: Earle, April 2016.

214   **"Dave Watt from MCA Canada"**: ibid.

215   **"We'd never played it before"**: ibid.

216   **"Gordon wasn't sure"**: Sylvia Tyson, November 2015.

217   **"At the time, he was renaissance Gord"**: McLauchlan, September 2015.

218   **"It really rubbed me the wrong way"**: quoted in Brian D. Johnson, "A Troubadour Tracks into the Heartland," *Maclean's*, March 16, 1987.

218   **"Not at all. I could tell"**: Caldwell, April 2016.

218   **"I have a picture of Gord"**: ibid.

220   **"We were all exhausted"**: David Suzuki, *David Suzuki: The Autobiography* (Douglas & McIntyre, 2006).

221   **"There wouldn't be a 'Pussywillows'"**: quoted in Mark Bisset, "Lightfoot Comes Home," *Orillia Packet & Times*, December 20, 1989.

221   **"I felt so guilty"**: quoted in Jean Sonmor, "Lightfoot: The Way I Feel," *Toronto Sun*, November 10, 1996.

222   **"I've been called arrogant"**: quoted in Liz Braun, "Hey, Don't Worry Gord," *Toronto Sun*, November 6, 1986.

223   **"I told him how thankful I was"**: Ringwald, April 2016.

223   **"Mostly we'd just go places"**: Eric Lightfoot, April 2016.

224   **"I could see she was beautiful"**: quoted in Jean Sonmor, "Lightfoot: The Way I Feel," *Toronto Sun*, November 10, 1996.

224   **"Liz likes to say I spent my honeymoon"**: Lightfoot, March 2014.

15: A PAINTER PASSING THROUGH
Author interviews with Bernie Fiedler, Ingrid Lightfoot, Rick Haynes, Jim Cuddy, Rick McGinnis.

228   **"I'm getting into a more ethereal thing"**: quoted in Dan Hulbert, "Gordon Lightfoot Still Has Tales to Tell in His Songs," *Atlanta Journal-Constitution*, July 15, 1990.

228   **"I played it for Bob"**: ibid.

229   **"whimsical and philosophical"**: Patrick Kampert, "Detours Behind Him, Lightfoot on Road Again," *Chicago Tribune*, September 5, 1991.

229   **"It's funny—as you get older"**: quoted in Patrick Kampert, "Lightfoot Has Lighter Touch," *Chicago Tribune*, July 1, 1991.229
"changed remarkably little": Stephen Holden, "Pop/Jazz in Review," *The New York Times*, October 3, 1991.

230   **"Your songs are our songs"**: CBC Radio *Morningside* interview with Peter Gzowski, November 8, 1991.

231   **"Gordon was the most fun guy"**: Fiedler, April 2016.

231 **"I got in this exercise class"**: quoted in Patrick Kampert, "Lightfoot Has a Lighter Touch," *Chicago Tribune*, July 1, 1991.

232 **"The world doesn't necessarily need"**: quoted in Peter Howell, "Lightfoot Springs Back," *Toronto Star*, November 10, 1991.

232 **"I can't be a politician"**: ibid.

232 **"preachy"**: ibid.

232 **"I didn't want him to sing it"**: Ingrid Lightfoot, February 2017.

232 **"It's as chauvinistic as hell"**: quoted in Peter Howell, "Lightfoot Springs Back," *Toronto Star*, November 10, 1991.

232 **"wasn't just a reasonable facsimile"**: Mike Joyce, "Gordon Lightfoot, in Perfect Form," *Washington Post*, September 19, 1992.

233 **"matinee"**: Haynes, February 2015.

233 **"Lightfoot's songs were always part"**: Cuddy, June 2003.

233 **"Its harmonic resonance"**: Greg Keelor, "The Birth of Blue Rodeo," *The Globe and Mail*, November 16, 2004.

233 **"I have a history of similar problems"**: Lightfoot interview on CBC TV's *News at Six*, July 9, 1992.

234 **"I was so awestruck"**: Lightfoot interview on CBC TV's *Hockey Night in Canada*, 2012.

234 **"Here's this rich guy making me a coffee"**: McGinnis, December 2016.

235 **"They were a really loose band"**: ibid.

235 **"His most consistently good"**: Peter Howell, "Lightfoot's Songs Outlast Musical Fads," *Toronto Star*, April 10, 1993.

235 **"there is a classic Lightfoot sound"**: James Marck, "Canadian Music's Favourite Institution Mounts a Fresh Assault," *Now*, March 11, 1993.

235 **"most personal songs he has ever written"**: "Lightfoot Back in Spotlight," Canadian Press, November 10, 1993.

235 **"Lightfoot has rediscovered the virtues"**: Geoffrey Himes, "Lightfoot Is Back with a Light Touch," *Washington Post*, July 16, 1993.

235 **"among the most honest"**: Buddy Seigal, "For Lightfoot, the Waiting's Over," *Los Angeles Times*, June 16, 1993.

235 **"it's comforting to know"**: Billy Altman, *Rolling Stone*, September 2, 1993.

236 **"I had a dry spell there"**: quoted in Seigal, "For Lightfoot, the Waiting's Over," *Los Angeles Times*, June 16, 1993.

236 **"I'm not worthy"**: quoted in Nick Krewen, "Lightfoot at 54," *Hamilton Spectator*, November 6, 1993.

238   **"In my first family"**: quoted in Sid Adilman, "If You Could Read His Mind . . . ," *Toronto Star*, March 12, 1995.

240   **"little trip down shrink alley"**: quoted in "Lightfoot's Ballads Give Goosebumps," *Green Bay Press-Gazette*, September 26, 1997.

240   **"Conversation lurches around unexpected corners"**: Jean Sonmor, "Canada's Most Famous Folk Singer Still an Intense Artist," *Toronto Sun*, November 10, 1996.

240   **"I've made a few mistakes"**: quoted in Peter Howell, "Lightfoot Rediscovers His Muse," *Toronto Star*, November 14, 1996.

241   **"aural Pierre Berton"**: Tom Hopkins, "Inside Gordon Lightfoot," *Maclean's*, May 1, 1978.

241   **"Gordie is a taciturn kind of guy"**: quoted in "Gord's Gold Mined from Soul," Christopher Guly, *The Globe and Mail*, November 10, 1997.

243   **"My mum had been sick"**: Lightfoot, July 2014.

244   **"The move went well"**: quoted in Brad Webber, "Gordon Lightfoot Still Serious About Songwriting," *Chicago Tribune*, October 15, 1999.

245   **"As a voyage of rediscovery"**: Max Bell, "Voyage of the Mind Reader," *Mojo*, August 1999.

245   **"magnificent"**: Kit Aiken, *Uncut*, August 1999.

16: INSPIRATION LADY

Author interviews with Rick Haynes, Barry Keane, Murray McLauchlan, Fred Lightfoot, Ingrid Lightfoot.

246   **"I don't want a beer commercial"**: Lightfoot interview on CBC TV's *The National*, May 10, 2004.

246   **"I don't have as much time"**: quoted in Neil Baron, "For the Sake of the Song," *Reno Gazette-Journal*, April 18, 2000.

247   **"Each concert is another challenge"**: quoted in Martin Griffith, "Gordon Lightfoot 'Still Out There,'" Associated Press, December 4, 2000.

247   **"Everybody [in the band] loves to play"**: quoted in Ben Elder, "Highway Songs," *Acoustic Guitar*, January 2000.

248   **"Sometimes we were criticized"**: Haynes, February 2017.

248   **"the same laconic appeal"**: Ann Powers, "Sailing Far from the Edmund Fitzgerald," *The New York Times*, August 12, 2000.

249   **"It's a song I just can't walk away from"**: quoted in Jim Slotek, "Full Steam Ahead," *Toronto Sun*, November 9, 2001.

249   **"It's my way of showing my worth"**: quoted in Kirk Baird, "Seeing the Light," *Las Vegas Sun*, August 17, 2001.

250   **"probably an unhealthy affection"**: quoted in Derk Richardson, "He Writes the Songs: Ron Sexsmith Finds Comfort in Songcraft, Gordon Lightfoot," *SFGate*, June 14, 2001, www.sfgate.com/music/article/He-Writes-The-Songs-Ron-Sexsmith-finds-comfort-3265731.php.

251   **"Gord went into some kind of convulsion"**: Haynes, February 2015.

252   **"Elizabeth wanted to keep it all quiet"**: ibid.

252   **"I've known Gord for thirty-five years"**: quoted in *Orillia Today*, September 10, 2002.

253   **"On the morning I woke up"**: Lightfoot, March 2015.

254   **"I plan to fight my way back"**: quoted in Bernard Heydorn, "The Comeback from Death's Door," *Toronto Star*, April 19, 2003.

254   **"the ginger shuffle of someone taking care"**: Erin Anderssen and James Adams, "Gordon's Song," *The Globe and Mail*, October 11, 2003.

256   **"Over the last four decades"**: Tim Sheridan, *Mojo*, August 2004.

256   **"That would've been worse than death"**: Keane, February 2017.

257   **"It was funny"**: McLauchlan, September 2015.

257   **"This was a proud man"**: Keane, February 2017.

258   **"a little short of wind"**: James Adams, "Gord and His Baritone Are Thin, but He's Back," *The Globe and Mail*, May 19, 2005.

259   **"Mom was definitely not the senior type"**: Ingrid Lightfoot, www.corfid.com/vbb/showthread.php?t=13721, November 17, 2006.

260   **"I was asked by [promoter] Michael Cohl"**: Lightfoot, February 2014.

260   **"He was way better than anybody"**: quoted in Frank Matys, "Lightfoot Thrills Old Friends," *Orillia Today*, December 7, 2005.

261   **"It was a bit of an inconvenience"**: quoted in John Swartz, "Back in Fighting Form," *Orillia Packet & Times*, November 14, 2009.

261   **"He lives to work"**: Ingrid Lightfoot, February 2017.

17: GOING THE DISTANCE

Author interviews with Fred Lightfoot, Ingrid Lightfoot, Eric Lightfoot, Meredith Moon, Rick Haynes, Wanda Hawkins.

264   **"It's rather amusing, actually"**: quoted in Jane Stevenson, "Lightfoot Amused by Death Hoax," *Toronto Sun*, February 19, 2010.

265   **"Dad really cherishes his space"**: Eric Lightfoot, October 2016.

266 **"Too many young people and not enough jobs"**: quoted in Peter Kuitenbrouwer, "Occupy Toronto Survives Another Day," *National Post*, November 15, 2011.

266 **"One of the things that I admire about him"**: Moon, May 2016.

267 **"There's been a lot of controversy"**: quoted in Bill DeYoung, "If You Could Read His Mind," *Connect Savannah*, March 2, 2010.

268 **"Gordo's been around as long as me"**: quoted in Bill Flanagan, "Bob Dylan Exclusive Interview," *Huffington Post*, May 16, 2009.

269 **"That's why I missed my chance"**: Lightfoot, July 2014.

270 **"Terry was a terrific guy"**: quoted in Nick Patch, "Gordon Lightfoot Remembers Late Guitarist Clements as One of His Best Friends," Canadian Press, February 28, 2011.

270 **"He was messing up real bad"**: Haynes, February 2017.

271 **"Despite [Lightfoot's] frail appearance"**: http://tapeunit.com/gordon-lightfoot-visits-the-grammy-museum-after-sundown-photos, March 26, 2013.

272 **"She said, 'Daddy, it's not'"**: quoted in Karen Hilfman Millson, "Interview with Gordon Lightfoot," *United Church Observer*, June 2013.

272 **"He listened to me"**: Ingrid Lightfoot, February 2017.

274 **"Every year you see him"**: Ron Sexsmith, quoted in "Superfans" video, ZoomerMedia, May 25, 2011.

275 **"I could've played something schmaltzy"**: Lightfoot, September 2014.

276 **"Gordon has always been kind of shy"**: Wanda Hawkins, January 2016.

276 **"When I found out"**: quoted in "Gordon Lightfoot Honoured with Tribute Sculpture in Orillia," Canadian Press, October 23, 2015.

277 **"[The Queen] told me how much she loved"**: quoted in Martin Chilton, "The Queen Likes My Canadian Railroad Trilogy Song," *Daily Telegraph*, January 21, 2016.

278 **"once velvet voice"**: John Aizlewood, "Hushed Tones of a Great Survivor," *Evening Standard*, May 25, 2016.

Bibliography

BOOKS

Adria, Marco. *Music of Our Times: Eight Canadian Singer-Songwriters.* Toronto: James Lorimer, 1990.

Bidini, Dave. *Writing Gordon Lightfoot.* Toronto: McClelland & Stewart, 2011.

Boyd, Liona. *In My Own Key: My Life in Love and Music.* Toronto: Stoddart, 1998.

Collins, Maynard. *Lightfoot: If You Could Read His Mind.* Toronto: Deneau, 1988.

Einarson, John, with Ian Tyson and Sylvia Tyson. *Four Strong Winds: Ian & Sylvia.* Toronto: McClelland & Stewart, 2011.

Gabiou, Afrieda. *Gordon Lightfoot.* Toronto: Gage, 1979.

Jacobson, Cliff. *Canoeing Wild Rivers: The 30th Anniversary Guide to Expedition Canoeing in North America.* Guildford, CT: Falcon Guides, 2015.

Jennings, Nicholas. *Before the Gold Rush: Flashbacks to the Dawn of the Canadian Sound.* Toronto: Viking, 1997; Penguin, 1998.

———. *Fifty Years of Music: The Story of EMI Music Canada.* Toronto: Macmillan, 2000.

———. *Gordon Lightfoot: Master Craftsman of Canadian Song.* Liner notes to *Songbook.* Los Angeles: Rhino, 1999.

Laing, Dave, et al. *The Electric Muse: The Story of Folk into Rock.* London: Methuen, 1975.

Marcus, Greil. *Like a Rolling Stone: Bob Dylan at the Crossroads.* New York: PublicAffairs, 2005.

Melhuish, Martin. *Oh What a Feeling: A Vital History of Canadian Music.* Kingston, Ontario: Quarry Press, 1996.

Richmond, Randy. *The Orillia Spirit: An Illustrated History of Orillia.* Toronto: Dundurn, 1996.

Rizzo, Dennis, and Ross Greenwood, eds. *Mariposa Exposed, Volume 1: Stories for the Sesquicentennial*. Orillia, Ontario: Le Temps H&S Times, 2016.

Schneider, Jason. *Whispering Pines: The Northern Roots of American Music . . . From Hank Snow to the Band*. Toronto: ECW Press, 2009.

Smith, Cathy. *Chasing the Dragon*. Toronto: Key Porter Books, 1984.

Suzuki, David. *David Suzuki: The Autobiography*. Vancouver: Douglas & McIntyre, 2006.

Treece, Tom. *But What Do I Know?* Maitland, FL: Xulon Press, 2007.

Wainwright, J.A. *Blazing Figures: A Life of Robert Markle*. Waterloo, Ontario: Wilfrid Laurier University Press, 2010.

Wald, Elijah. *Dylan Goes Electric!: Newport, Seeger, Dylan, and the Night That Split the Sixties*. New York: Dey Street Books, 2015.

Yorke, Ritchie. *Axes, Chops & Hot Licks: The Canadian Rock Music Scene*. Edmonton: M.G. Hurtig, 1971.

Young, Peter. *Let's Dance: A Celebration of Ontario's Dance Halls and Summer Dance Pavilions*. Toronto: Natural Heritage, 2002.

SECONDARY BOOKS

Barris, Alex. *The Pierce-Arrow Showroom Is Leaking: An Insider's View of the CBC*. Toronto: Ryerson Press, 1969.

Bender, Carole, and Bob Gibson. *Bob Gibson: I Come for to Sing*. Gretna, Louisiana: Firebird Press, 2001.

Colby, Bob, with Bob Fitzpatrick. *The Bitter End: Hanging Out at America's Nightclub*. New York: Cooper Square Press, 2002.

Colling, Herb. *Turning Points: The Detroit Riot of 1967, a Canadian Perspective*. Toronto: Natural Heritage Books, 2003.

Cullen, Don. *The Bohemian Embassy: Memories and Poems*. Hamilton: Wolsak and Wynn, 2007.

Dylan, Bob. *Chronicles: Volume One*. New York: Simon & Schuster, 2004.

Foster, David, with Pablo F. Fenjves. *Hitman: Forty Years Making Music, Topping Charts & Winning Grammys*. New York: Pocket Books, 2008.

Goodman, Fred. *The Mansion on the Hill: Dylan, Young, Geffen, Springsteen and the Head-On Collision of Rock and Commerce*. New York: Random House, 1997.

Hadju, David. *Positively 4th Street: The Lives and Times of Joan Baez, Bob Dylan, Mimi Baez Fariña and Richard Fariña*. New York: Macmillan, 2011.

Houghton, Mick. *Becoming Elektra: The True Story of Jac Holzman's Visionary Record Label*. London: Jawbone, 2010.

Hunter, Tommy, with Liane Heller. *Tommy Hunter: My Story*. Toronto: Methuen, 1985.

Leacock, Stephen. *Sunshine Sketches of a Little Town*. Toronto: Bell & Cockburn, 1912.

Leigh, Spencer. *Frank Sinatra: An Extraordinary Life*. Camarthen, Wales: McNidder and Grace, 2015.

Rosenthal, Elizabeth J. *His Song: The Musical Journey of Elton John*. New York: Watson-Guptill, 2001.

Rutherford, Paul. *When Television Was Young: Primetime Canada, 1952–1967*. Toronto: University of Toronto Press, 1990.

Sloman, Larry. *On the Road with Bob Dylan*. New York: Three Rivers Press, 2002.

Warhol, Andy. *The Andy Warhol Diaries*. Edited by Pat Hackett. New York: Grand Central Publishing, 1991.

Weintraub, Jerry, with Rich Cohen. *When I Stop Talking, You'll Know I'm Dead: Useful Stories from a Persuasive Man*. New York: Hachette, 2010.

Woodward, Bob. *Wired: The Short Life and Fast Times of John Belushi*. New York: Simon & Schuster, 1984.

ARTICLES

Batten, Jack. "I Just Write Songs I Think People Will Dig." *The Canadian*, February 5, 1966.

———. "The Vulnerability of Gordon Lightfoot." *Saturday Night*, July 1974.

De Villiers, Marq. "Gordon Lightfoot: Hurtin' All the Way to the Bank." *Toronto Life*, June 1968.

Harris, Marjorie. "Gordon Lightfoot: Folk Singer with a Message." *Maclean's*, September 1968.

Henthoff, Nat. "On the Road with Bob Dylan, Joan Baez and the Rolling Thunder Revue." *Rolling Stone*, January 15, 1976.

Hopkins, Tom. "Inside Gordon Lightfoot." *Maclean's*, May 1, 1978.

Johnson, Brian D. "A Troubadour Tracks into the Heartland." *Maclean's*, March 16, 1987.

King, Paul. "Movie Finds Flip Side of Gordie Lightfoot." *Toronto Star*, January 3, 1981.

Lacey, Liam. "For Gordon Lightfoot, Top 40 Radio Is the Brass Ring." *The Globe and Mail*, March 12, 1983.

Macfarlane, John. "Lightfoot: The Lyrical Loner." *The Globe and Mail*, June 18, 1966.

Markle, Robert. "Early Morning Afterthoughts." *Maclean's*, December 1971.

Markle, Robert. "Knowing Lightfoot: A Friend's Portrait of the Artist at Work and Play." *The Canadian*, April 16, 1977.

McDonald, Marci. "The Shy, Withdrawn Singer Whose Music Spans Canada." *Toronto Star*, March 11, 1972.

Naglin, Nancy. "Gordon Lightfoot Rises After Sundown." *Crawdaddy*, April 1975.

Ochs, Phil. "The Ballad of Gordon Lightfoot." *Broadside*, July 15, 1965.

Vallance, Jim. "Tears Are Not Enough." *Canadian Music Blog*, May 30, 2011.

Discography

SINGLES

All singles released in Canada and the United States, plus additional countries as stated.

1962 – "Lesson in Love" / "Sweet Polly" – Quality Records (1395x) (recorded as a member of the Two Tones)

1962 – "Daisy Doo" / "Remember Me (I'm the One)" – Chateau Records (ABC-Paramount in the US) (10352) Canada (10352)

1962 – "Remember Me (I'm the One)" / "Daisy Doo" – Decca Records (UK) (f11527) Chateau Records (Canada) (142)

1962 – "Adios, Adios (I'll Meet You in Michoacan)" / "Is My Baby Blue Tonight" – Chateau Records (152)

1962 – "It's Too Late, He Wins" / "Negotiations" – Chateau Records (ABC in the US) (10373) Canada (148) – also released in the UK

1963 – "Day Before Yesterday" / "Take Care of Yourself" – Chateau Records (156) – also released in the UK

1965 – "I'm Not Sayin'" / "For Lovin' Me" – Warner Brothers (WB) Records (5621)

1965 – "Just Like Tom Thumb's Blues" / "Ribbon of Darkness" – United Artists (UA) Records (0929)

1966 – "Spin Spin" / "For Lovin' Me" – UA Records (50055)

1966 – "Early Morning Rain" / "The Gypsy" – UA Records (35274) – UK only release

1967 – "Go Go Round" / "I'll Be Alright" – UA Records (50114)

1967 – "The Way I Feel" / "Peaceful Waters" – UA Records (50152) – with picture sleeve

1967 – "Movin'" and "Talkin' Freight" - Peterson Custom Record Productions – PRC 5000
— as part of *Movin' / Allons-y!* with Jean-Pierre Ferland for CN Rail – with picture sleeve

1968 – "Black Day in July" / "Pussywillows, Cat-Tails" – UA Records (50281) – also released in France with picture sleeve

1968 – "Bitter Green" / "Does Your Mother Know" – UA Records (50447) – also released in Italy – with picture sleeve

1970 – "Me and Bobby McGee" / "The Pony Man" – Reprise Records (0926) – also released in Germany and the UK – with picture sleeve

1970 – "If You Could Read My Mind" / "Poor Little Allison" – Reprise Records (0974) – also released in Japan, Australia, the UK, France, Germany, Greece and the Netherlands – also released in Italy and Portugal with picture sleeve and in Spain b/w "Me and Bobby McGee"

1971 – "This Is My Song" / "Sleep Little Jane" – AME Records (102x)

1971 – "If I Could" / "Softly" – UA Records (3938-50765)

1971 – "Talking in Your Sleep" / "Nous Vivons Ensemble" – Reprise Records (1020) – also released in New Zealand, Portugal, France and the Netherlands – with picture sleeve

1971 – "Summer Side of Life" / "Love and Maple Syrup" – Reprise Records (1035)

1971 – "If You Could Read My Mind" / "Me and Bobby McGee" – Hispanvox Records (Spain) (h-702) – with picture sleeve

1971 – "Baby It's Alright" / "Me and Bobby McGee" – Reprise (R21-155) – South Africa only release

1972 – "Beautiful" / "Don Quixote" – Reprise Records (1088) – also released in Brazil

1972 – "That Same Old Obsession" / "You Are What I Am" – Reprise Records (1128) – also released in Japan – with picture sleeve

1972 – "Christian Island" / "Beautiful" – Reprise Records (K14176)

1973 – "Can't Depend on Love" / "It's Worth Believin'" – Reprise Records (1145) – also released in the UK

1974 – "Sundown" / "Too Late for Prayin'" – Reprise Records (1194) – also released in Japan, Spain, France, Portugal and the Netherlands – with picture sleeve

1974 – "Carefree Highway" / "Seven Island Suite" – Reprise Records (1309) – also released in Holland with picture sleeve – also released in Germany b/w "Cotton Jenny" with picture sleeve

1975 – "Rainy Day People" / "Cherokee Bend" – Reprise Records (1328) – also released in New Zealand, Spain, Portugal and the UK – with picture sleeve

1975 – "Cold on the Shoulder" / "Bells of the Evening" – Reprise Records (14390) – also released in France and Germany – with picture sleeve

1976 – "The Wreck of the Edmund Fitzgerald" / "The House You Live In" – Reprise Records (1369) – also released in Australia, Germany, Spain, Italy and the UK – with picture sleeve – re-released in Spain b/w "Race Among the Ruins"

1976 – "Race Among the Ruins" / "Protocol" – Reprise Records (1380) – also released in Spain with picture sleeve b/w "The Wreck of the Edmund Fitzgerald"

1976 – "Summertime Dream" / "Spanish Moss" – Reprise Records (14-442) – Germany only release with picture sleeve – also released in Japan b/w "Protocol" with picture sleeve

1978 – "The Circle Is Small" / "Sweet Guinevere" – Warner Brothers (WB) Records (8518) – also released in the UK

1978 – "Daylight Katy" / "Hangdog Hotel Room" – WB Records (8579) – also released in the UK and New Zealand – also released in Germany b/w "Sweet Guinevere" with picture sleeve

1978 – "Dreamland" / "Songs the Minstrel Sang" – WB Records (8644)

1980 – "Dream Street Rose" / "Make Way for the Lady" – WB Records (49230) – also released in the UK

1980 – "If You Need Me" / "Mister Rock of Ages" – WB Records (49516)

1981 – "If There's a Reason" / "The Wreck of the Edmund Fitzgerald" - WB Records (K17833) – Ireland only release

1982 – "Baby Step Back" / "Thank You for the Promises" – WB Records (50012) – also released in the UK

1982 – "Blackberry Wine" / "Shadows" – WB Records (7-29963) – also released in the UK

1982 – "Shadows" / "In My Fashion" – WB Records (7-29859)

1983 – "Knotty Pine" / "Salute (A Lot More Living to Do)" – WB Records (7-29511)

1983 – "Without You" / "Someone to Believe In" – WB Records (7-29466)

1983 – "Whispers of the North" / "Gotta Get Away" – WB Records (92-9399) – Netherlands release only – with picture sleeve

1986 – "Anything for Love" / "Let It Ride" – WB Records (92 86557) – with picture sleeve

1986 – "Stay Loose" / "Morning Glory" – WB Records (92 85537)

1987 – "East of Midnight" / "I'll Tag Along" – WB Records (92 84227)

1987 – "Morning Glory" / "Ecstasy Made East" – WB Records (7-28222)

1993 – "I'll Prove My Love" – Reprise Records

1993 – "Waiting for You" / "Fading Away" – Reprise Records (PRO 800) – Germany only release

1998 – "A Painter Passing Through" – Reprise Records

2004 – "Inspiration Lady" – Linus Records (0204) – also released in the Netherlands – with picture sleeve

2016 – "Plans of My Own" – Warner Music Canada

ALBUMS

All albums released in Canada and the United States, plus additional countries.

STUDIO RECORDINGS

1964 – *The Canadian Talent Library* – Canadian Talent Library (S5049)
Habour Le Cou|The Auctioneer|Betty Mae's a Good Time
Gal|Long River|Turn, Turn, Turn|Cod Liver Oil

1966 – *Lightfoot!* – United Artists (UA) Records (UAS 6487) Mono (UAL 3487)
Rich Man's Spiritual|Long River|The Way I Feel|For Lovin'
Me|The First Time Ever I Saw Your Face|Changes|Early Morning
Rain|Steel Rail Blues|Sixteen Miles (to Seven Lakes)|I'm Not
Sayin'|Pride of Man|Ribbon of Darkness|Oh, Linda|Peaceful Waters

1967 – *The Way I Feel* – UA Records (UAS 6587) Mono (UAL 3587)
Walls|If You Got It|Softly|Crossroads|A Minor Ballad|Go Go
Round|Rosanna|Home from the Forest|I'll Be Alright|Song for a
Winter's Night|Canadian Railroad Trilogy|The Way I Feel

1968 – *Did She Mention My Name* – UA Records (UAS 6649) Mono (UAL 3649)
Wherefore and Why|The Last Time I Saw Her|Black Day in
July|May I|Magnificent Outpouring|Does Your Mother Know|The
Mountains and Maryann|Pussywillows, Cat-Tails|I Want to Hear
It from You|Something Very Special|Boss Man|Did She Mention
My Name

1968 – *Back Here on Earth* – UA Records (UAS 6672)
Long Way Back Home|Unsettled Ways|Long Thin Dawn|Bitter
Green|The Circle Is Small (I Can See It in Your Eyes)|Marie
Christine|Cold Hands from New York|Affair on 8th Avenue|
Don't Beat Me Down|The Gypsy|If I Could

1970 – *Sit Down Young Stranger* (later *If You Could Read My Mind*) –
Reprise Records (RS 6392) (CD 6392-2)
Minstrel of the Dawn|Me and Bobby McGee|Approaching
Lavender|Saturday Clothes|Cobwebs and Dust|Poor Little
Allison|Sit Down Young Stranger|If You Could Read My
Mind|Baby It's Alright|Your Love's Return|Pony Man

1971 – *Early Lightfoot* (recorded in 1962) – AME Records (AME 7000)

Remember Me (I'm the One)|Daisy Doo|Adios, Adios|Is My Baby
Blue Tonight|Sleep Little Jane|Long Haired Woman|It's Too Late,
He Wins|Take Care of Yourself|This Is My Song|Negotiations

1971 – *Summer Side of Life* – Reprise Records (MS 2037) (CDW 45686)
Ten Degrees and Getting Colder|Miguel|Go My Way|Cotton
Jenny|Talking in Your Sleep|Nous Vivons Ensemble|Same Old
Lover Man|Redwood Hill|Love and Maple Syrup|Cabaret|Summer
Side of Life

1972 – *Don Quixote* – Reprise Records (MS 2056) (CDW 45687)
Don Quixote|Christian Island (Georgian Bay)|Alberta
Bound|Looking at the Rain|Ordinary Man|Brave
Mountaineers|Ode to Big Blue|Second Cup of Coffee|Beautiful|
On Susan's Floor|Patriot's Dream

1972 – *Old Dan's Records* – Reprise Records (MS 2116)
Farewell to Annabel|Same Old Obsession|Old Dan's Records|Lazy
Mornin'|You Are What I Am|Can't Depend on Love|My Pony Won't
Go|It's Worth Believing|Mother of a Miner's Child|Hi'way Songs

1973 – *Sundown* – Reprise Records (MS 2177) (CD 2177-2)
Sundown|Somewhere U.S.A.|High and Dry|Seven Island
Suite|Circle of Steel|Is There Anyone Home|Watchman's
Gone|Carefree Highway|The List|Too Late for Prayin'

1975 – *Cold on the Shoulder* – Reprise Records (MS 2206) (CDW 45688)
Bend in the Water|Rainy Day People|Cold on the Shoulder|The
Soul Is the Rock|Bells of the Evening|Rainbow Trout|Tree Too
Weak to Stand|All the Lovely Ladies|Fine as Fine Can Be|Cherokee
Bend|Now and Then|Slide on Over

1976 – *Summertime Dream* – Reprise Records (MS 2246) (CD 2246)
The Wreck of the Edmund Fitzgerald|Race Among the
Ruins|I'm Not Supposed to Care|I'd Do It Again|Never
Too Close|Protocol|The House You Live In|Summertime
Dream|Spanish Moss|Too Many Clues in the Room

1978 – *Endless Wire* – Warner Brothers (WB) Records (KBS 3149)
(CDW 45685)
Daylight Katy|Sweet Guinevere|Hangdog Hotel Room|If
There's a Reason|Endless Wire|Dreamland|Songs the Minstrel
Sang|Sometimes I Don't Mind|If Children Had Wings|The Circle
Is Small (I Can See It in Your Eyes)

1980 – *Dream Street Rose* – WB Records (XHS 3426)
Sea of Tranquility|Ghosts of Cape Horn|Dream Street Rose|On
the High Seas|Whisper My Name|If You Need Me|Hey You|Make
Way for a Lady|Mr. Rock of Ages|Auctioneer

1982 – *Shadows* – WB Records (XBS 3633)
14 Karat Gold|In My Fashion|Shadows|Blackberry Wine|Heaven
Help the Devil|Thank You for the Promises|Baby Step Back|All I'm
After|Triangle|I'll Do Anything|She's Not the Same

1983 – *Salute* – WB Records (92 39011)
Salute (A Lot More Livin' to Do)|Gotta Get Away|Whispers of
the North|Someone to Believe In|Romance|Knotty Pine|Biscuit
City|Without You|Tattoo|Broken Dreams

1986 – *East of Midnight* – WB Records (92 54821) (CD 9 25482-2)
Stay Loose|Morning Glory|East of Midnight|Lesson in
Love|Anything for Love|Let It Ride|Ecstasy Made Easy|You Just
Gotta Be|Passing Ship|I'll Tag Along

1993 – *Waiting for You* – Reprise Records (CDW 45208)
Restless|Ring Them Bells|Fading Away|Only Love Would
Know|Welcome to Try|I'll Prove My Love|Waiting for You|Wild
Strawberries|I'd Rather Press On|Drink Yer Glasses Empty

1998 – *A Painter Passing Through* – Reprise (CDW 46949)
Drifters|My Little Love|Ringneck Loon|I Used to Be a Country
Singer|Boathouse|Much to My Surprise|Painter Passing
Through|On Yonge Street|Red Velvet|Uncle Toad Said

2004 – *Harmony* – Linus Entertainment (CD 2 70027)
Harmony|River of Light|Flyin' Blind|No Mistake About It|End
of All Time|Shellfish|The No Hotel|Inspiration Lady|Clouds of
Loneliness|Couchiching|Sometimes I Wish

LIVE RECORDINGS

1962 – *Two Tones at the Village Corner* – Canatal Records (4026)
We Come Here to Sing|Fast Freight|The Fox|Dark as a
Dungeon|Sinnerman|This Is My Song|Kilgarry Mountain|Calypso
Baby|Summer Love|Children Go Where I Send Thee|Copper
Kettle|Lord I'm So Weary

1969 – *Sunday Concert* – UA Records (UAS 6714) EMI reissue (CD E2-
53299-2-0)

In a Windowpane|The Lost Children|Leaves of Grass|I'm Not Sayin'/Ribbon of Darkness|Apology|Bitter Green|Ballad of Yarmouth Castle|Softy|Boss Man|Pussywillows, Cat-Tails|Canadian Railroad Trilogy

2012 – *All Live* – WEA (CD 2-614790)
14 Karat Gold|If You Could Read My Mind|Fine as Fine Can Be|Baby Step Back|Early Morning Rain|Restless|A Painter Passing Through|Rainy Day People|Ringneck Loon|Shadows|Sundown|Carefree Highway|Christian Island|The Wreck of the Edmund Fitzgerald|Canadian Railroad Trilogy|Let It Ride|Blackberry Wine|Song for a Winter's Night|Old Dan's Records

COMPILATIONS

1975 – *Gord's Gold* – Reprise Records (2RS 2237) (CD 2237-2) – released by Rhino 2005

1988 – *Gord's Gold II* – WB Records (CD 25784) – released by Rhino 2005

1992 – *The Original Lightfoot: The United Artists Years* – UA Records (S2 80748) (S2 80749) (S2 80750)

1993 – *The United Artists Collection* – EMI Records (E2-27015)

1999 – *Songbook* box set – Warner Archives/Rhino (R2 75802)

2002 – *Complete Greatest Hits* – WB/Rhino (WTVD 78287)

Acknowledgments

In 1999, I received a phone call from Barry Harvey at Early Morning Productions. He wanted to know if I would write extensive liner notes for Gordon Lightfoot's *Songbook* box set. The origin of this book dates back to that phone call. This biography evolved from there, with numerous stops and starts along the way.

I want to thank Gordon Lightfoot for entrusting his life story to me. For a man so intensely private, such openness took tremendous faith and courage. Over the course of a dozen years, off and on, Gord invited me to his Toronto home for interview sessions and to look at photographs from his collection. Sometimes I'd pull into his driveway and he'd be outside, sitting on his folding lawn chair with tattered webbing, having a quiet cigarette. Inside, he'd offer to make old-style "bush coffee" on his stove. Then we'd get down to business, either in his spacious kitchen—always with sports or CNN on the TV in the background—or his elegant living room, with its *Edmund Fitzgerald* gallery, or his cozy music study, a dark sanctuary filled with guitars, notebooks, amplifiers and tape recorders. The interviews usually went long, and Gord was always generous with his time.

I greatly appreciate the trust that members of the Lightfoot family showed in speaking with me, especially Kim Lightfoot, Meredith Moon, Eric Lightfoot, Fred Lightfoot and Ingrid Lightfoot. I also want to thank Anne Leibold, who keeps Early Morning Productions on an even keel and helped make my job easier, along with Bernie Fiedler and the late Barry Harvey. While on the road with Gordon, I was always made to feel welcome by his tour manager, Warren Toll, crew and band members, including Carter Lancaster. The longest serving Lightfoot sidemen, Rick Haynes, Mike Heffernan and Barry Keane, put up with my frequent questions and phone calls. Their ability to remember key details going back over forty years with Gord was invaluable.

The community of "Lightheads" is a faithful and enthusiastic collection of fans around the world who regularly convene online. The research for this book was assisted in no small part by the contributions of administrators Wayne Francis (www.lightfoot.ca), Val Magee (www.gordonlightfoot.com) and Florian Bodenseher (www.corfid.com), whose popular websites do a great job chronicling the Lightfoot history.

Thank you to Alexander Mair, Ron Sexsmith and Murray McLauchlan for providing ongoing counsel, a talk in the park and an inspiring late-night canoe ride. Others, such as fellow music biographers Barney Hoskyns, Sylvie Simmons and David Yaffe, shared useful contacts, while Rob Caldwell, Cathy Coonley, John Corcelli (CBC), Marc Coulavin, Bob Dion, Carl Kenneally (BBC Archives), Pat LaCroix, Doug McGarvey, Jennifer Murrant (Orillia Public Library), Len Rosenberg, Duane Sauder, Joan Schafer, Tiziano Vanola (Toronto Public Library), Dave Watt, Char Westbrook, John Willans (Royal Albert Hall Archives) and friends Brian Reagan, Renée Langlois and Audrey O'Brien all aided in archival and audio-visual research. Thanks also to Steve Kane, Greg Morris, James Findlay and Steve Waxman at Warner Music Canada for discography help, and to Tony Quarrington for his insights into Lightfoot's guitarists.

Nino Ricci, Dale Reagan and especially Ian Pearson all generously read different versions of the manuscript and gave critical advice and suggestions. Robin Budd provided design assistance on the original proposal, while friend Roger Gibbs, my sister Christina

Jennings and son Callum Jennings were constantly supportive. The book was written in various locations, including the farm belonging to my sister Ali Jennings and brother-in-law Paul DeGuzman and the hospital room of my father-in-law Roy Hay. The great spirits of Paul and Roy live on in this work.

I have a long history with two key individuals on this project. I first met my agent, Westwood Creative Artists' Jackie Kaiser, when she served as the editor on my first book, *Before the Gold Rush*, in the 1990s. Her belief in this book never wavered, and her support kept me positive when I needed it most. Diane Turbide and I worked together for many years at *Maclean's* magazine, so I was thrilled to team with her as my editor at Penguin Random House. She kept a close eye and steady hand on all stages of the manuscript. In addition, my appreciation goes to Alex Schultz for his careful copyediting. Diane, it really is true that it takes a community to create a book.

Finally, and most significantly, I was extremely fortunate to have had two immediate family members at my side throughout the process. My son Duncan Jennings, a musician himself, fearlessly dove in and studiously transcribed every single interview for this project. I couldn't have done it without him. And my wife, Carol Hay, read every draft of the manuscript, listened as I worked through various elements and provided crucial direction that helped shape the book. I am grateful beyond words.

N.J.

March 2017

Permission Acknowledgments

REMEMBER ME (I'M THE ONE)
Words and Music by GORDON LIGHTFOOT
Copyright © 1962 (Renewed) WB MUSIC CORP.
All Rights Reserved
Used By Permission of ALFRED MUSIC

SONG FOR A WINTER'S NIGHT
(THAT'S WHAT YOU GET) FOR LOVIN' ME
EARLY MORNIN' RAIN
Words and Music by GORDON LIGHTFOOT
Copyright © 1965 (Renewed) WB MUSIC CORP.
All Rights Reserved
Used By Permission of ALFRED MUSIC

CANADIAN RAILROAD TRILOGY
Words and Music by GORDON LIGHTFOOT
Copyright © 1967 (Renewed) WB MUSIC CORP.
All Rights Reserved
Used By Permission of ALFRED MUSIC

BLACK DAY IN JULY
CIRCLE IS SMALL
AFFAIR ON EIGHTH AVENUE
Words and Music by GORDON LIGHTFOOT
Copyright © 1968 (Renewed) WB MUSIC CORP.
All Rights Reserved
Used By Permission of ALFRED MUSIC

IF YOU COULD READ MY MIND
Words and Music by GORDON LIGHTFOOT
Copyright © 1969, 1970 (Copyrights Renewed) WB MUSIC CORP.
All Rights Reserved
Used By Permission of ALFRED MUSIC

Index

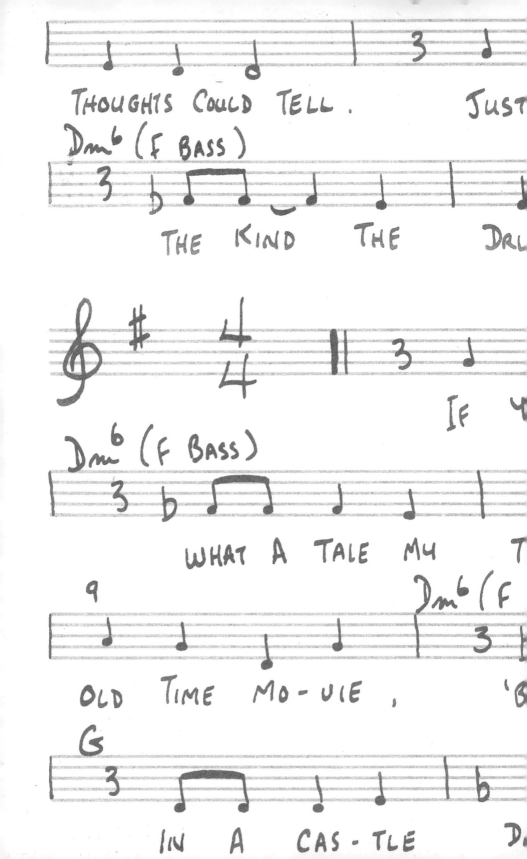